Cosmo Nelson Innes

Scotland in the Middle Ages

Sketches of early Scotch history and social progress

Cosmo Nelson Innes

Scotland in the Middle Ages
Sketches of early Scotch history and social progress

ISBN/EAN: 9783337411596

Printed in Europe, USA, Canada, Australia, Japan

Cover: Foto ©ninafisch / pixelio.de

More available books at **www.hansebooks.com**

SCOTLAND

IN THE MIDDLE AGES

SKETCHES OF EARLY SCOTCH HISTORY

AND SOCIAL PROGRESS

BY

COSMO INNES

PROFESSOR OF HISTORY IN THE UNIVERSITY OF EDINBURGH

EDINBURGH
EDMONSTON AND DOUGLAS
1860

PREFACE.

These Sketches were read in the shape of Lectures to a class in this University; but it cannot be said they thereby received much publicity.

In now publishing them, I have something to disclaim. I trust the origin of the little work may be a sufficient excuse, if it be found wanting in that originality of facts or views without which no one would deliberately compose a book of History. The same cause may obtain pardon for some unacknowledged plagiarism, which it might savour of ostentation more specifically to point out.

If the Sketches have any merit, it is in teaching that true History is best to be learnt from the study of its genuine materials, and not from the twice-told tale of the historians of the book-shelves. Here, as in other studies,

> . . . . Juvat integros accedere fontes
> Atque haurire.

I would warn the young student of history against translations; against abridgments. Let him not think that he learns history by committing a big table of contents to memory. If he takes my advice, his will be the pleasure as well as the gain. He will find endless amusement in the contemporary chronicler, and his rough and vivid pictures of events, which fall very flat and dull, even in the elegant summary of Hume, and the glittering narrative of Gibbon. But books are not all. The history of a nation has to do with things which books never quite supply; the manners of the people, their modes of life, action, and thought. We know more of old Rome from a day among its ruins—from a visit to Herculaneum or Pompeii—than from all the compilations of modern historians, or even the mythical narrative of Livy, charming as it is.

Above all, look to the real evidence, as the lawyers call it. Judge a people by their institutions and laws; by the cultivation of their soil; by their literature; by their achievements in science and art; by what they have done for civilization, and the happiness of the world.

———

After these Sketches were printed, my friendly publishers, taking, I fear, an exaggerated view of their importance, urged me to prefix some Maps that might serve to illustrate my notions of old Scotland, and its progress. I saw the danger, and it was not without reluctance that I complied. As was to be expected, the Maps led to explanatory Notes and Lists of Places, and other topographical apparatus, which now form such a bulk of preliminary matter. I am not willing to think that the labour bestowed has been useless. Indeed, I believe the information here brought together has not been collected in print before, and may be serviceable to many readers; and, if so, perhaps I should not be much concerned though critics may discover that my little craft was not built or rigged for such a ponderous freight.

No one can hold the book at a lower rate than I do, but that must not prevent me from mentioning the names of some of those who have assisted me, and on whom lies none of the blame of any shortcoming.

Mr. Joseph Robertson, my old friend and fellow labourer, has now, as always, been as ready to give, as I to ask assistance. He would be a rash man who should write on Scotch charters or records, or on Scotch church architecture, without taking counsel with Mr. Robertson. Dr. Reeves of Lusk, the historian of St. Columba, who has shamed our Scotch scholars by the light he has thrown upon the christianizing of our western shores, has also assisted me cordially and cheered me on. Mr. W. F. Skene, a Celtic scholar and antiquary of the first order, whose fault is that he will not give his collections to the world, has not withheld them from me. To the last two gentlemen I am indebted for learned and ingenious suggestions upon early Scotch geography, and I feel that I ought to explain why I have not availed myself of them. I am, unfortunately, quite ignorant of the Celtic languages, and the only expositors in whom I have confidence not being entirely at one, I have thought it best not to set down on my map what I could not personally verify.

EDINBURGH, *January* 1860.

NOTES ON THE MAPS.

1. SCOTLAND IN THE *TENTH CENTURY.*

The settlement and early geography of Scotland have given rise to much war and calling of hard names; and the collision of the Goths and the Celts, blinded with their fury, has not had the effect which sometimes results from such conflicts, of throwing light for the bystanders. I cannot extract any satisfactory conclusions on this subject from the erudition of Pinkerton, or the industry of Chalmers. The profusion of unusual learning of the late Mr. Algernon Herbert,[1] can scarcely be said to have cleared the matter; and we shall probably get as near the truth by turning to the slender materials which those writers successively used, drawing from them opposite conclusions.

I do not seek at present to go farther back than the century preceding the great movement of southern settlers to the north—the period preceding the age of Malcolm Canmore—preceding the Norman conquest of England—just before the commencement of Lord Hailes's Annals.

Let it be remembered then, that the Roman power and all memory of Roman provinces had long passed away. To the native tribes, barbarous and fluctuating, without letters or monuments to preserve their history or their changing limits, the descriptions and inferences of Cæsar and Tacitus were now inapplicable. Nor are the ancient geographers of more use. We may possibly recognize the sounds of a few rivers and firths in Ptolemy, but placed all confusedly; while his names of the tribes and their cities give us

[1] Notes on the Irish Nennius, 1848, etc.

no information at all.¹ His nomenclature joins on to nothing before or after. Ptolemy no doubt built on a foundation of truth, and may have known as much of our island, as a London map-maker does of the interior of Japan or Patagonia. Richard of Cirencester, if not a pure modern invention, cannot be quoted as an authority.

I do not find, then, that we have anything very reliable, till we rest on the solid foundation of the venerable Bede. Even the venerable Bede must be taken with a grain of reservation. Believe him as a true witness to what he saw and heard, but no more. For his ancient history, remember when and where he lived. A Benedictine monk of Jarrow, on the coast of Northumberland, writing in the middle of the eighth century, might well be proud of his scholarship, and was content to describe his Britain after Pliny, Eutropius, Solinus, and Orosius. For his more modern events, remember what he tells us himself. " I beseech my reader, if he find in my writings things other than true, he impute not that to me, since I have done that which is the true rule of history, simply noted down for the instruction of posterity those things which I have gathered from common report *(fama vulgante)*." Nothing can be more honest, but let us take warning from the author's own testimony, which is not over-stated. The district of Lindessei (part of Lincoln), though almost adjoining his own country of Northumbria, was not connected with it politically or ecclesiastically, and consequently Bede was quite ignorant of the contemporary transactions of that district. Again, the account which he gives of the arrival of the Saxons and Angles, and their settlement in England, is purely fabulous, being " not in fact," says his last editor, " the history, but the tradition of the Jutish kingdom of Kent." ²

When moderate distance of time and of place thus interfered with the accuracy of the venerable historian, it requires discrimination

---

¹ For instance, on the north coast the *Nouantai* dwelling beside a promontory of their own name, had the following cities (πολεις) *Loucopibia Retigonion*. The *Selgouai* had four: the *Damnioi* six *cities;* not one of which is identified.

² Stevenson's preface, p. xxiii-vii.

to turn his information to account for matters more remote. Let us not be surprised if we have to correct his narrative in his first fact of our history. He tells us Columba obtained his little refuge of Hii from Bridius son of Meilochon, a most powerful king of the Picts. Now we have this Brude son of Malcolm, in our poor roll of Pictish kings, and his reign corresponds with the ascertained era of Saint Columba. Indeed, we know from the best authority, that the saint visited his court, somewhere beyond Loch Ness; but it would overthrow our most settled notions of geography and history, to allow that Iona was of the Pictish territory. It was in the very heart of that district which Bede himself and all our authorities require us to believe was the original seat of the Scots on their arrival from Ireland. And we cannot read Adomnan's history, otherwise than as establishing that Iona was subject to the princes of the Scots. There it was that St. Columba inaugurated Aidan, king of the Scots; there St. Columba with his monks pray for victory to king Aidan as their sovereign.[1] But little recked the monk of Jarrow whether the green islet, "placed far amid the solitary main," belonged to one kingdom of heathens or another. Little dreamt he of the trouble his careless words would cause to his countrymen, a thousand years later, trying to build a national history on the foundation of his "common report."

Thus driven from Bede's account, and Adomnan giving no certain sound in the matter, we fall back on the Irish annalists, and have no scruple to believe that Iona was given to Saint Columba, by Conal son of Comghall, king of the Scots.

But when Bede narrates things of his own time and country, things of such a character too as must have impressed any intelligent man, we take him as our guide with all confidence. He tells us then of Ecgfrid, king of the Northumbrians, in the year 685, cut off with all his army, in an expedition into the country of the Picts, and that the Picts from that time, and down to Bede's own time—only 46 years later—had recovered and kept their old

[1] Innes, p. 89.

possessions which the Angli had held, and the (British) Scots and Britons also recovered their freedom. He describes, as a consequence of that defeat, the retreat to Whitby of " the man of God, Trumuin," who had been bishop over the Picts, though making his residence at Abercurnig (*Abercorn*) situate indeed in the country of the Angli, but close to the firth (*in vicinia freti*) which separates the lands of the Angli and the Picts. The country of the Angli then, Bede's own countrymen of Northumbria, met the country of the Picts at our firth, in the eighth century. Here there can be no mistake. The firth was the proper established boundary, though the success of the Picts had made Abercorn an unsafe dwelling for the bishop and his clerics.

In another passage, Bede, relating the migration of the Scots from their native country, Ireland, to the western shore of our highlands, says that colony was anciently (*antiquitus*) divided from the Britons by the Firth of Clyde, and the strong fortress of Alcluith: and afterwards, explaining what he meant by styling the Scots and Picts *transmarine* nations, says, it was not that they were settled out of Britain, but were separated from the Britons by two arms of the sea, one entering from the east, the other from the west, but not meeting—the former having in its midst the town Giudi (*in medio sui urbem Giudi*), while the western firth has on its right bank the city called Alcluith, which in their tongue (the tongue of those two peoples?) signifies Clyde rock *(Petra Cluith)* because it is on the river of that name. As if to make the southern boundary more precise, Bede tells us of the Roman wall between those two firths, of which plain remains were to be seen in his day, beginning at two miles west from Abercurnig, at a place which, in the language of the Picts, is called *Peanfahel*, and in that of the *Angli* Penneltun, and stretching westward till it terminates beside the city Alcluith.

One passage more, and we have all that Bede affords for our present purpose. The venerable historian informs us that the southern Picts had already, long ago (about 150 years earlier, we know), received the true faith by the preaching of St. Ninian, when, in the year 565, Columba crossed from Ireland on his mission for converting the northern Picts, separated from the southern Picts by ridges of high and rugged mountains.

Such is the northern geography of Bede. In his time, the Picts, now wholly christianized, were a powerful and growing people, possessing all the lowlands of Scotland beyond the Forth, and giving an uneasy border even to their great Northumbrian neighbours. The bishopric of St. Ninian was Pictish too; and the Galwegians, if not the whole inhabitants of Cumbria, are, down to comparatively modern times, spoken of as Picts.[1]

There is less difficulty with regard to the Scots. Without seeking to fix the period of their immigration from the old "land of Scots," Ireland—which was undoubtedly gradual, beginning, perhaps, in the third or fourth century—as soon as they had assumed the coherence of a kingdom, we find them inhabiting Argyll, the Western isles, and the western highlands, marching with the Picts on the mountains which form the water-shed to east and west. Bounded to the south as Bede has limited them, their other boundaries were not doubtful. "Fergus son of Erch, first reigned in Scotland beyond Drumalbane to Slough Munt and to Inchgall." It is a chronicler of St. Andrews who thus writes,[2] and, looking at our map from his point of view, he would give the Scots the boundaries of the sea and isles to the south and west—the Breadalbane or rather Drumalbane range to the east—and the ridge of the Monad-lia, which skirts the upper valley of Spey, to the north.

From the time of Bede to the middle of the tenth century, two hundred years had elapsed, a long dark period indeed, but not altogether without light. In the middle space, the Scots and Picts were united under Kenneth Macalpin, and from thenceforward, by a strange process, the name of the Picts as a nation disappears from history. The change, however, was only one of dynasty and

A.D. 842.

---

[1] In twelfth century, Richard of Hexham, etc.

[2] *Excerpta ex registro S. Andreæ* (i.e., from the great register of the priory, now lost). *Innes*, p. 797, and preface to the printed register of St Andrews, p. 11.

national name. The king of the (British) Scots, acquiring, in addition, and apparently by succession, the kingdom of the Picts, chose to be still called king of Scots; and his kingdom, made up of the two nations, in a short time began to be called after his people, by its present name of Scotland. The inhabitants do not yet appear to have suffered a change. Our eastern seabord was still called Pictland (*Pictavia*) by the Latin chroniclers. Its inhabitants still, as heretofore, pressing for enlargement against the English border, encroached at different times quite to the Tweed; and in the middle of the tenth century, Indulf, the king of the whole country now called Scotland, obtained a formal cession from the Saxon monarch, of the town of Edinburgh (*oppidum Eden*).

That is the state of occupation which the first map tries to represent.

While the names of "Northern and Southern Picts" are given, after Bede, and according to my reading of his geography, I need hardly explain that this does not here, as with Bede, express the existence of two Pictish kingdoms. The whole country — all Pict-land and Scot-land — was now under one government; though, as I have said, I think the population remained nearly unchanged from Bede's time.

In like manner, the names of Cumbria, Strathcluyd, Bernicia, Deira, are rather the shadows of former petty kingdoms than actual existing separate governments. The first two left their names to known districts, and to a peculiar people — peculiar in laws, manners, and language; the others had long ago disappeared, leaving the limits of their territories a matter for conjecture, and their people so mixed and scattered, that even in the tenth century they had no known representatives.

It may be thought that I have restricted too much the portion of the "Norsemen," as in the tenth century; but I cannot find evidence of their colonizing or steady government, for any space to be noticed in a map, beyond their known and recognized earldoms of Orkney and Caithness (including Sutherland). Down the

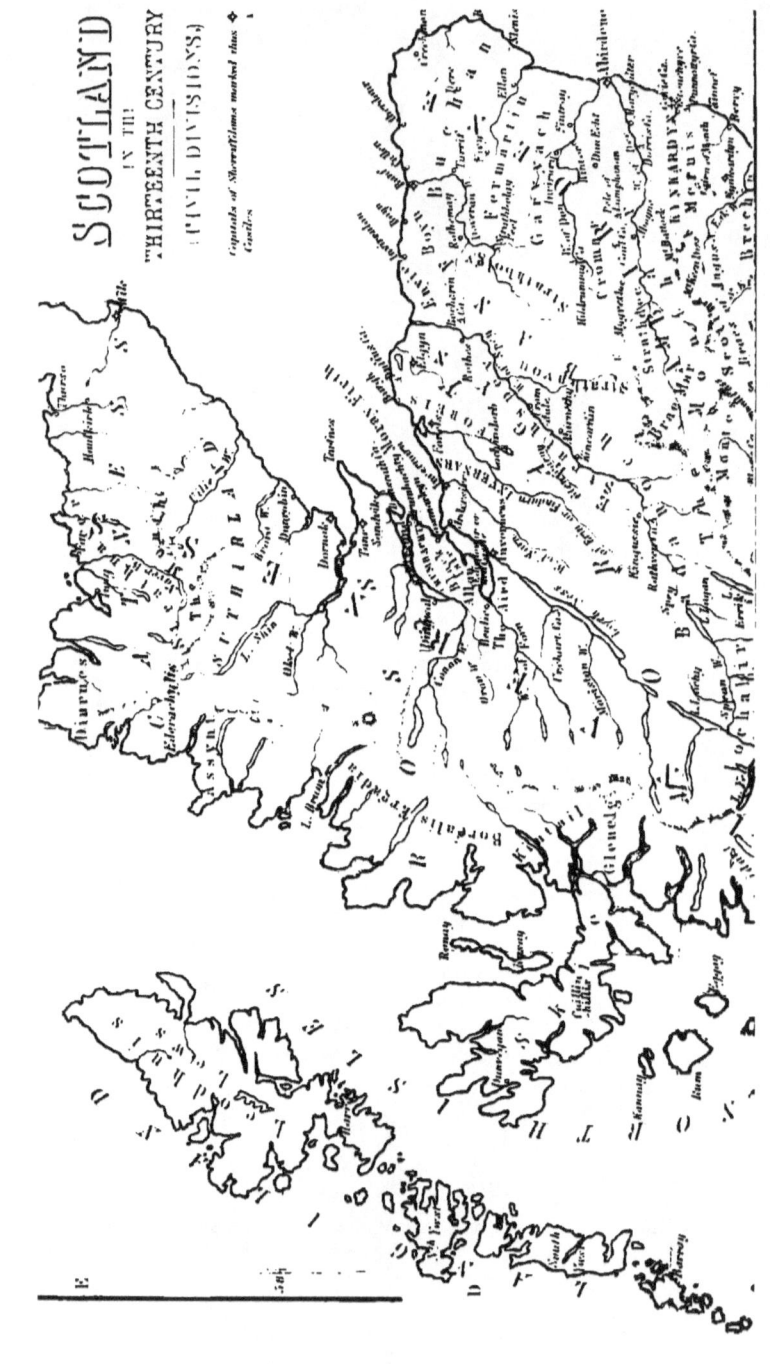

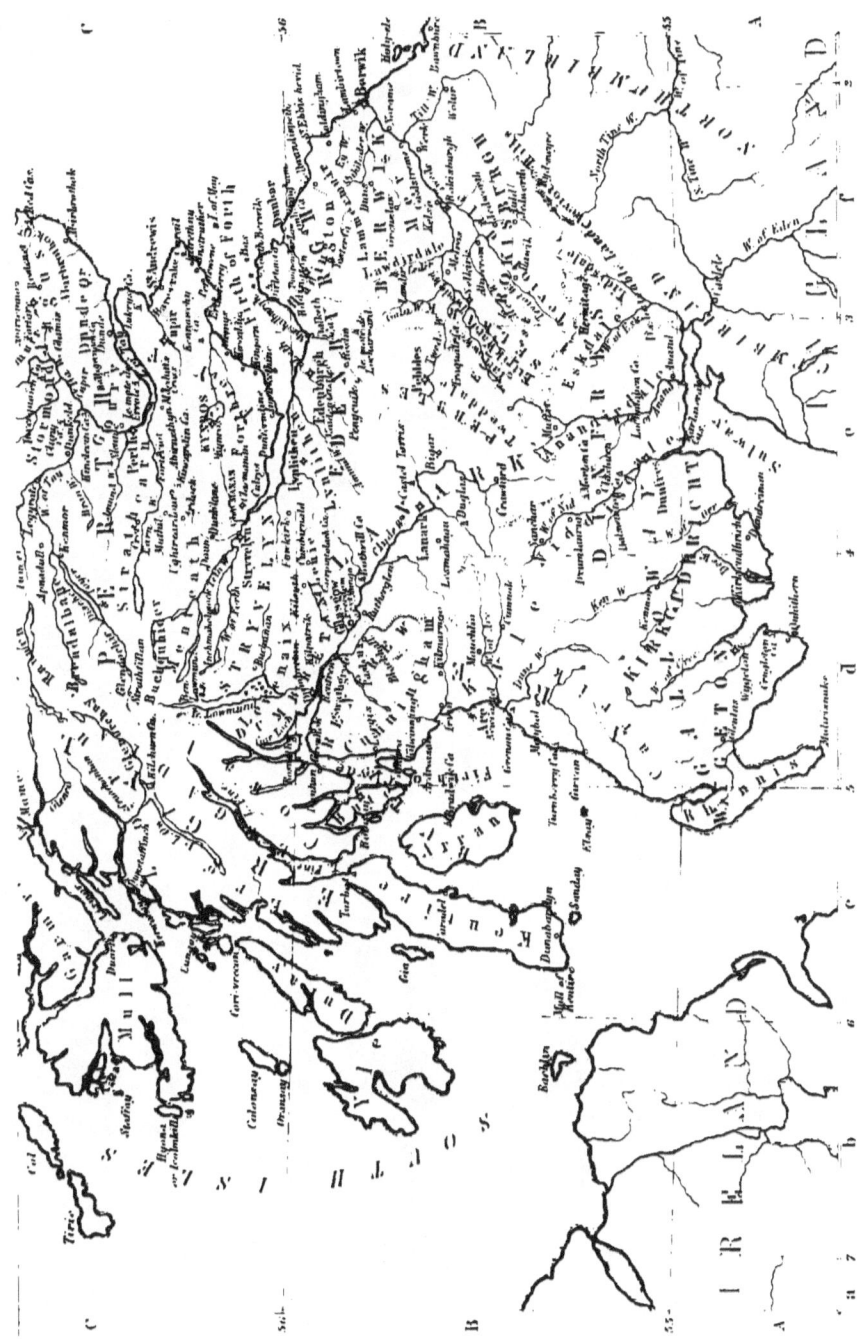

east coast, their occupation was temporary, and almost predatory. Even on the west coast, and among the western isles, where their power was little resisted or disputed, except among themselves, their dominion was that of a continuous stream of pirates successively plundering the country and each other, and scarcely yet approaching to settled and civilized government.

I have ventured to put down our own city of Edinburgh in this map of Scotland of the tenth century. I wish I could also give the local habitation for the city of Giudi, which Bede tells us was *in medio* of our firth; or find names for the capitals of the two nations of the Picts, one of which apparently was low down in the valley of Stratherne, and the other somewhere on the short run of the Ness.

Places indicated in the Map of Scotland in the Tenth Century.

ABERCURNAIG (Abercorn).
Aberdeen
Abernethy.
Alcluid (Dumbarton).
BERNICIA.
Brebanburg (Bamborough).
Brechin.
CLUYD WATER.
Coludesburh (Coldingham).
Cullenros (Culross).
Cumbria.
DEIRA.
Drumalbyn.
Dunkeld.
EDWYNESBURG.
FORTEVIOT.
GALLOWAY (Terra Pictorum).
Glasghu.
HY.

KINNEIL.
Kylreymont (St. Andrews).
LINDISFARN.
Lodene (Lothian).
MAILROS (Melrose).
Mann, Isle of.
Meigle.
NORTH ISLES.
Northern Picts.
Northumbria.
ORKNEYAR.
QUHITHERN (Whithorn).
SCOTS.
Southern Picts.
Stennes.
Strathcluyd.
Sudureyar.
TYREE.

II. SCOTLAND IN THE *THIRTEENTH CENTURY*.

A great change had taken place in the last two centuries. The English tendencies of the sovereigns from Malcolm Canmore downwards, and the stream of southern settlers that overspread the land, had introduced new institutions for distributing justice, protecting trade, property, and person, and along with these, though

b

in some respect opposed to them, the fortified dwellings of the new feudal chivalry.

Though by no means the oldest, the division into sheriffdoms had now become the most important of the civil divisions. Their introduction in Scotland is at least as old as the very beginning of the reign of David I. In 1305—when we find them enumerated in a public ordinance—they already amounted to twenty-five (without counting some shires omitted in the list).

The present map is intended to mark those sheriffdoms, and their subordinate districts; and also those ancient districts, the memory of which has been preserved historically and in the popular use, though unconnected with sheriffdoms, or any existing legal jurisdictions.

And first, with regard to the sheriffdoms, which stand now as they stood in the thirteenth century, with few exceptions—

The northern counties of Caithness, Sutherland, and Ross, were of old under the jurisdiction of the sheriff of Inverness. The act for disuniting them was passed in 1503, but did not take effect till 1641.

Elgin and Forres were anciently separate sheriffdoms.

The sheriffdom of Forfar had four bailiaries, called
1. The Quarter of Dundee,
2. The Quarter of Kirriemuir,
3. The Quarter of Brechin,
4. The Quarter of Arbroath,

each having a *Mair* to whom the sheriff directed his precepts for execution.

The great sheriffdom of Perth had in like manner a division into Quarters, viz.—
1. The Quarter of Stormont,
2. The Quarter of Athol,
3. The Quarter above Isla (*supra Ylef*),

4. The Quarter below Isla (*sub Ylef*),
5. The Quarter of Stratherne,

besides the Quarter of the seven shires of Perth (*quarterium septem schirarum de Perth*) the signification of which, who can tell?—Menteith and Stratherne were separate as to jurisdiction and taxation till last century.

The sheriffdom of Fife was sometimes divided into *quarters :*—
1. The Quarter of Eden.
2. The Constabulary of Craill.
3. The Quarter of Leven.
4. The Quarter of Inverkeithing.
5. The Quarter of Dunfermline.

Linlithgow and Haddington were constabularies comprehended under the sheriffdom of Edinburgh principal.

Lanark, or Clydesdale, had, and still has, three *Wards*,—
1. The Over Waird.
2. The Middle Waird.
3. The Nether Waird.

Ayrshire has for a very long period been divided into the *Bailiaries* of—
1. Kyle.
2. Carrick.
3. Cuninghame.

The upper district of Selkirk is known as The Forest, or Ettrick forest. It had doubtless of old a separate judicial establishment, and we know it was again divided into three *Wards*, called—
1. The Ward of Ettrick.
2. The Ward of Yarrow.
3. The Ward of Tweed.

Berwick is divided into three districts (I know not, if legal divisions),—
1. Merse.
2. Lammermoor.
3. Lauderdale.

The first gave their title to the great Earls of March, who sometimes took their style, and latterly their name, from their castle of Dunbar. Lauderdale was a bailiary, and retained its independent jurisdiction, probably from the ancient regality of the De Morvilles, its old lords.

Argyll has four such districts,—

    1. Lorn,
    2. Argyll proper,
    3. Cowall,[1]
    4. Cantyre,

of which the first two were the lordships of the great ancient families of De Ergadia and Lorn.

With regard to other old districts preserved in popular memory, or historically—

Caithness was an ancient earldom of the Norsemen, from which Sutherland was separated by King Alexander II., and then was made an earldom for the family of De Moravia, who still hold it.

Ross was an ancient mormaership and earldom. Its western shore is called in charters *borealis Ergadia*, North Argyll.

Moray, an ancient mormaership and earldom in the family through which Macbeth claimed the crown of Scotland, was revived as an earldom for Thomas Ranulph, Bruce's nephew. As limited in Ranulph's charter, the earldom extended from the mouth of Spey to the Beaulie, and westward to the west sea, including Glenelg.

Buchan and Marr were ancient mormaerships and earldoms.

The district of Mearns, which also perhaps gave the title of mormaer, seems equivalent to the sheriffdom of Kincardine; perhaps at one time "The Mearns" was limited to the district south of "The Mount," still known as the "Howe of the Mearns."

---

[1] Standing, one day, on the north head of Arran, looking across the firth to Cowall, I asked some Loch Ranza fishermen what was the name of that coast. They pointed to the mouth of Loch Fyne, and said, all from thence to about Dunoon they called "Kerry." Suspecting I misheard. I asked one of them to spell the name, which he did quite scholarly, as here given. I cannot account for the local name.

Angus, an ancient earldom, appears to have been equivalent to the sheriffdom of Forfar. The old earls, perhaps originally mormaers, whose dwelling seems to have been at Kerymore, ended in an heiress, Countess Maud, who, in the thirteenth century, carried the earldom into the house of De Umframvil, great lords of the English border; the same family which held Redesdale *per potestatem gladii*.

Fife, a very ancient earldom.

Lothian, besides the three shires still popularly known as East, West, and Mid-Lothians, included at various times an undefined territory, extending from the Firth of Forth to the English border, and even some way into England.

Lennox (Levenax, or the basin of the Leven) is an ancient earldom, perhaps nearly equivalent to the sheriffdom of Dumbarton.

Stratherne, a very ancient earldom, and in later times a county palatine.

Garviauch, Atholl, Menteith, were ancient earldoms.

The great district of Galloway, within the period of record, continued to be governed with almost independent sway by its native lords; and even after their overthrow, under its ancient customary laws. It was popularly, and perhaps legally, divided into Galloway above Cree, and Galloway below Cree.

In the thirteenth century, the earldom of Carric had grown out of that old lordship, and was now in the family of Bruce, the lords of Annandale.

A word of the castles most noted in the thirteenth century:—

Dunskaith, beside Cromarty, and Edirdouer (now Red-castle), in Ardmanoch, were built by king William the Lion in 1179 for repressing the insurrection in Ross.

Urquhart castle on Loch Ness, at the mouth of its beautiful valley, was at an early period a royal castle, of which successively Durwards, Chisholms, and Lauders are known as keepers.

Duffus and Bocharm were castles of the great lords of Moray.

Ruthven was the head castle of the lordship of Badenoch, for a great part of the thirteenth century, in the hands of John the Red Cumyn.

Lochindorb was a castle of the same great lordship.

The peel of Strathbolgie, the chief castle of the great family of that name, and head of the lordship and district known as the Eight and Forty Davach of Strathbolgie, now Huntly—a name imported by the Gordons from their original country on the Borders.

Fyvie, at an early period a royal castle *and burgh*. The castle passed through the hands of the Prestons and Meldrums, before it acquired its present grandeur from the Chancellor Seton.

Ellon was the *caput comitatus* of Buchan.

Inverury was the head of the Garioch, an earldom in the person of Robert Bruce, by succession to earl David.

Migveth, conjectured by some to have been the *caput comitatus* of the earldom of Mar.

Kildrummy, a magnificent castle on Don side. Sir R. Gordon says it was built by Bishop Gilbert de Moravia, for the Crown. It is best known as a residence of Bruce, who held it apparently in right of his nephew, the Earl of Mar.

Lumphanan, a peel curiously seated near the upper end of the "loch of Lumphanan." Macbeth was slain about a mile to the north of it.

Coul, the chief castle of the great family of Durward.

Durris, a royal residence and royal park, as early as the reign of Alexander III.

Cowie, a royal castle *and burgh*. Charters of the fourteenth century are extant, granting lands for maintaining the causey through the "mount," between Cowie and Aberdeen.

The castle, afterwards known as the craig of Dunnotter, does not appear in charters so early as the period of this map.

Kincardin castle, in the Mearns, a royal castle *and burgh*. Its *park* was enlarged by Bruce. Some of the village tofts and tenements, both here and at Cowie, preserve the names which they acquired from being appropriated to the officers and domestics of the royal court.

Brechin was a castle in the hands of the family of De Brechin, illegitimate descendants of earl David.

The Red-castle on the shore of Lunan bay, was a seat of the De Berkeleys, and in the thirteenth century had come to the Balliols.

Forfar, Glammis, Kinclevin, all royal castles.

Balligernoch, or the Red-castle, a seat of the Cambruns, stood on the verge of what are now the grounds of Rossie priory.

The "Mote of Errol" was a seat of the Hays before they established themselves in Buchan.

Leuchars, a castle of the De Quincys. Their estates fell, in the middle of the thirteenth century, to co-heiresses, two of whom were married to De Ferrers and La Zouche.

Crail a royal castle.

St. Andrews, a bishop's castle, founded in 1206, by bishop Roger (De Leicester).

Kennoquhy and Cupar were castles of the earls of Fife.

Dumbarton castle, a seat of royalty in early times, was the head castle of the earls of Lennox, at the first period of record. It was surrendered to king Alexander II., by earl Maldouen, and has remained a royal castle.

Inch-mahome was an ancient castle, and head of the earldom of Menteith.

Stirling always a royal castle.

Linlithgow castle or "peel," a royal manor and strength.

Carpentoloch, vulgarly Kirkentulloch, an old castle of the Cumyns.

Bothwell, a castle of a family of De Moravia.

Castel-tarres (Carstairs), a fortified house of the bishop of Glasgow. Edward I. granted pardon to the bishop for fortifying it without licence.

Douglas, the head castle of the original lordship of that illustrious name.

Morton, a castle of the thirteenth century, by evidence of its architecture. It was the head castle of Nithsdale, and was granted to Ranulph by king Robert I.

Dalswinton, a castle of the Cumyns. Here, Red John Cumyn resided when Bruce sent Niel and Thomas, his brothers, to bring him to Dumfries.

Lochmaben, the head castle of the great lordship of Annandale.

Crugelton, a castle of the Cumyns. The lead for its roof was brought from the mines of Man, by grant of Edward I.

Turnberry, Bruce's castle, probably the head castle of the earldom of Carric.

Rothesay, a royal castle and fortress from the beginning of the thirteenth century.

Edinburgh, always a royal castle.

Lochorwart (now Borthwick), a castle, first of the Lynes, afterwards of the Hays of Errol. The present building is comparatively modern, being of the fifteenth century.

Lamberton, a castle of the Lindesays, who styled it their "court" (*curia nostra*), and had a private chapel there, before 1212, jealously watched by the parish church.

Whittinghame, a manor of the earls of Dunbar. It was perhaps here that Earl Patrick, in 1231, kept the feast of Christmas, surrounded by his family and neighbours, and bidding them all adieu, received extreme unction and died.

Dunbar, the head castle of the great earldom of March.

Yester, the castle of the Giffords. The present building dates from 1268.

Roxburgh, a royal castle *and burgh*, one of the chief strengths of the kingdom.

Jedburgh, a royal castle, manor, and park, in the time of Alexander III.

Hawic, a castle of the Lovels, who afterwards changed their residence to Angus.

It may be stated, generally, that there was originally a royal castle at every ancient royal burgh.

SCOTLAND IN THE THIRTEENTH CENTURY. XXV

Places indicated in the Civil Map of Scotland of the Thirteenth Century.

[The situation of the place is indicated by *letters*, corresponding to similar *letters* on the margin of the Map.]

Aberdour	Df	Brechin	Cf	Discher	Cd	
Abirbrothok	Cf	Brora Water	Ed	Diurnes	Ed	
Abirdene	Df	Brum Loch	Dc	Don Water	Df	
Abirdene, Sheriffdom of	Df	Buchan	Df	Dornok	Dd	
		Buchanan	Cd	Doveran Water	Df	
Abir Loch	Cc	Buchannes	Dg	Doun	Cd	
Abirlemno	Cf	Buchquhider	Cd	Drumlanrig	Bc	
Abirnethy	Dc	Burgh	De	Duart	Cc	
Abirnethyn	Ce	Bute, Sheriffdom of	Bc	Duffus Castle	De	
Aboyne	Df			Duglas	Be	
Aird, The	Dd	CÆRPINTOLACH		Dumbretan	Bd	
Ale Water	Bf	CASTLE	Bd	Dumbretan, Sheriffdom of	Bd	
Allan	Dd	Cairn of Month	Cf			
Alnecrom	Bf	Caldstreme	Bf	Dunbar	Cf	
Amund Water	Ce	Carail	Cf	Dunbardyn	Bc	
Anand	Be	Carndel	Bc	Dunblane	Cc	
Anandirdale	Be	Carnwall Pass	Cc	Dunde	Cf	
Andrewis, St.	Cf	Carrik	Bd	Dundreinan	Ae	
Angus	Cf	Castel Tarris	Bc	Dun Echt	Df	
Angus, Braes of	Cc	Catness	Ed	Dune Water	Bd	
Anstruther	Cf	Cheviot Hills	Bf	Dunfermline	Cc	
Apnadull	Cd	Clacmanan	Cc	Dunfres	Bc	
Ardersier	Dd	Clacmanan, Sheriffdom of	Ce	Dunfres, Sheriffdom of	Be	
Ardnamorchin	Cb					
Ardoch	Ce	Closburn	Be	Dungalsby	Ef	
Ardrossan	Bd	Col	Cb	Dunhun	Bd	
Are	Bd	Colbrandispeth	Bf	Dunnottyr Castle	Cf	
Are, Sheriffdom of	Bd	Coldingham	Bf	Dunpender Law	Bf	
Are Water	Bd	Colonsay	Cb	Dunrobin	Ec	
Arran	Bc	Conan Water	Dd	Duns	Bf	
Assynt	Ec	Cori-vrecan	Cc	Dunscath Castle	De	
Athol	Ce	Coul Castle	Df	Dunstaffinch Castle	Cc	
		Cowal	Cc	Dunvegan	Db	
BADANOCH	Dd	Cowie Castle	Df	Duray	Bc	
Balligernach Castle	Ce	Crawfurd	Be	Durris Castle	Df	
Banf	Df	Crechmond	Dg			
Banf, Sheriffdom of	De	Cree Water	Ad	EARN WATER	Cc	
Bares-rake	Cf	Cref	Ce	Ebbis-hevid, St.	Bf	
Barray	Ca	Cromar	Df	Edenburgh	Bc	
Bas Rock	Cf	Cromdale	De	Edenburgh, Sheriffdom of	Be	
Battock Mount	Df	Cruachanban	Cc			
Bawnburch	Bg	Crugleton Castle	Ad	Ederachylis	Ed	
Ben Lowmund	Cd	Crumbachty	Dd	Edirdovar or Red Castle	Dd	
Ben Nevis	Cd	Crumbachty, Sheriffdom of	Dd	Eggay	Cb	
Berwik	Bg					
Berwik, Sheriffdom of	Bf	Cupir (Angus)	Ce	Elgyn	De	
Bervy	Cf	Cupir (Fife)	Ce	Elgyn, Sheriffdom of	De	
Beulie	Dd	Cuillin-hillis	Db	Ellon	Df	
Bigar	Be	Cullen	Df	Elsay	Bc	
Black Isle	Dd	Culros	Ce	Enyie	Df	
Blackhall	Bd	Cumbra	Bd	Ergadia	Cc	
Blare Castle	Ce	Cumnok	Bd	Erin or Findarn Water	Dd	
Bocharin Castle	De	Cuningham	Bd	Ergyle, Sheriffdom of	Cc	
Borealis Ergadia	Dc			Erlisferry	Cf	
Bothvill Castle	Bd	DALKETH CASTLE	Be	Errick Loch	Cd	
Boyn	Df	Dalswinton Castle	Be	Errole, C mote de	Ce	
Braemar	De	Dee Water	Df	Eskdale	Be	
Bradwik Castle	Bc	Dere	Df	Ettrik Forest	Be	
Bran Water	Ce	Dingwall	Dd	Ettrik Ward	Be	
Breadalbane	Cd	Dirleton Castle	Cf	Ey Water	Bf	

Far	Ed	Jedworth	Bf	Lumphanan Pele	Df
Fawkirk	Ce			Lungay	Cc
Fermartin	Df	Kannay	Db	Lynlitheu	Be
Fine Loch	Cc	Karlaverak Castle	Ae	Lynlitheu, Sheriffdom of	Be
Fintray	Df	Kelso	Bf		
Fivy	Df	Kenmor	Bd	Macduff's Cross	Ce
Forcis	De	Kenmor	Ce	Mamor	Cc
Forcis, Sheriffdom of	De	Ken Water	Bd	Maryculter	Df
Forfare	Cf	Kentire	Bc	Mauchlin	Bd
Forfare, Sheriffdom of	Cf	Kerwaray	Cc	May, Isle of	Cf
Forn Water	Dd	Kerymuir	Ce	Maybol	Bd
Forteviot	Ce	Kyle	Bd	Melros	Bf
Forth, Firth of	Cf	Kynkardyn	Cf	Menteath	Cd
Forth Water	Cd	Kynkardyn, Sheriffdom		Mernis	Cf
Forthrev	Cc	of	Cf	Mers	Bf
Foyer	Cd	Kynros	Cc	Month, The (Montes	
Freedom of St. Mungo	Bd	Kynros, Sheriffdom of	Cc	Scotiæ)	Ce
Fyf, Sheriffdom of	Ce	Kilchurn Castle	Cd	Moray	De
		Kilmarnoc	Bd	Moristan Water	Dd
Gala Water	Bf	Kilpatrik	Bd	Morton Castle	Be
Galloway	Bd	Kilrethny	Cf	Mount Keen Pass	Cf
Gar Loch	Cd	Kilsyth	Bd	Moffet	Be
Garmoran	Cc	Kildrummy Castle	Df	Muidart	Cc
Garvyach	Df	Kincardin	De	Mulirisnuke	Ad
Gia	Bc	Kincardin Castle	Ce	Mull	Cb
Girvan	Bd	Kinclevin Castle	Ce	Mull of Kentire	Bc
Glamis	Cf	Kingorn	Ce	Munross (Montrose)	Cf
Glasgow	Bd	Kingussie	Dd	Muskilburgh	Bc
Glenco	Cc	Kinnef	Cf	Muthil	Ce
Glendochir	Cd	Kinneil	Ce	Mygveth	De
Glencarny	De	Kintail	Dc		
Glenelg	De	Kintor	Df	Narn Water	Dd
Glenlus	Ad	Kircaldie	Ce	Ness Loch	Dd
Glenurchay	Cd	Kirkwall	Ef	Niddisdale	Be
Goury	Ce	Kirkcudbright	Ad	Norame	Bf
Grenan Castle	Bd	Kirkcudbright, Sheriff-		North Berwick	Cf
Grenelaw	Bf	dom of	Bd	North Esk Water	Cf
				North Isles	Db
Hadington	Bf	Lambirtown	Bf	North Ywst	Da
Haey	Ee	Lammermuir	Bf		
Haly-elend	Bg	Lagan Loch	Cd	Okel Water	Ed
Haulkirk	Ee	Lanark	Be	Orkney Isles	Ef
Harray	Db	Lanark, Sheriffdom of	Bc	Oran Water	Dd
Hawik	Bf	Lang Island	Da	Oronsay	Cb
He	Bb	Largis	Bd	Orr Water	Ae
Hermitage	Bf	Lawdir	Bf	Ow, Loch	Cc
Huarf	Ed	Ledir Water	Bf		
Hyona	Cb	Leuie	Bd	Pasley	Bd
		Lesmahagu	Be	Peebles	Be
Icolmkill	Cb	Leth	Be	Peebles, Sheriffdom of	Be
Ila Water	Ce	Lawdirdale	Bf	Penycuik	Bc
Inchmaholmock	Cd	Lismor	Cc	Perth	Ce
Invernarn	De	Leodhuis (Lewis)	Eb	Perth, Sheriffdom of	Ce
Invernarn, Sheriffdom		Levenaix	Cd	Petlandisfiord	Ec
of	De	Lidisdale	Bf	Petnewene	Cf
Inverness	Dd	Lochabir	Cd		
Inverness, Sheriffdom		Locharward, C mote de	Bc	Quhitader Water	Bf
of	Dd	Lochindorb	Dc	Quhithern	Ad
Inverquoich Castle	Ce	Lochmaben Castle	Bc	Quhitingham Castle	Bf
Invirculan	Df	Lochy Loch	Cd		
Invirkethine	Ce	Logyrate	Ce	Ranach	Cd
Invirlochy Castle	Cd	Lorn	Cc	Rasay	Db
Iuvirury	Df	Lowmund, Loch	Cd	Red Castle	Cf
Irvin	Bd	Lukrys Castle	Cf	Red Castle	Dd
				Renfrew	Bd

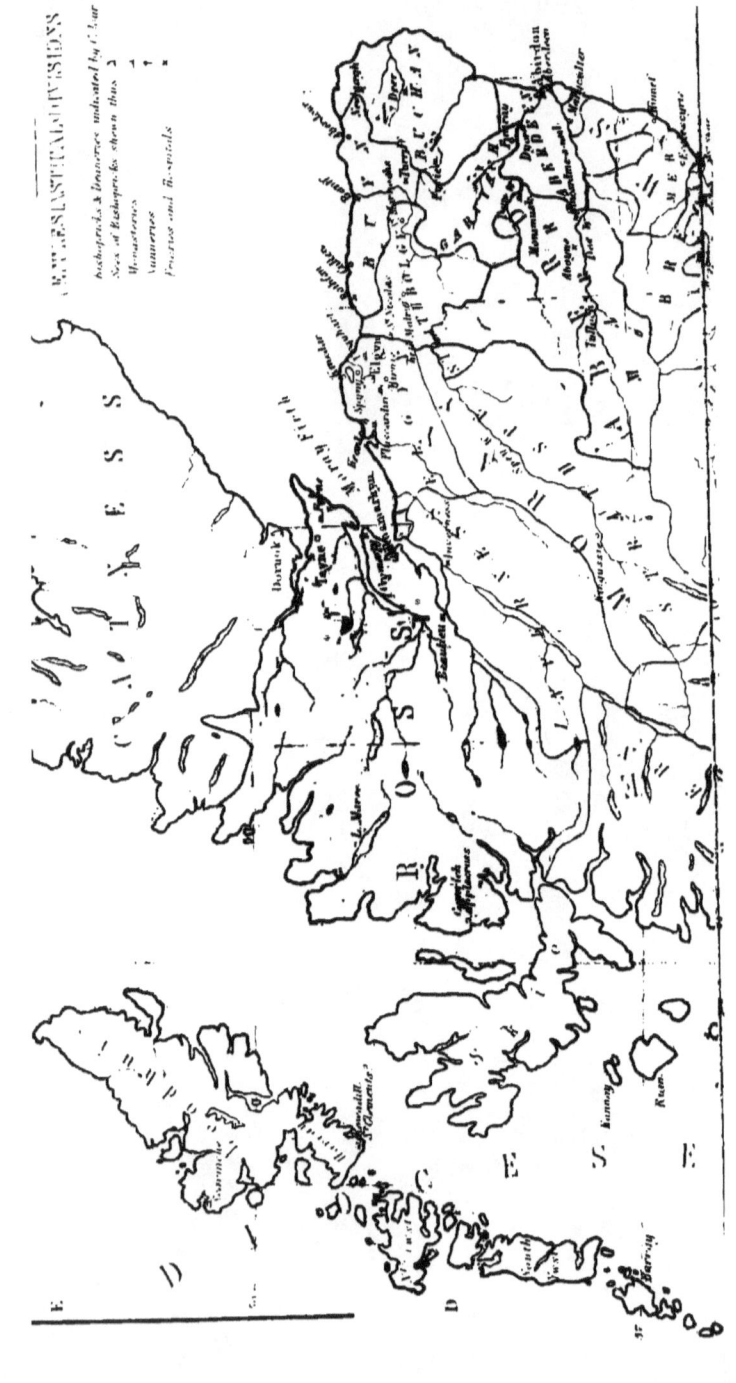

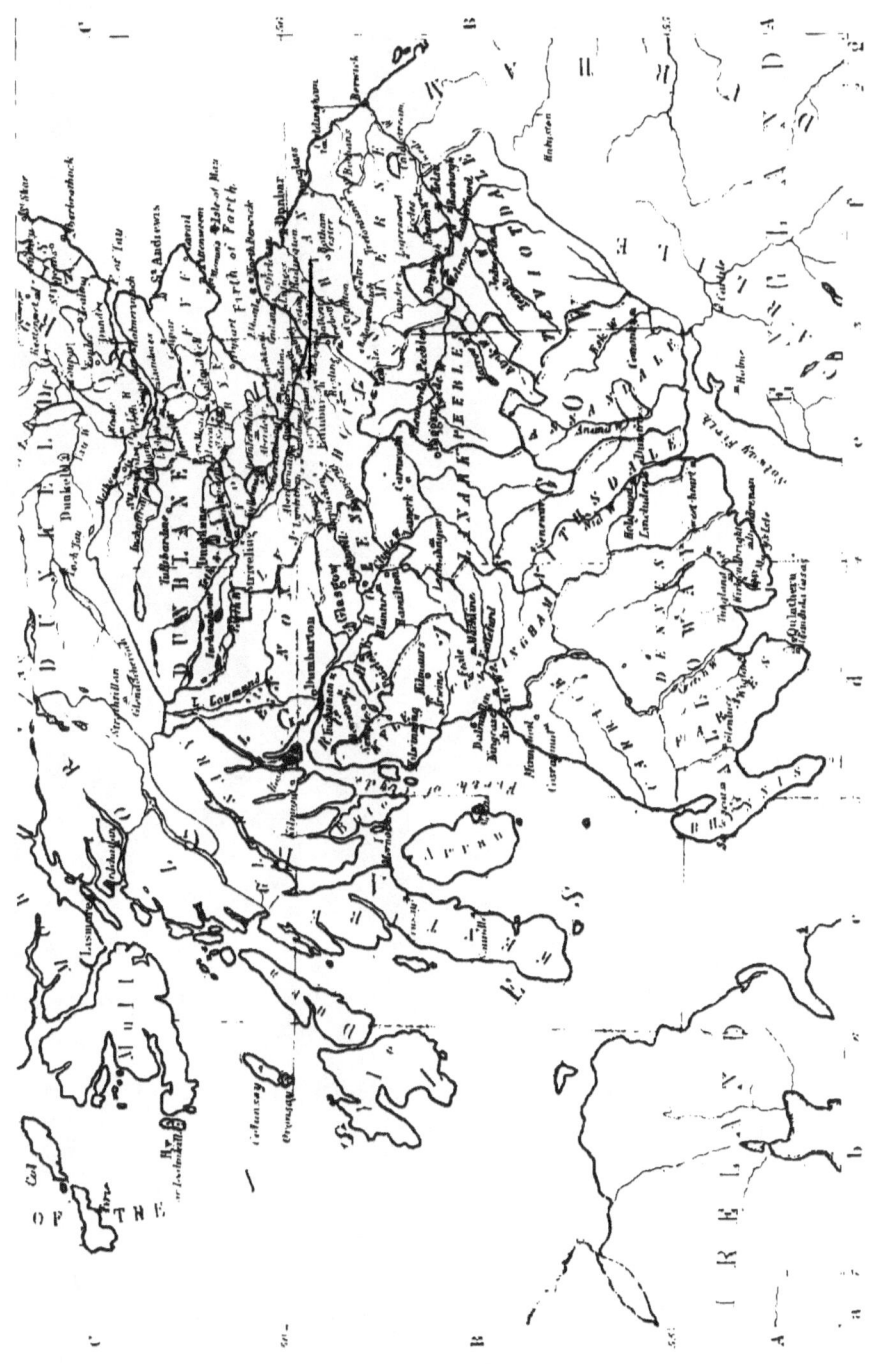

SCOTLAND IN THE THIRTEENTH CENTURY. xxvii

Renfrew, Sheriffdom of	Bd	Skie	Db	Teth Water	Cd
Restenet	Cf	Skune	Ce	Teviotdale	Bf
Rhynnis	Ac	Sleuis Castle	Dg	Thurso	Ee
Roguvaldsay	Ef	Spean Water	Cd	Till Water	Bf
Rokisburgh	Bf	Spey Water	De	Tirie	Cb
Rokisburgh, Sheriffdom of	Bf	South Esk Water	Cf	Traquair Castle	Be
		South Isles	Bb	Tumel Water	Cd
Ronay	Dc	South Ywst	Da	Tung	Ed
Roslin	Be	Staffay	Cb	Turnberry Castle	Bd
Rosmarkyn	Dd	Stonehyve	Cf	Turrif	Df
Rosueth	Cd	Stormond	Ce	Tweddale	Be
Ross	Dc	Strathavon	De	Twede Water	Bf
Rothemay	Df	Strathbolgy	Df		
Rothes	De	Strathbolgy Peel	Df	UILIE WATER	Ee
Rothsay	Bc	Strathdee	De	Ughtreardour	Ce
Rum	Cb	Strathearn	Ce	Ulva	Cb
Rutherglen	Bd	Strathfillan	Cd	Urchart Castle	Dd
Ruthven Castle	Dd	Strathgryfe	Bd		
Ryd-swyre	Bf	Strathnaver	Ed	WEMYS	Ce
		Strathspey	De	Werk	Bf
SANCHAR	Bc	Stryvelyn	Ce	Wik	Ee
Sanday	Bc	Stryvelyn, Sheriffdom of		Wolur	Bf
Sandvik	De		Cd	Wygeton	Ad
Schie Water	Ce	Suthirland	Ed	Wygeton, Sheriffdom of	Ad
Selkirk	Bf				
Selkirk, Sheriffdom of	Bf	TARBAT	Bc		
Sheil Loch	Cc	Tarfnes	De	YARROW WARD	Be
Shin Loch	Ed	Tane	Dd	Yell Loch	Cc
Sikirsund	Dd	Tay Water	Ce	Yester Castle	Bf

III. SCOTLAND IN THE *THIRTEENTH CENTURY*

With its Ecclesiastical Divisions.

The dioceses are—

1. ST. ANDREWS, a bishoprick of unknown, but very high antiquity, being a continuation of a Pictish bishoprick, perhaps of a different see, perhaps of a jurisdiction without settled seat.[1] The chapter, at first Culdees, were afterwards canons regular of St. Austin. The diocese was divided by the firth into the Archdeaconries of—

(1.) St. Andrews principal, comprehending the rural deaneries of—

   1. Fife.
   2. Fothrif.
   3. Gowrie.
   4. Angus.
   5. Mearns.

[1] The bishops of St. Andrews were made primatial about 1470.

(2.) Lothian, having jurisdiction over the rural deaneries of—
1. Lothian or Haddington.
2. Linlithgow.
3. Merse.

2. The bishoprick of DUNKELD, also of high and mysterious antiquity and authority. Engrafted on an ancient Columbite foundation, and especially after the destruction of Hy, wielding the authority of St. Columba, this bishoprick was, until the thirteenth century, of great extent, embracing the whole of Argyll. Even after the diocese of Argyll was taken out of it, Dunkeld, for the love and reverence of its patron, reserved to itself the island of Hy, though so far removed, and the island of St. Colm in our firth, besides several parishes on both sides of the firth.[1] The chapter at first consisted of Culdees and canons regular.

This diocese was divided into the rural deaneries of—
1. Atholl and Drumalbane.
2. Angus.
3. Fife, Fothrif, and Stratherne.
4. South of the Firth (*in partibus australibus*).

3. The bishoprick of ABERDEEN, founded in the middle of the twelfth century at Aberdon (now old Aberdeen), by David I., who transferred to it the property and some of the respect of an old monastery at Mortlach in Glenfiddich. The patron is Saint Machar, a follower of Saint Columba. In the thirteenth century, the diocese of Aberdeen contained three rural deaneries—
1. Mar,
2. Buchan,
3. Garviauch,

which were afterwards arranged into five: Aberdeen, Mar, Garviauch, Buchan, and Boyne.

4. MORAY, a bishoprick before the time of David I. At first, the diocese had no defined see. After being successively changed

---

[1] The connection of Dunkeld with its churches in Lothian and Fife, would form a very curious subject of research.

to Birny, Kinneddor, and Spynie, it was settled in the church of the Holy Trinity, beside Elgin, in 1224; and then was begun that glorious cathedral, which has survived through fire and violence and long neglect, to recall some memory of the taste and religious feeling of an age called unenlightened. The diocese of Moray was divided into four rural deaneries:—

    1. Elgin.
    2. Inverness.
    3. Strathspey.
    4. Strathbolgy.

5. BRECHIN, the seat of an old abbey of Culdees, whose abbots had become hereditary, was erected by David I. into a bishoprick in the middle of the twelfth century; the Culdees forming the bishops' chapter. The diocese was small, and had no subordinate divisions for rural deans.

6. DUNBLANE, sometimes called the bishoprick of Stratherne. An old Culdee house and a previous bishoprick, had fallen into decay, when, at the beginning of the thirteenth century, Gilbert, earl of Stratherne, restored or founded the bishoprick of Dunblane. The chapter was of Regulars. The property of the bishops was held *in capite* of the great earls down to the fifteenth century, when their rights merged in the Crown.

7. Ross. This bishoprick was founded or restored by David I. early in the twelfth century, the cathedral at Rosmarkie being under the invocation of Saint Peter and Saint Boniface. The diocese of Ross met the bishoprick of Moray at the "water of Forn" (Beaulie.)

8. CAITHNESS. This diocese, including the whole *ancient* earldom of Caithness, had for its cathedral and see, the church of St. Fymbar of Dornoch. The date of its foundation is not known, but it existed in the beginning of the twelfth century.

9. GLASGOW, one of the bishopricks restored and re-endowed by David I., while still only Prince of Cumbria, c. 1116. At that time the jury of the *seniores homines et sapientiores totius Cumbriæ*,

tracing back the first institution of the see to Saint Kentigern, in the sixth century, declared its right to numerous possessions, in virtue of that primæval institution; and their verdict received effect. Glasgow had two archdeaconries :—

(1.) Glasgow proper, comprehending the rural deaneries of—
    1. Rutherglen.
    2. Lennox.
    3. Lanark.
    4. Kyle and Cuninghame.
    5. Carric.

(2.) The archdeaconry of Teviotdale, including the deaneries of—
    1. Teviotdale.
    2. Peebles.
    3. Nithsdale.
    4. Annandale.[1]

10. GALLOWAY. The see was Whithern (*candida casa*), and the bishop took his Latin style from that church, founded and dedicated to Saint Martin of Tours by St. Ninian, the apostle of the Picts, in the fifth century. The chapter was composed of the canons regular of the priory of Whithern. The diocese had three deaneries, the names of which are now almost forgotten :—
    1. Desnes.
    2. Farnes.
    3. Rinnes.

11. ARGYLL, sometimes called the diocese of Lismore from its episcopal see, was erected in the beginning of the thirteenth century out of the great bishoprick of Dunkeld. It contained the deaneries of—
    1. Kintyre.
    2. Glassary.
    3. Lorn.
    4. Morven.

---

[1] Glasgow was made an archbishoprick in 1491; its suffragans being the bishops of Dunkeld, Dunblane, Galloway, Argyll, and Isles.

SCOTLAND IN THE THIRTEENTH CENTURY. xxxi

12. ISLES. The bishoprick of the Isles at first included Man with all the western isles, and was subject and suffragan to the archbishops of Drontheim. After coming for a time under the jurisdiction of Scotland, it again suffered a change in the fourteenth century, when the other western isles (*the Sudoreyar*) were separated from Man, which was now subject to England. The abbey church of Hy, or Iona, in the fifteenth century became the cathedral and bishop's see of the Scotch bishoprick called the bishoprick of the Isles or Sodor.

Places indicated in the Ecclesiastical Map.

ABERBROTHOK (now Arbroath), an abbey of Tyronensian Benedictines and Burgh   Cf
Abercurnaig (Abercorn), ancient monastery and seat of a Pictish bishop in Bede's time   Ce
Aberdeen, deanery of diocese of
Aberdon   Df
Aberdour (in Fife), a Franciscan nunnery   Ce
Abernethy, a house of Culdees, and probably an ancient bishop's see. In 13th century a priory of canons regular under Inchaffray   Ce
Aboyne, a house of the Knights Templars, afterwards of the knights of St. John   Df
Ayr   Bd
Andrews, St., diocese of   Cf
Andrewis, St., a priory of canons regular, coming in place of Culdees   Cf
Angus, deanery of   Cf
Annandale, deanery of   Be
Applecross (Apurcrossan, Comrich), an ancient foundation of St. Malruve.   De
Ardchattan, a priory of Cistercians of the order of *vallis caulium*   Ce
Arniston, *see* Balantradoch

BALANTRADOCH (now Arniston). A house of the Templars, and later, of the Knights of St. John of Jerusalem   Be
Ballincrieff, an hospital dedicated to Saint Cuthbert   Be
Balmerinach, an abbey of Cistercians   Cf
Banff, a convent of Carmelite friars   Df
Beaulieu, a priory of Cistercians of *vallis caulium*   Dd
Berwick, an hospital of Trinity friars   Bf

Berwick, North, a convent of Cistercian nuns   Cf
Biggar   Be
Birnie   De
Blantire, a priory of canons regular subject to Holyrood   Bd
Botham   Bf
Botham's, St. (Abbey St. Bathan's), a convent of Cistercian nuns   Bf
Bothwell   Bd
Brechin, deanery of   Cf
Buchan, deanery of   Df
Buyn, deanery of   Df

CAITHNESS, diocese of   Ed
Cambuskenneth, an abbey of canons regular   Ce
Candida Casa   Ad
Canonby, a priory of canons regular subject to Jedburgh   Bf
Carail.   Cf
Carlisle, diocese of   Af
Carnwath   Be
Carrick, deanery of   Bd
Carlile   Af
Clements, St.   Db
Coldingham, anciently a nunnery, afterwards a priory of Benedictine monks subject to Durham   Bf
Colmoc, St., a priory of canons regular subject to Cambuskenneth.   Cd
Coldstream, a convent of Cistercian nuns   Bf
Colme Inch, *see* Inchcolme   Ce
Colonsay, a priory of canons regular subject to Holyrood   Cb
Comrich, *see* Applecross   De
Corstorphin   Be
Crichton   Bf
Cromarty   Dd
Crosragmol (Crossregal), an abbey of Cluniac Benedictines   Bd
Cullen   Df

Culross, a Cistercian abbey　Ce
Cupar (in Angus), an abbey of Cistercians　Ce
Cupar (in Fife), a convent of Dominican friars　Ce

DALKEITH　Be
Dalmullin, a monastery of canons and nuns of the order of Simpringham; afterwards belonging to Paisley. Also a convent of Benedictine nuns　Bd
Deir, an ancient Columbite house. Afterwards an abbey of Cistercians　Df
Desnes, deanery of　Bd
Dirleton　Cf
Dornock, an hospital of Trinity friars　Dd
Dryburgh, an abbey of Præmonstratensian Augustinians　Bf
Dumfries, a convent of Franciscan friars　Be
Dumbarton　Bd
Dumfermling, an ancient Culdee house. Afterwards an abbey of Benedictines　Ce
Dunbar, an hospital of Trinity friars, and a convent of Carmelite friars　Cf
Dunblane　Ce
Dunblane, diocese of　Cd
Dundee, an hospital of Trinity friars. A convent of Franciscan friars　Cf
Dundrenan, an abbey of Cistercians　Ae
Dunglas　Bf
Dunkeld, diocese of　Ce
Durham, diocese of　Bg
Dyce　Df
Dysart　Ce

ECCLES, a convent of Cistercian nuns　Bf
Ecclescyric　Cf
Edinburgh　Be
Ednam, an hospital dedicated to Saint Laurence　Bf
Elbottle, a convent of Cistercian nuns　Cf
Elchow, a convent of Cistercian nuns　Ce
Elgyn　De
Elgyn, deanery of　De
Erusay　Be

FAILEFURD, an hospital of Trinity friars　Bd
Farnes, deanery of　Ad
Feale, a priory of Cluniac monks; a cell of Paisley　Bd
Ferne, an abbey of Præmonstratensian Augustinians　De
Fintray　Df
Fothryf, deanery of　Cf
Foulis　Ce
Fyf, deanery of　Cf

Fyvie, a priory of Tyronensians; a cell of Arbroath　Df

GALLOWAY, diocese of　Bd
Garuiach, deanery of　Df
Germains, St., a house of Knights Templars, afterwards of Knights of St. John, latterly granted to King's College, Aberdeen　Bf
Glasgow, diocese of　Be
Glassary, deanery of　Ce
Glendocheroch　Cd
Glenluce, an abbey of Cistercians　Ad
Goury, deanery of　Ce
Gulane, a convent of Cistercian nuns　Cf
Guthry　Cf

HADDINGTON, a convent of Franciscan friars; a convent of Cistercian nuns　Bf
Halyston, a priory of Benedictine nuns　Bf
Hamilton　Bd
Holme-Cultram, a monastery of Cistercians　Ae
Holyrood, an abbey of canons regular　Be
Holywood (Dercongal) Sacri nemoris, de sacro bosco. An abbey of Præmonstratensian Augustinians　Be
Howston, an hospital of Trinity friars　Bd
Hy (Iona, Icolumkille). The ancient foundation of St. Columba having been destroyed, an abbey was founded in the twelfth century, of Cluniac Benedictines; also a nunnery of canonesses of St. Augustin　Cb

INCHCOLME, an abbey of canons regular, founded by King Alexander 1.　Cb
Inchaffray, an abbey of canons regular, founded by Gilbert, Earl of Stratherne　Ce
Inchkeith　Ce
Inchmahome, a priory of canons regular subject to Cambuskenneth　Cd
Inchynan, a house of Templars, afterwards of Knights of St. John of Jerusalem　Bd
Inverkeithing, a convent of Franciscan friars　Ce
Inverness, deanery of　Dd
Irwine, a convent of Carmelite friars　Bd
Isles, diocese of the　Cb

JEDBURGH, an abbey of canons regular　Bf

KINLOSS, an abbey of Cistercians　De

SCOTLAND IN THE THIRTEENTH CENTURY. xxxiii

Kelso, a great abbey of Tyronensian Benedictines, originally seated at Selkirk — Bf
Kentire, deanery of — Bc
Keth Malruf — De
Kilmaures — Bd
Kilmund — Cd
Kilwinning, an abbey of Tyronensian Benedictines — Bd
Kincardine-o-neil, an hospital — Df
Kinedar — De
Kinef — Cf
Kingcase, an hospital — Bd
Kingussie — Dd
Kirkcudbright, a convent of Franciscan friars — Ad
Kirkwall — Be
Kyle and Cunningham, deanery of — Bd

LANARK, deanery of — Be
Lanark, a convent of Franciscan friars; an hospital dedicated to St. Leonard — Be
Lauder, an hospital — Bf
Leith, priory of canons of St. Anthony — Be
Lennox, deanery of — Cd
Leonards, St. (beside Edinburgh), an hospital — Be
Leonards, St. (beside Peebles), a convent of Cistercian nuns; an hospital — Be
Lesmahagow, a priory of Tyronensians; a cell of Kelso — Be
Leven, Loch, a house of Culdees, and afterwards a priory of canons regular — Ce
Lincluden, a convent of Benedictine nuns — Be
Lismore — Cc
Ligerswood, an hospital — Bf
Lorn, deanery of — Cc
Louthian, deanery of — Bf
Lufness, an hospital of Trinity friars — Cf
Lundores, an abbey of Tyronensian Benedictines — Ce
Lynlithcu, a convent of Carmelite friars; an hospital of Lazarites dedicated to St. Mary Magdalene — Be
Lynlithcu, deanery of — Be

MACHLINE, a Cistercian house; a cell of Melrose — Bd
Magdalene — Be
Manuel, a convent of Cistercian nuns — Be
Maree, L. — Dc
Marnochs, St. — Df
Marr, deanery of — Dc
Maryculter, a house of the Templars, afterwards of the Knights of St. John of Jerusalem — Df
Mary, St., isle (S. Mariæ de Trayll), a priory of canons regular subject to Holyrood — Bd

May, isle of, of old a cell of Reading, in England; afterwards a priory of canons regular, dedicated to St. Adrian — Cf
Maybole (Minniboil) — Bd
Melross, a Columbite monastery in the time of Bede; afterwards an abbey of Cistercians — Bf
Mernis, deanery of — Cf
Mernoch, L. — Bc
Merse, deanery of — Bf
Methven — Ce
Minniboil (Maybole) — Bd
Molas, L. — Bc
Monans, St., a convent of Dominican friars — Cf
Monimusk, a house of Culdees; later, a priory of canons regular subject to St. Andrews — Df
Montrose — Cf
Moray, diocese of — De
Morvern, deanery of — Cc

NEWBOTTLE, an abbey of Cistercians — Be
Newburgh (in Buchan), an hospital — Df
Nithsdale, deanery of — Be

OGGERSTON, a house of the Templars; afterwards of the Knights of St. John
Orkney (diocese of) — Ee
Oronsay, a priory of canons regular subject to Holyrood — Cb

PAISLEY, a great abbey of Cluniac Benedictines — Bd
Peebles the Ministry or Cross Church, a hospital of Trinity friars — Be
Peebles, deanery of — Be
Pentlandisflord — Ee
Perth — Ce
Pittenweem, a priory of canons regular subject to St. Andrews — Cf
Pluscardin, at first a priory of Cistercian monks of *Vallis caulium*; afterwards a cell of Dunfermline — De
Port Moack, a priory of canons regular; a cell of St. Andrews — Ce

QUEENSFERRY, a convent of Carmelite friars — Ce

RESCOBIE — Cf
Restalrig — Be
Restennot, a priory of canons regular subject to Jedburgh — Cf
Rhynnis, deanery of — Ad
Rosline — Be
Roseneth — Cd
Rothfan, a leper hospital — Df
Rowadill, a priory of canons regular subject to Holyrood — Db
Roxburgh, a convent of Franciscan friars. An hospital or Maison Dieu — Bf

c

Rutherfoord, an hospital dedicated to St.
 Mary Magdalene   Bf
Rutherglen, deanery of   Bd

St. Margaret's Inch. (Forfar)   Cf
Saundle (Sadael), a Cistercian abbey   Bc
Scarinche, a priory of canons regular
 subject to Inchaffray   Ea
Scone, an abbey of canons regular   Ce
Scotland Well, an hospital of Trinity
 friars   Ce
Semple   Bd
Senewar (Sanquhar), an hospital   Bc
Serf, St.   Ce
Seton   Bf
Skae, St.   Cf
Soltra, an hospital for poor and sick, and
 for travellers   Bf
Souls-seat, an abbey of Præmonstraten-
 sian Augustinians   Ad
Spey, St. Nicolas, at the bridge of, an
 hospital for poor travellers   De
Spyny   De
Strathfillan, a priory of canons regular
 subject to Inchaffray   Cd
Strathbolgy, deanery of   De
Strathspey, deanery of   De
Striveling, hospital of St. James, at the
 end of the bridge   Ce
Suggeden (Seggieden), an hospital dedi-
 cated to St. Augustin   Cc
Sweetheart, an abbey of Cistercians   Ae

Tay, Loch, a priory of canons regular   Cd

Tayne   Dd
Tealing   Cf
Temple, a house of the Knights Tem-
 plars; later, of the Knights of St.
 John of Jerusalem   Be
Teviotdale, deanery of   Bf
Torphicen, an hospital, preceptory and
 chief house of the Knights of St.
 John of Jerusalem in Scotland   Be
Trefontain, a convent of Cistercian
 nuns   Bf
Tullibardine   Ce
Tullilum, a convent of Carmelite
 friars   Ce
Tulloch, a house of Templars, after-
 wards of Knights of St. John of
 Jerusalem   De
Tungland, a monastery of Præmonstra-
 tensian Augustinians   Bd
Turriff, an hospital for twelve poor
 men   Df

Urquhart, priory of Benedictines, subject to Dunfermline   De

Vigeans, St.   Cf

Whithern (Candida Casa), a priory of
 Præmonstratensian Augustinians,
 who were the chapter of the Cathedral   Ad
Wigton   Ad

Yester   Bf

CONTENTS.

CHAPTER I.

INTRODUCTORY 1

Modern political society originating with the era of Charlemagne—The state of Europe in his time—The population — Celts — Franks — Sclaves — Wends — Bavarians — Northmen or Danes—Saxons—Teutonic races—Superstitions of the Northmen—Virtues of the Germans—Saint Boniface's Catechism—Pagan Saxon prayer—The Moors — Their accomplishments — Their activity and enterprise—The Lombards—Rome—Her missions and adoption of co-operating missionaries—Her danger from the Arian heresy—The Church, its influence and power—Used for the advantage of mankind—Constantinople and the Eastern empire—The dominions of Charlemagne—Vestiges of Roman Institutions—Municipia—Defects of those institutions for patriotic union—Charlemagne himself, his appearance, habits, dress, arms, ornaments—The amount of his education—His buildings, fleets, his ordinances, his country houses—His gardens, flowers, fruit trees, poultry, game—His ordinance for schools—Keeping of Sunday—Preaching—Charlemagne the champion of Christianity—Saxon Resistance—Duke Radbod—Witikind—Final subjugation of the Saxons—Charlemagne's other triumphs—Harun-el-Rashid's, and the Greek Emperor's embassies—Crowned as Cæsar—His achievements.

CHAPTER II.

INTRODUCTORY 35

Growth of the feudal system—Later Carlovingians without power—The feudal vassals become independent—Counts of Paris—Hugh Capet crowned king of the French—Settlement of the Normans in France—Old Britain; what remains of Ante-Roman Britain—Language, Institutions—The Normans in France—Their change of manners when settled—Readily adopt feudalism and the privileges of seignory—The Romans in Britain—Their civilization—Roman villas in Britain—Roman towns, roads, bridges——Britain Christianized—Roman colonization gave no independence or self-government—Roman civilization obliterated—The Saxons in Britain—Hengist and Horsa apocryphal—Jutes—Angles—Saxons—Other Teutons—Frisians—King Arthur the only British hero—Anglo-Saxon institutions—King—Hereditary nobility, Thane, Alderman—Churl—Serf—Property of the soil—Folcland—Bocland—Subdivisions and meetings—*Scir-gemot*—Great assembly of the nation—Christianity restored—Wholesale conversions—Edwin of Northumbria—Caefi, the high priest—Rome endeavours to win over the British Bishops—In vain—Saxon missionaries on the Continent—Alfred—Cnut—The Danes and English—The Norman conquest—The Normans in England—Composition of the army of invasion—Causes of its success—Why the Anglo-Saxon language and institutions prevailed over those of the conquerors.

CHAPTER III.

SCOTLAND—EARLIEST HISTORY 77

Earliest Writing—Charters—Chronicles—Old Scotch collections of laws—The Berne MS.—The Ayr MS.—Materials of early history—State papers from Alexander III.—Records of Parliament from Robert I.—Barbour, Wyntoun, Fordun—Scotland in the twelfth century—Scots—Picts—Lothian—The Norse settlement—Strath-Clyde—Cumbria—Language of old Scotland, Celtic—After Malcolm Canmore, tendency to anglicize—Scotch princes anglicizing—The Scotch courtiers and settlers all Saxon or Teutonic—Northumberland under David I.—Walter Espec at the battle of the Standard—David's troops—The Galwegians—The Scots—Bruce at the battle of the Standard—Early Christianity—Saint Ninian—Columba—Iona—Conversion of Northumbria—The see of Lindisfarne founded—Ædan Bishop of Lindisfarne—St. Cuthbert—Iona the source of Christianity in Scotland—The Culdees—Their later irregularities—Ancient Bishoprics restored by David I.—Munificence to the Church—David I.—His character.

CHAPTER IV.

SCOTLAND IN THE TIME OF DAVID I. 118

Short period of prosperity under Macbeth—David's reign the beginning of a new policy and of long prosperity—Royal progresses—Great officers of state—The king's household—Sources of revenue—Demesne lands—Burghs—Feudal casualties—Customs and duties—Fines and escheats—Items of royal expenditure—Warlike defence—Hunting and hawking—Gardening—The king's tailor—Gascon wine—Meat—Salted marts—Fish—Country life of the king—Royal parks—At Stirling—At Jedburgh—Nobles of the Scotch court—Great earls of Stratherne—The Bruces—The Stewarts and their followers—Knightly occupations—War—The chase—The Stewarts' preserved forest and park—Studs of horses—The Church — The secular clergy — Parish churches bestowed on monasteries—The Church—Monachism in Scotland—Monasteries—Their education—Schools—The arts and trades practised in the Convent—Life in the Convent — Early rental of Kelso — Rural population under the monks—Nativi—Serfs—Price of serfs—Serfs emancipated by the Church—Some light on the condition of serfs—Emancipation of serfs—Agriculture—Roads—Carriages—Mills—Agriculture of the monks.

CHAPTER V.

Scotch Burghs 148

Roman Institutions remaining after the overthrow of the Roman power—Municipal Institutions—Spanish Fueros—German free cities—Hanse Towns—English burghs—Scotch burghs—The Scotch laws of the burghs founded on old customs of English and Scotch burghs—Election of Magistrates—Who were the electors?—Scotch burghs more ancient than any charters—Berwick—St. Andrews—Edinburgh—Rutherglen—Perth—Perth burgh charter—Aberdeen—Inverness—Ayr—Churchmen's burghs—Glasgow—Court of the four burghs—Beauty of Scotch towns—Burgesses.

CHAPTER VI.

Vestiges of Ancient Law 175

Ancient, customary, and common law—Celtic law of succession—Celtic marriages—No general change of law—*Æstimatio personarum*—Ancient law of compensation—Criminal law—Wager of battle—Compurgators—Trial by battle—Trial by fire and water—Law of ordeal—Proof by witnesses gradually admitted—Penalties of theft—Penalty of slaughter—Four pleas of the Crown—Laws of Galloway—Galloway customs—Law of sanctuary—Church girth — Famous sanctuaries — Stow in Wedale—Lesmahago—Inverlethan—Tyningham.

CHAPTER VII.

Ancient Constitution of Scotland 199

Early Tenures—Bruce charter—Dundas charter—Charter to the Steward—The Stewarts' charters—Legal fiction that all property belonged to the Crown—First Stewart charters—Early tenures—The Baron's court—Suit, and service — Composition of the king's court — National Council; its composition in early times—*Communitas regni*—Taxes, how imposed of old—Parliament, when first so called—Burgesses in Parliament—Grant of aid—Conditions of the grant—Committees of Parliament—Committee of Articles—Judicial committee—Institution of Court of Session—The Lords of the Articles—Representation of small freeholders—Representation of burghs—Officers of state with seat in Parliament—All sat together—Defects of the Scotch Parliament.

CHAPTER VIII.

Page

EARLY DRESS AND MANNERS . . . 227

Early utensils—Cups of glass—Boats and galleys—Scotch pearls valued in the twelfth century—Costly horse trappings and armour—Early manufactures—Ancient herring fishery—Mines of gold, silver and iron, worked—Early trade—Riches of the burghs—Berwick—Cnut the Opulent—Munificence of the burgesses of Berwick and Roxburgh—Ship-building at Inverness in the thirteenth century—Coal worked—Merchandise—Commodities traded in, in the twelfth century—Duties of export and import—Customs of Scotch ports in the fourteenth century—Old burgher life—Magistrates—Merchants' ledger of the fifteenth century—Halyburton, a Scotch merchant settled at Middleburgh—His correspondents, persons of all ranks in Scotland, up to the Prince, Bishop of St. Andrews—Scotch goods consigned to him—Wool—Hides—Skins—Salmon—"Claith"—Returns in Wine—Malvoisie—Claret—Rhenish—Canvas—Fustian—Velvet—Damask—Satin—Spices—Roman Bulls of dispensation for marriage—Tayssillis—Soap—Rice—Sugar valans—Scroschats—Sugar lacrissie—Sugar candy—Feather beds—Candlesticks and hanging chandeliers—Pewter dishes—Dornyck—Table linens—Arras coverlets, pots, and pans—Ryssil broun (cloth) satin—Bugles, silk and gold thread (for embroidery)—Bear—Almonds—Raisins—Figs—Olives—Apple oranges—A signet of silver, and one of gold—The bishop's round seal and long seal—Silver chalices—Board cloths with towels and serviettes—Flanders cloths—Bonnets—Caps—An orloge mending—Raised work—

A gown of ypres, black lined with say—Doublet of camlet—Pair of hose—Kist of iron work—Plate—A mat for the Bishop's chamber—Tiles for his chamber floor—Woad and Bryssell—Books of both laws—Review of Scotch trade.

CHAPTER IX.

LANGUAGE AND LITERATURE 251

Origin and formation of Scotch language—At first the same language as the English—English south and north of Trent—The Northern a well cultivated speech—The separation and progressive diversity of Southern and Northern English—The latter called Scotch—Earliest written Scotch—As found in charters—Earliest literary compositions — Lays or ballads — Ossianic poetry — Never influenced our national literature—Early Northern romances — Remaining Scotch of fourteenth century in writing of that period—Barbour's poem composed then—Earliest copies extant not *written* for a century after—Scotch used in Parliament at end of fourteenth century — Letters of correspondence then written — Wyntoun's chronicle written about 1420—Preserved in MS. almost of that date — Progress of Scotch literature in poetry and prose — How far the people capable of appreciating it—Education of the people—Scarcity of books—Modes of instruction—Universities—The pulpit—Ælfric's homilies of the eleventh century—Library of the Culdees of Lochleven of the twelfth century—Catalogue of Glasgow Cathedral library 1432—Burgh schools—Act of Parliament 1496—Old grammar schools—Grammar school of Aberdeen 1520—Andrew Simpson's school at Perth before the Reformation—Introduction in Scotch schools of Greek and Hebrew—Scotch Universities—St. Andrews, Glasgow, and Aberdeen—Founded in the fifteenth century—Popular tendency of our authors.

CHAPTER X.

Dwellings—Architecture and Arts Connected with it . 276

Early dwellings—Caves—Subterranean built chambers—Galleries in Orkney—Early strongholds of wood—Circular hill forts—Some very remarkable—Cathertun—Barmekyn of Echt—Vitrified forts—Picts' houses—"Druid's circles"—Some of their purposes—Sculptured monuments—Symbols of unknown meaning—Limitation of the sculptured monuments, as to place (Lowland Scotland) and time (eighth and ninth centuries)—Earliest Christian buildings—Round towers—History of art depending on architecture—Attempt to fix eras of architectural style—Old Whithern and Iona quite gone—First style extant, Norman or Romanesque—Its date—Next, " First Pointed"—Third, " Middle Pointed"—Later style—Collegiate churches—Ornamental arts subserving architecture—A word about heraldry—Stained glass—Symbolical meaning of church architecture—Workmanship in iron and wood—Timber roofs—Stucco ceilings—Wood carving—Dunblane—King's College, Aberdeen—Tiles—Ancient seals, baronial and ecclesiastical—Coins—A charter of 1159 with portraits of David I. and Malcolm IV.—Hoard of silver ornaments found in Orkney—Its date fixed to the ninth century—Architectural art as applied to domestic buildings—Scotch castles of the time of David I. and earlier, all gone—

Remains of those of the thirteenth and fourteenth centuries—Kildrummy—Lochindorb—Bothwell—Baronial tower of the fifteenth century—Causes of its poor style—Subsequent additions—Ornate style introduced by James IV. and James V.—Stirling—Linlithgow—New style of castle mansion—Lord Dunfermline and Earl of Strathmore its leaders—Fyvie—Pinkie—Glammis—Spread especially in Aberdeenshire—Castle Fraser—Craigievar—Crathes—Craigston, etc.—Dwellings of the people—Never retrograding—Change and improvement—Constant and still continuing—Burgh domestic architecture.

POSTSCRIPT 321
APPENDIX—
  I. Capitular of Charlemagne, *De villis imperialibus* . 327
 II. Aelfric's homilies in Anglo-Saxon . . 331
 III. Library of the Culdees of St. Serf's . . . 333
 IV. Lease between the Abbot of Scone and Hay of Leys 334
 V. Catalogue of Books in Glasgow Cathedral . . 336
 VI. James Melvill's Diary . . . 340
GLOSSARY 343
INDEX 347

ERRATA.

Page 184, line 16, for *theft's* read *thief's*.
Page 193, footnote, line 9, for *xxx* read *xx*.
Page 224, line 14, for *offices* read *officers*.
Page 237, line 2, for *woald* read *woad*.

SKETCHES

OF

EARLY SCOTCH HISTORY.

CHAPTER I.

INTRODUCTORY.

In laying before the public these Sketches, I may be permitted to explain that their original purpose was merely to engage the interest of young men in the study of history. I offer no ambitious disquisitions on political science; still less do I strive to crowd into a few pages the facts of a nation's history. I have thought it more useful to direct attention to the origin and progress of the complicated frame of modern society, the sources of our institutions, and the mixed foresight and accident that have fostered them. I would willingly show the stages through which European society has passed, not using the *a priori* speculations of theorists, but taking history and its materials as our guides.

CHAP. I.

I trust it will not be unacceptable if, in tracing up the great stream of civilization, I follow the little tributary branch that rises and flows through our own valleys. The same results for science may be derived from the research, as if it were extended over a much wider field; and the very familiarity of the scenes, and the interest you cannot avoid feeling in them, will, at any rate, help to keep up your attention, which might flag in more general discussions. For my part, I shall have obtained my utmost object if, in pointing your observation to the structure of our political society, and to the domestic history of our ancestors—to their modes of thought, feeling, and action—I can awake some taste for historical research and speculation, or assist, in however humble a degree, to promote the love of reasonable liberty, of truth, and of virtue.

A.D. 768-814.

In such an inquiry, I think I have gone high enough in beginning at the era of Charlemagne. Most of our institutions—I may say, all the peculiar institutions of the existing body politic of Europe—have arisen within that limit. Then, too, we begin to have some of the authentic materials of history. We have original letters and state papers; bodies of laws, rude indeed, but most characteristic; we have chroniclers, meagre and undiscriminating, but still giving facts as they appeared to common men at the time, and deriving value even from the exhibition of the prepossessions and prejudices of the relater; and, finally, we have lives of great men, written by their familiars. Unfortunately, at that time the history of our own country is a blank; and we are left to conjecture that similar institutions, and manners not materially different when they first fall within the light of history, have had a similar origin, and passed through the same stages of progress.

After examining the structure of Christendom under Charlemagne, and the fragments into which it was broken when no longer sustained by his wisdom and power, I propose to leave the general European history at the period of the Norman conquest of England, and to direct your attention to the state of Britain at that era. That is an important point in the history of England, which then first becomes one of the members of the Continental family—a state of the great commonwealth of Europe; and it may be said to be the beginning of Scotch history.

Soon after that period, we may derive materials from our own records that will enable us to throw light upon the state of our country, feeble at first, and uncertain, but gradually brightening into the fulness of perfect history.

Modern politicians are in the habit of claiming for their own time the dignity and interest of a great political *crisis;* but the student of history, looking back through the cool vista of a thousand years, will find no crisis so important in European affairs as the era of the accession of Charlemagne. We should take a narrow and mistaken view if we regarded the wars of that time as the struggle for superiority of men or of nations—as a dispute whether Charles or Witikind should reign—whether the Saxons or the Franks should be the dominant tribe. If we examine more attentively, we shall find the elements of a different war. The great fight then began, which has continued ever since, now slumbering, now blazing out anew—often asleep, never dead—the struggle between order and anarchy, between civilization and barbarism. Setting out of view the interposition of an over-ruling Providence (which a historian has no right to limit as a cause of any *particular* issue), it is owing to the wisdom and vigour of Charlemagne, and to the success of that party of which he was the leader and the type, not only that the Germanic race is lord of the ascendant in Europe, but, perhaps, that Europe has set up the standard of mind against brute force—has identified its existence with Christianity; instead of the worship of the groves and of Odin, or the doctrine of the prophet of Islam.

We shall understand this better if we bestow a

little attention upon the state of society in Europe at that important era when Charlemagne ascended the throne of the Franks. Thirty-six years before, his grandfather, Charles Martel, mayor of the palace of the Merovingian kings, had set a limit to the progress of the invading Moors of Spain, in a three days' fight near Poictiers, which has been exaggerated and surrounded with romantic marvels, as was natural and almost fitting for a battle upon which depended the fate of the Christian world. Twenty years after that victory, Pepin, the son of the conqueror, already king in power and authority, became King of the Franks by the solemn election of the free German nation, in an assembly or parliament held at Soissons, when he was proclaimed King, and the degraded Childeric deposed and sent as a shaven monk to drag out the remainder of his life in a monastery at St. Omers. On Pepin's death again, the people immediately elected his sons Charles and Carloman as his successors. The Pope Zacharias had sanctioned the setting aside of Childeric III., the last of the ancient Merovingian kings, in favour of the more vigorous race, whose arms he trusted to engage in the service of the Church, then sore bestead. Pepin immediately showed his gratitude by bestowing on the Roman See its first great territorial possessions, the provinces of Romagna and the march of Ancona, wrested by him and his hardy Franks from the Lombards, whom the languid Emperors of the East allowed to possess the fairest provinces of Italy. And there began that intimate alliance of the Church and the State, which, cultivated at first, perhaps, for political or even selfish ends, had the effect for many centuries of giving unity to Christendom and predominance to the Papal power; and of engaging the successive rulers of Europe to propagate and support the doctrines of the Church.

It is not necessary to dwell upon the short period of double rule of Charles and his brother Carloman, and I only advert to it to call your attention to two facts—first, the partition of the inheritance, so contrary to the notions of after-feudalism, and in reality so dangerous to the existence of the kingdom, but so established in the customs of the time, that neither Charles Martel, Pepin, nor Charlemagne himself, ventured to controvert it. Secondly, we must not omit to notice, that whatever the destination of the deceased monarch might be, and however influential in guiding the succession, still the absolute election and right of choice lay in the people.

Observe how Europe was peopled at that time. The original Gaulish people had experienced the fate which seems to attend the Celtic race when brought in collision with Teutonic nations. A part had submitted to the fortune of war, and as bondmen tilled the soil which they had formerly possessed; and part had been pushed back into the defiles of Armorica, or disappeared among the gorges of the Alps and the Jura, and while they have left interesting traces of their manners and their language, they may, without much injustice to history, be discounted as an independent people from the politics of Europe.

The swarms of many named Teutonic barbarians before whom they had retired, soon filled the land from the Mediterranean to the North Sea, introducing every where a new element into European society, the sentiment of personal independence and passion for individual liberty, which you will find on reflection was unknown among the Romans, and which formed no part of the feeling or instruction of the Christian church.

The leading band of the barbarians, who had at an early time inhabited the district of the Lower Rhine and Weser, but after their combination occupying the country from the Rhine to the Somme, and including Holland, Brabant, Flanders, Gueldres, all the ancient states, afterwards the kingly dukedom of the Burgundian princes, had, long before the time of Charlemagne, united for common defence, and assumed the common name of Franks. Their bond of union consisted in a common Teutonic tongue, and a similarity at least of national customs

About A.D. 240, soon after Maximin's slaughter, which was in 238.

Chap. I. and laws; and latterly the conversion of their leaders to Christianity, and the gradual propagation of its doctrines through the people, had given them another principle of union, and drew upon them doubly the enmity of the other Germanic and Eastern pagans, who already envied them for their power and the occupation of the fairest provinces of Europe.

Of many of these pagan hordes on the eastern frontier of the Frank kingdom, we know nothing but the names.

The Sclaves, the Wends, the Bavarians—so formidable under their dukes Odilo and Tassilo—are known to us only as the inveterate enemies of the Franks and of Christianity, and we are left to conjecture the extent of their power from the mighty efforts which it cost to subdue them.

Farther to the north, swarming from their native forests of Scandinavia, Jutland and Saxony, were the numerous peoples who called themselves the sons of Odin, and who worshipped Thor and Odin. Of this people, who crowded thick and threatening along the eastern and northern frontiers of Christian Europe, I should mislead you if I pretended to trace the remote original. From the East, our common cradle, they had long migrated, and themselves preserved but a faint and uncertain tradition of Asgard and Asaland, and an Asiatic origin. One branch of this great family had already become known under the name of Northmen or Danes, a race of warriors despising the arts of peace, and loving war for its danger no less than its plunder. These were the *Vikingr*, the men of the Bays, the pirates of the North, the sea-kings, and the terror of every coast in Europe where a prey was to be taken.

Kindred to them in blood and language, and resembling them in manners and religion, was the nation which is to us the most interesting of all the Teutonic peoples. Their favourite weapon, the Saex, or long knife, gave them the name they have handed down to a sturdy race, who have already spread their Saxon language and love of freedom over half the world. Some centuries before the era of Charlemagne, the Saxons had established their colonies in England, respectable in strength and intelligence, but removed by their position from the active struggle of the Continent. They left behind them in their native forests of Saxony, Friesland, and Jutland, the most obstinate and formidable of the opponents of the Christian empire.

Of the religion and superstition of these northern and eastern Teutons, we know somewhat from the Frankish Royal Ordinances, denouncing the varieties of paganism, as well as from the remains of the remarkable men who devoted their lives to their conversion; and more from that extraordinary literature of the north, one class of which, the Edda, has preserved to us their mythology, and another their historical and romantic narratives, the Sagas. "The Saxons," says Einhard, "like almost all the nations inhabiting Germany, are of fierce nature, and devoted to the worship of demons, and most hostile to our religion." No people perhaps has ever so realized their rude ideas of another state of being, and the presence and interference of their deities. These, indeed, were rather deified heroes, raised into gods by antiquity; men, only more powerful than the mortals of a degenerate time. Like the Greek deities of the Homeric age, they often mixed in human affairs, and were sometimes met by mortal heroes in not unequal combat. The joys of their Olympus or Valhalla were to be opened to the valiant warrior after death, who was to employ his days in warlike exercises, to feast on the everlasting boar's flesh, and revel in horns of ale and mead. Over these hero gods was the eternal being, the Alfader, the creator and ruler, not only of the earth and heaven, but also of those interposed godheads kindred to humanity, and which, in the absence of revelation, seem necessary for its support. They had the reverence for woods and groves and fountains, natural to man in his unenlightened state, and many of their heathen observances were connected with them. Charlemagne himself ordained, "that any one who made a vow or offering, after the manner of the pagans, to fountains, or trees, or groves, or made sacrifices in honour of demons, should be fined according to his rank, or if unable to pay, be given to the service of the church till the fine be made up; that the bodies of the Christian Saxons should be taken for burial to the church cemeteries, and not to the tumuli of the pagans; and that sorcerers and diviners should be given over to the church and the clergy." Their practice of eating horse flesh was not a mere indulgence of taste, but was connected with their national superstitions. Pope Gregory, in one of his epistles, enjoins the zealous Boniface to repress it by every means as a foul and execrable practice. A more monstrous enormity prevailed among some of the Thuringians, who, having themselves nominally embraced Christianity, yet ministered to their native superstitions in their worst forms, by selling slaves to the unconverted pagans for the purpose of sacrifice.[1] This is denounced by the Pope as an impious offence, and to be visited with the same penance as homicide. Procopius assures us, indeed, that many of the Germanic tribes, even those professing Christianity, adhered to the rites of their ancient idolatry, and sacrificed human victims.[2]

A.D. 540.

[1] Quidam ex fidelibus ad immolandum Paganis sua venundant mancipia. [2] Thierry, 52.

While we notice these monstrous superstitions, let us not pass over the savage virtues of our German forefathers, and their abhorrence of some kinds of immorality. In a curious letter of Boniface to Ethelbald, king of Mercia, reproving him for his licentious life, he appeals to the usages even of Pagan Germany as enforcing his precepts. His words are,—"Not only by Christians, but by Pagans also, such conduct is esteemed a dishonour and shame; for the very Pagans, though ignorant of the true God, observe in this matter, by nature, the things of the law, and keep what God has from the beginning ordained. For they respect their conjugal engagements, and punish paramours and adulterers. In old Saxony, if a young woman pollutes her paternal name by impurity, or a wife violates her marriage obligations, they sometimes compel her to strangle herself, and hang the seducer over the funeral pile of her burning body. Sometimes they assemble a crowd of women, who whip the offending female from village to village, scourging her with rods, tearing her clothes from her sides, and lacerating her body with knives, till she is left dead or dying, that others may feel a salutary fear of adultery and wantonness." I have given the words of the letter, that you may observe the minute details and differences which, I think, prove it to be written from the Bishop's own observation, and not merely copied from a passage of Tacitus, where he describes similar manners among the ancient Germans. This is confirmed by his adding a further illustration of conjugal fidelity, in the practice of the *Suttee*, which we know to have then prevailed among the Wendish or Sclavonian tribes, who were neighbours of the Saxons on the East. " Even the Wends," continues the Anglo-Saxon missionary, " who are the vilest and most degraded of mortals, so zealously adhere to the bond of marriage, that the wife, when her husband dies, refuses to survive him; and she is considered the most exemplary of her sex who inflicts her death-wound with her own hand, and perishes upon the same pile with her husband." There is reason to believe that the same practice was at least in occasional observance among the early Germans, and vivid traces of it appear in the heroic poems of Scandinavia; but it cannot be affirmed that it continued to prevail down to the period of their known history.

A fragment, found in a MS. of the Vatican, gives us the form of the catechism of the new converts of the Thuringians and Saxons brought into the Church by St. Boniface and his companions in the middle of the eighth century, which, while it indicates a multitude of their prevailing superstitions contains a very remarkable specimen of the language then spoken by the governing people of Northern Europe. It is

A.D. 743.

plain that it was the common language of Frank, Saxon, and Thuringian; and it is interesting to find that it is understood, without difficulty, eleven hundred years later, by Germans, Dutch, Scandinavians, Scots, and English—all the people who speak a genuine Teutonic language.

Forsachistu diobolæ? Forsakest thou the devil?

A. *Ec forsacho diobolæ.* I forsake the devil.

End allum diobolgeldæ? And all devil worship?

A. *End ec forsacho allum diobolgeldæ.* And I forsake all devil worship.

End allum dioboles uuercum? And all the devil's works?

A. *End ec forsacho allum dioboles uuercum end uuordum, Thunaer ende Woden ende Saxnote, ende allem them unholdum the hira genotas sint.* And I forsake all the devil's works and words, Thor and Woden and Saxnot, and the unclean spirits that are their comrades.

Gelobistu in Got Alamehtigan Fadaer?

A. *Ec gelobo in Got Alamehtigan Fadaer.*

Gelobisto in Crist Godes suno?

A. *Ec gelobo in Crist Godes suno.*

Gelobistu in Halogan Gast?

A. *Ec gelobo in Halogan Gast.*[1]

There is preserved a vow or prayer offered up by the Saxon army, apparently after the slaughter

[1] Pertz, Monumenta Germaniæ, tom. iii. p. 19.

at Verden:—" Holy great Woden, deliver us and our Prince Witikind from the most foul Charles— woe to that butcher!—and I will give to thee a wild bull (*urus*) and two sheep, and the spoils, and I will kill to thee all my prisoners in thy sacred hill of Artishberka."

On the other side of the territory occupied by the new Frankish nation, on the Pyrenean frontier, were the Moors of Spain, a formidable enemy, checked by the defeat at Poictiers, but still warlike, active, and zealous for extending their dominion and faith. These were beyond doubt the most enlightened as well as the most refined people of Europe at that time. They cultivated letters, science, and some of the arts with a taste and success which we do not find among the nations of Christendom for ages afterwards. We owe to them our modern system of arithmetic, and our earliest acquaintance with astronomy, which their forefathers had studied in the plains of Bagdad and Sinaar. To that study they were partly led by the belief of the influence of the stars upon the actions and fortunes of men; and their zealous prosecution of chemistry, long before its first principles were understood in Christendom, might originate in the strange tradition which gave rise to the search after a mysterious agent that could convert the baser metals into gold, and bestow life and youth as well as wealth upon its possessor. But even the pursuit of such dreams bespeaks a diving into the mysteries of nature and a cultivation, far removed from the rudeness of the Germanic peoples. The remains of Moorish architecture, so rich and graceful, so suited for the enjoyment of that voluptuous climate, would alone convince us how far they had outstripped our ancestors in the arts of life. But nothing appears to me to show better what civilization owes to the Moors, than the unquestionable etymology of some of those terms now so familiar in our mouths—words connected with the foundation of our knowledge of the properties of numbers, the calculations of astronomy, and the science and art of chemistry.[1]

This people, so ingenious, of so fine and subtle a nature, were not less active and enterprising. They had already run down all the southern coast of the Mediterranean, and colonised from the sea to the ridge of Atlas. They had made themselves a home in the Spanish peninsula, and were clustering round the Pyrenean passes, ready to send off a swarm into France. They were unrivalled at sea, at least in that sea which served as their road of communication with their fatherland. Along its waters they brought to Spain the produce of Asia, and of the

[1] As almanack, algebra, cypher, zenith, nadir, azimuth, alembic, alkali.

unknown regions of Central Africa. Other peoples Chap. I. of the same stock and religion soon became even more dangerous, and in spite of the awe of the great Emperor, devastated the coasts of Italy, seized upon Sardinia and Sicily, and established a colony within the territory of the Frank empire on the coast of Provence.

On the south side of the Alps the Longobardi were the most formidable of the rivals of the Franks, though they had more than once given way before the prowess of the ancestors of Charlemagne.

Beyond their kingdom, on the banks of the Tiber, on the hills whence Rome once sent out its legions, was that old city, no longer imperial nor the centre of civil dominion, but swaying the minds of men with an authority more awful. It was not merely the respect for the seat of the chief Christian bishop—venerated as the scene of the preaching and suffering of the greatest of the Apostles—seen indistinctly through the misty distance—with a name still associated with universal dominion. In those ages Rome made her existence be felt by sending her missionaries to the most dangerous and distant fields of exertion, and by winning over to co-operation and unity the most zealous preachers of Christianity who had not drawn their zeal or their commission from herself, at least directly. By the A.D. 596. mission of Augustine she had reclaimed Saxon

CHAP. I. England from utter Paganism; and in another age, when the English neophytes proved their gratitude by spreading Christianity among the Frisians and Saxons of their German fatherland, Wilbrord and Boniface in succession—names now unfamiliar to our ears, but long venerated as the English apostles of the faith amongst the Germans—at the height of their success, and while bringing within the pale of Christianity whole provinces by their preaching, consented to bow to the majesty of Rome and to accept at her hands the consecration of their Episcopal office. In the time of the Carlovingian princes, Rome had to struggle almost for her existence. The mighty Arian heresy which began in Egypt at the beginning of the fourth century, and was spread through all the Eastern churches, had inundated Europe also, with the irruption of the Goths, the Vandals, the Burgundians and the Lombards, all tainted with the prevailing Arian doctrines. Against it, Rome had to contend almost alone, and scarcely was she finally victorious in

A.D. 660. that struggle, when another dispute embroiled her with the Eastern emperors, and obliged her to turn for refuge and support to a new, a rising, and a more energetic ally.

And here it is necessary to speak of the Christian Church, its influence and its effects. I cannot go into the more ancient history of the organisation of the clergy, but must regard it as it had become shortly before our era, a completely organised society, separated from the laity by celibacy, extending from one centre and embracing all Christendom; comprehending in its ranks nearly all of intelligence, literature, and science that then existed; having alone some communion with the mind of immortal antiquity, and having in view, when rightly considered, the noblest and most elevating objects of man's exertions. It is not surprising that by their office the clergy should possess a large share of influence; but when we consider the general want of that discipline of mind necessary for common affairs, we find an additional cause for the crowd of secular business thrown upon the churchmen in the middle ages. The bishops of all the cities of Gaul were administrators of the civil and Imperial authority under the Lower Roman emperors.[1] "It is not quite fair to accuse the clergy of usurpation in this matter," says Guizot, "for it fell out according to the common course of events. The clergy alone possessed moral strength and activity; and the clergy everywhere succeeded to power—such is the common law of the universe."

How did the Church wield this vast power? It is a large subject, and I cannot be expected here to go into the discussion. I have studied it, however,

[1] They were called papas or patres.—*Leg. Arcad. et Theodor.*

Chap. I. with some care, and as I am not aware of any prejudice or prepossession, I will not withhold from you the results.

I think it could be shown that up to the era of Charlemagne, and for some time afterwards, the Church was in a state of continual progression of intelligence, and high views. It attacked barbarism at every point, to civilize and to rule over it. Notwithstanding its denial of the exercise of individual judgment—notwithstanding its claim to the right of compelling submission—its tendency was ever popular. It protected the weak against oppression. It supported the poor. It emancipated the slave. It admitted into its own bosom all comers of all ranks. With its mighty moral power it saved the world, when there was a danger of its falling a prey to brute force. I use the words of a Protestant and a true philosopher when I say,—" humanly speaking, it was the Christian Church that saved Christianity."[1]

In this rude numbering of the elements of European society, I have not alluded to that shadow of ancient empire, which yet brooded over the Bosphorus. The emperors of Constantinople had still some footing in the exarchates of Italy (though even there, the Lombards were fast encroaching on them); but of Europe beyond the Alps, they had neither influence nor knowledge. They despised

[1] Guizot.

the country which they stamped as barbarous, and knew nothing of the power which was rising out of the ruins of their old Gaulish provinces. The Byzantine writers of the sixth century speak of the Western inhabitants of Europe, even of the mighty league of the Franks, as something indistinct and all but fabulous. We cannot imagine that the barbarians were more informed regarding the city and its emperors; and all the records we have of them, show that it formed no object of their respect or thoughts. It was indeed impossible that the fame of Charlemagne should not reach even to Constantinople; and we have records of several embassies sent to him by the Byzantine emperors; but the distance prevented any collision or political intercourse; and it was not till the time of the Crusades, that the wily Greeks learned to respect or fear the iron-handed men of the North.

At the death of Pepin, the father of Charlemagne, the empire of the Franks consisted of the three kingdoms of Neustria, Burgundy, and Austrasia; in other words, of three-fourths of France, Holland and Belgium, Switzerland, the Grand Duchy of the Lower Rhine, Wurtemberg and Bavaria, and the small states of the German Confederacy. It extended from the Loire to the frontiers of modern Austria and Bohemia—from the German Sea to the Mediterranean. I have already said that the Franks—a Teutonic confederacy—were the predominating people. They occupied the territory between the Rhine, the Seine, and the Loire. The Gauls, the former possessors of a great proportion of the territory, were still, perhaps, found scattered over their former possessions, though united and in strength chiefly in the Orleanois, the central district of modern France. The Visigoths occupied Languedoc, and all the country from the Loire to the Pyrenees. The Ostrogoths were seated in Provence; the Burgundians between the Loire, the Rhone, and the Rhine, from Avignon to Basel. Brittany had its own Celtic inhabitants, reinforced by large additions from Britain in the middle of the fifth century, when the Roman province was overrun by the barbarians. A large territory on the right bank of the Rhine can scarcely be held as adding strength to the kingdom of the Franks. The Thuringians, the Alimanni, and its other inhabitants, had, indeed, more than once been reduced to submission by the predecessors of Charlemagne; but these were mere barbarians, constantly fluctuating, and yielding a mere nominal obedience.

The Roman power may be said to have been finally destroyed in Gaul by the victory of Clovis at Soissons; but we must not suppose that the Roman civil dominion of many ages, over every part of Europe, had left no permanent effects on its society. These were chiefly seen in the cities; for the Romans of the provinces seem to have lived altogether in towns, while their barbarian invaders, on the contrary, either at once, or soon after their settlement, took their seats chiefly in the open country. In the time of Charlemagne, Roman cities still remained over all Germany, maintaining a sort of tolerated independence, using their own customs, and having the election of the managers of their local affairs. The effect of such communities, where order was preserved and property protected, must have been very great even upon the rude settlers of the open country round, and they were soon imitated as models in the cities which grew up round the princes and bishops of the new peoples. A writer[1] of the fifth century describes the Visigoths on the west of the Rhone, and the Burgundians on the east, living on the most friendly terms with the Romanised Gauls, "not as if with subjects, but with brothers."[2] In the sixth century, Alaric, a king of the Visigoths of Toulouse, collected and published a body of Roman laws, a fact which speaks the continued influence of Roman manners, long after the downfall of the power of Rome. We should overrate the power of this element, however, if we did not observe that whilst the Roman institutions, still

---

[1] Paulus Orosius.   [2] Non quasi cum subjectis sed cum fratribus.

remaining amongst the new peoples, gave the experience of order and security, they inculcated little of real patriotism. When cut off from Rome, they had no common bond of union; each city stood alone, with no natural connection even with other free communities, still less with the government, under which it existed by sufferance.

Of such materials, with little of adherence in their structure, and hemmed in on the East and West by the most dangerous enemies, was composed the empire of the Frankish princes, the ancestors of Charlemagne.

Charles, whom we know best by the name of Charlemagne, was twenty-six years old when he succeeded his father in the western provinces, and three years afterwards, the death of his brother Carloman left him undisputed lord of the Frankish empire.

We owe the description of his person to his contemporary and friend Einhard. He was large of limb, strong bodied, tall, but yet not more than seven times the length of his own foot, which his biographer considered the just proportion. His eyes were large and quick, his nose somewhat too long. He had fine fair hair. His countenance was gay and cheerful. He had a dignified presence, whether standing or walking, though his neck was too thick and short, and his belly somewhat prominent. His gait was firm, and his whole appearance manly; but his voice, though clear, was scarcely full enough to suit his great size. He was always in good health, until the last four years of his life. He was fond of riding and hunting, and passionately fond of swimming. The same author describes his dress as that of his nation—a linen shirt and breeches, and above them a tunic bordered with a fringe of silk. His legs were bandaged with stripes of cloth, and he wore low leather buskins. In winter he defended his shoulders and chest with a jacket of otter and marten skins. Over these, he had a blue cloak, and always wore a sword, the hilt and belt of which was of gold or silver. Sometimes he put on a jewelled sword, but that was only at the great feasts of the Church, or at the reception of foreign ambassadors. He rejected all foreign garments, however beautiful, and only on two occasions, at Rome, he was persuaded to use the Roman garb. On great festivals he wore a robe woven with gold and buskins ornamented with jewels, with a gold clasp for his cloak, and on his head a diadem of gold and gems. On common days, his dress was simple, and differed in nothing from that of his people. He was moderate in his food, and still more temperate in his drink, and hated drunkenness. His common dinner consisted of four dishes; but the meat he liked best was the little roast which the hunters brought him fresh killed, and presented

Chap. I. on the spit. Whilst he was at table, he liked to hear reading, and it was the history of old times, and the great deeds of his forefathers, which he generally chose to hear. He also liked the works of St. Augustine, particularly his "City of God." In summer, at his mid-day meal, he would eat some apples, take one draught of wine, and he then undressed, and lay down to sleep for two or three hours. At night his sleep was broken, and he often got up and dressed four or five times during the night. In the morning, whilst he was dressing, he admitted his friends; and if any law cause of great importance was pending, he had the parties brought before him, and decided it himself.

Einhard praises his eloquence, in language borrowed from Suetonius' characters of Augustus and Titus. He knew Latin perfectly, and spoke it like his own language; but Greek he did not pronounce so well as he understood it. He studied Grammar —which word then comprehended some classical learning—and Dialectics, as they were then taught under Peter of Pisa, and our countryman Alcuin, who was considered the paragon of all learning and accomplishment of his time. He studied Astronomy, and was skilful in computing the courses of the stars. Lastly, he tried anxiously to learn to write, but with little success, although he used to carry writing materials about with him, and endeavour to trace the written characters even in bed.

He loved the society of strangers, and entertained all comers with the most royal hospitality. He commenced two sumptuous palaces; but he bestowed his attention chiefly upon building and repairing churches throughout his vast dominions. He built fleets in all the rivers which run into the Northern Ocean, for repelling the invasions of the Northmen, and had a navy in the Mediterranean, for protecting his coasts against the pirate Moors.

Einhard tells us much of his charity and alms, and that he adhered most religiously to the Christian faith, which he had learned in his youth. But for this and some other matters, I may be permitted to bring under your notice a few passages from his own ordinances, preserved among the capitularies of the ancient Frankish kings. Some of these give the most minute descriptions of the court life of the eighth century. The one prescribing the order to be observed in the imperial country houses is perhaps the most curious, and illustrates the home life of the castles of the period, its comforts and luxuries, scattered as they were in a country but half reclaimed from the original forest. We have careful arrangements for vintage, harvest, and hay-making; provisions for the feeding and proper fattening of poultry, and for a supply of swans, of peacocks, pheasants, and winged game, "*pro dignitatis causa*," and innumerable regulations applicable to a country life, like that on which we now pride ourselves in England. The Emperor's care descended even to the plants which were to be cultivated in his garden. His list of flowers began, as was fitting, with the lily and the rose, and extended through an immense catalogue of names, which are rather puzzling to modern gardeners, while some of them undoubtedly belong rather to the produce of the kitchen and herb garden, and others may have served as charms against witchcraft and sorcery.

Of trees, he ordered apple trees of different kinds, with very hard names;[1] some for keeping through the winter, others for summer use; pears of three or four different kinds, and plums, medlars, chesnuts, peaches, and quinces; almond trees and mulberries; walnuts and varieties of cherries. Finally, the gardener was to have upon the roof of his own house the plant which, in Charlemagne's time, bore the name of *Jove's beard*, and which is well known to us by the name of *house-leek*, a sort of domestic plant, to which I believe some superstition has always attached. Nothing could bring the scene of a thousand years ago more freshly to our mind than these curious ordinances now collected with the accuracy and care they deserve. We see the great

[1] Gozmaringa, Geroldinga, Crevedella, Spiranea.

Emperor among his fruits and his flowers, his harvests, his poultry and his game, surrounded by men of science and letters, by the high officers of his crown and dignified churchmen, with his palace crowded with strangers, dispensing his charity with profusion, leading the life of the opulent and well educated country gentlemen of our own time.[1]

It has been said that the famous constitution of Charlemagne, for instituting schools in every bishopric and monastery, was the cause of the restoration of letters and learning in France and Germany. In that, perhaps, there is some overstatement, but I cannot now dwell upon the inquiry. I prefer giving you a specimen of an exhortation of Charlemagne, addressed to all persons, clerical and secular, in the year 789, which I cannot help thinking in every way most memorable; especially the latter clauses, which regard the keeping of Sunday, and the preaching of pastors. The king ordained, that according to the precept of the Divine Law, no servile works should be done on the Lord's day, particularly, that men should not work at country work, in the vineyard, or in ploughing, reaping, mowing, hedging, nor in grubbing wood, or cutting trees; that they should not build houses, nor work in their gardens, nor meet in law courts, nor hunt. It was not lawful to use cart or carriage

---

[1] See a notice of the capitular of Charlemagne *de villis imperialibus*, in the Appendix.

labour, except for three purposes:—for expeditions of war, for victuals, and thirdly, if it should be necessary, for burial. Women were prohibited from weaving on that day, from shaping or sewing clothes, and from embroidery and needlework, from carding wool, beating flax, public washing of clothes, and shearing of sheep. All were ordered to assemble at church for mass, to praise God for all the good things he bestowed upon us in that day.

The injunction with regard to preaching is more remarkable. Here are the words of Charlemagne himself:—"It is your duty to see, beloved and venerable pastors of the churches of God, that the priests whom you send throughout your parishes preach rightly and honestly, and that you allow none to preach to the people novelties, or things not canonical, according to their own sense, and not according to the Scripture, but do you yourselves preach what is useful, honest, and right, and such things as lead to eternal life; and instruct others to do the same.

"First of all, the preacher should instruct all generally, that they should believe that the Father, the Son, and the Holy Ghost are one God, Almighty, Everlasting, Invisible, who created Heaven and Earth, and all that in them is;" and so on through all the points of the Apostle's Creed, set down with great plainness and precision. Afterwards, he is enjoined to preach against the works of the flesh, for which men are punished in another life, "but," continues Charlemagne, "above all, admonish them concerning the love of God and their neighbour, of faith and hope in God, of humility and patience, of chastity and continence, of kindness and mercy, of alms, and the confession of sins, and the forgiving of debts."

Charlemagne was hereditarily attached to the Church, and to Rome. His family had risen as the champions of the Church. I believe he was firmly convinced of the truth of her doctrines, and of the virtue of unity. But other motives were not wanting to confirm his attachment. Surrounded by Pagan enemies, it was his policy to be Christian. In a church and society long distracted by schism, he saw the advantage of supporting and enforcing a standard of unity of doctrine. You have seen that with some inconsiderable exceptions in Europe, and excepting, of course, the Greek Empire, his kingdom was co-extensive with Christianity. Thus from policy as well as zeal, he marched to battle as the servant of the Cross. With him, all Pagans were enemies, and all Christians were both friends and subjects. Every battle he gained brought him not only new subjects, but new proselytes. Baptism was the necessary consequence of submission to Charlemagne. He compelled unity in the Empire and in the Church. By his creed there should be but one king and one faith! But while he converted with the sword, and baptized the conquered Pagans in their blood, he supported the zealous missionaries who used methods more suited to the doctrines they taught. The preacher of peace and the mighty warrior worked in harmony together, to bring new subjects within the pale of Christendom and the Empire.

We are not surprised that the rude freemen of Saxony long resisted such conversion. Radbod, a fierce chief of the Frisians, who had withstood the arms of Pepin Heristal, was at length almost gained over to Christianity, by the persevering entreaties and preaching of Wulframn and other missionaries. He was even brought to the sacred font. He had already one foot in the water, when he suddenly stopped—turned to Wulframn, and asked, whether there were more Frieslanders in heaven or in hell. The missionary could not hesitate, and told him that all his ancestors being unbaptized, were certainly in the latter place. The prince immediately drew back his foot from the font. "I cannot," he said, "give up the company of my ancestors even for the joys of heaven."[1] "And Duke Radbod," says the chronicler, "died unbaptized."

Charlemagne turned his whole power against the Saxons. His generals were defeated over and over again. He marched himself at the head of immense

[1] Pertz, II. 221.

armies against them. He won battle after battle, but still the stubborn people refused his rule, or only submitted while he was amongst them, to revolt whenever his force was withdrawn. Baptism had become a badge of slavery, which they were loath to undergo, and Witikind, their chief, resisted as long as nature could endure. It cost thirty-three years of war to the great emperor to complete the subjection of the Saxons. None of his other undertakings was so wasteful of blood and treasure, and yet it was no light task to stem the tide of barbarous nations, setting so strongly from the east to the west of Europe. We must not follow him through his lifetime of war and conquest, nor dwell upon the suffering occasioned to his subjects by his endless conscriptions and levies. He humbled the Moors of Navarre, and pushed his frontier beyond the Pyrenees to the Ebro. He won and wore the iron crown of Lombardy. He ruled the Western Continent of Europe from the Mediterranean and the Atlantic, to the Danube and the Oder, the Baltic Sea and the Eyder. He received suppliant embassies from the Emperors of the East, and the mighty caliph *Harūn-al-Rashīd* sent him ambassadors and presents—rich robes and perfumes of the east, and his only elephant,[1]

---

[1] We learn that he bore the name of *Ab-ul-Abas*, or "the father of destruction;" that he was brought into Italy in the year 802, and died in Lippenhein in 810—in all likelihood, the only elephant seen to the north of the Alps since the days of Hannibal.

Chap. I. which Charlemagne had expressed a desire to possess. Charlemagne reached the summit of earthly
A.D. 800. grandeur, when the Pope, placed on his head the crown of the Cæsars, and hailed him by the still unforgotten titles of Emperor and Augustus.

But more than this, he had effectually rolled back the hitherto constant tide of invasion, which had kept Europe barbarous since the first irruption of the Goths and Vandals. He had given steadiness to the society of his great empire. He had promoted sound religion and unity, while he discouraged superstition. He had done something for education by ordaining schools, colleges, and libraries, and patronising the teachers of the learning and science of that day. He had matured and defined the great system of feudalism, and introduced method into the laws of his people, and civilization into their manners of life. From him we date the first recognition of the existence of the great European Christian community and republic, with some mutual duties, common interests and principles of action, which among all the changes that have come over it, has never been entirely abolished or forgotten. From his era we trace the rise of feudalism, with all its consequences—the gradation of ranks—the growing attachment to the soil—the respect for women—in short, chivalry in its noblest acceptation.

CHAPTER II.

It was vain to hope that any other hand could wield the sceptre of the great emperor; and in the grasp of his feeble and divided successors, his power was rapidly dissipated. But though his kingdom fell to pieces, the effects of his institutions, the spirit of a reign of half a century, directed to the restoration of order and establishment of law, were not altogether lost to the world.

The unhappy system of partition of the succession, was the cause of civil war and unnatural dissension immediately upon the death of Charlemagne. The reign of his son, Louis le Debonnaire, presents the revolting spectacle of a continual struggle between the sons and the father, which resulted in the establishment of independent kingdoms, fluctuating so constantly in their dynasty and their territories, that it would serve but little purpose to enumerate their names. Out of the wrecks of Charlemagne's great Christian empire arose by slow degrees the kingdom and empire of Germany, the kingdom of France, the kingdoms of the Burgundies and Provence.

Chap. II.
A.D. 887.

After the deposition of Charles the Fat, the legitimate son of Charlemagne, and the death of Arnulph, an illegitimate descendant of the great Emperor, the German people, or in other words the five duchies of the Franks, the Swabians, the Bavarians, the Saxons, and the Lorrainers, chose for their emperor, Conrad of Franconia, who was succeeded by Henry the Fowler, Duke of Saxony; and the German throne was occupied by four generations in succession of that Saxon family—a great gain to the cause of civilization, and a proof that the desire of union and steady government planted by Charlemagne had not yet died.

During the confusion of that distracted period, the feudal institutions, which were in their infancy under Charlemagne, grew and spread over Europe with a rapidity that would be marvellous, if we did not consider how singularly adapted the system was, I had almost said how natural, to the circumstances of the dominant tribes in their new settlements. If you picture to yourself a victorious army, which has just won a province in a battle. The general is the first divider of the land. He portions it out among his captains. Each of them subdivides his portion among his subaltern officers. But the country, though won, is not secure. Each captain holds his land, therefore, subject to being summoned by the general, to do service against the enemy in its defence. He makes the same compact with his subalterns, now become his vassals; and you have already the rude outline of feudalism. I shall have an opportunity of entering into some of its details in our own country hereafter.

Charles the Simple, the grandson of Charles the Fat, and the undoubted male representative of Charlemagne, was acknowledged as king over the country now taking the name of France, in the end of the ninth century, and his descendants continued titular kings till 987. But they were kings in name only, for Brittany, Aquitaine or Guienne, Provence, uniting a part of the ancient kingdom of the Burgundians, had each secured a sovereign independence; and the great feudal vassals, the Counts of Flanders, Champagne, Normandy, Burgundy, Nivernois, the Duke of Gascony, the Counts of Anjou, Ponthieu, and Vermandois, the Viscount of Bourge, the Lords of Bourbon and Couci, exercised all the rights of independent sovereigns, and scarcely, perhaps, acknowledged the king as their feudal superior; so that the kingdom of the Gallo-Franks, or France, as it now began to be called, was limited by the Loire, the Meuse, the Scheldt, and the frontier of Brittany.

In the meantime, an influence was springing up, similar to that upon which the Carlovingian power was at first founded, and the Counts of Paris and

Chap. II. Orleans, after repeatedly controlling, if not filling, the throne, at length took the place of the descendants of Charlemagne. Hugh Capet was crowned
A.D. 987. at Rheims, King of the French, and handing down his crown to his descendants, gave somewhat of stability to the French monarchy.

The powerlessness of the degenerate descendants of Charlemagne had encouraged the settlement of the Northmen, first on the coast, and afterwards in the interior of France: for during the reign of the great Emperor, though that bold and adventurous people had already formed a permanent settlement in England, in France they were only known as the pirate scourges of the coasts. It is surprising how quickly the Northmen adopted the manners and language of the people among whom they had settled as masters. It was the end of the ninth century when the pirate band ascended the Seine. When the envoys of the French king wished to parley with those companions of Rollo or "Hrolf the ganger," who were making dangerous encroachments on his territory, they approached their camp from the opposite side of the river Eure—"Ho!" cried they, "what is your chief's name?" "We have no chief, we are all equal," replied the Northmen. "Why are you come into this country, and what do you want here?" "To drive out the inhabitants," said they, "or to subdue them, and make us a country to dwell in." On that occasion the opposite parties required an interpreter to communicate, and they found a fit one in the famous Hasting, a native of Champagne, who in his youth had joined a party of Northern pirates, and made himself a terrible renown as their leader in England and all over Europe, and afterwards struck a peace with the government of France, submitted to be baptized, and obtained the county of Chartres.

A few years afterwards, when that same colony has wrested from Charles the Simple, the direct descendant of Charlemagne, one of his greatest provinces, observe how their conduct has changed. Now they allow their leader Rollo to take the hereditary Seignory, and he consents to become the vassal of the French king. As part of the treaty, and as plain matter of compact, the new French duke and his followers, now his vassals, agree to receive baptism. A few years more, and Rollo, the old sea-king, pirate, and robber, has settled down into the peaceful and prudent Duke of Normandy. He was particularly distinguished as a great Justicer, and the severe represser of all wandering robbers. Only one small body of the Scandinavian sea-kings had some remaining scruples about baptism, and these were allowed to settle by themselves, round Bayeux, on the Eure, where their little colony, for a few generations, preserved some

A.D. 912.

traces of the old Norse faith and manners. The romance of "Rollo" makes them respond to the war-cry of the Norman chivalry—"Dieu aide!" (God to our help)—by their old country shout of "Thor aide!"

It was easier for the body of the Normans to adopt the system of vassalage and feudal tenures, which, while it placed a lord *over* them, placed *under* them the whole natives of the land as their vassals, tenants and serfs. It was with them as with the Franks of old. Every born Norman was esteemed a gentleman. He was free from tax and toll; privileged to kill the game of his forests and the fish of his rivers; privileged to wear arms, and to ride on horseback; privileged to exact service, and lord almost of the life and goods of the race whom the fortune of war had degraded into the tillers of his lands. It thus came to pass, that in an incredibly short space of time, the descendants of the Northmen had adopted the language of Northern France, and all its feudal customs, as well as the system of land tenures, even to an extreme rigour; and, before the period of the conquest of England—only 160 years after their arrival in France as rough and landless Scandinavian pirates, "who knew no country, owned no lord,"—they had adopted territorial styles of surname from their baronial chateaus in Normandy, practised the knightly fashions then coming into observance, and affected all the forms and language of infant chivalry.

I have hitherto avoided speaking of the affairs of Britain. During the times we have been passing under review, our island was little mixed up in the politics of Continental Europe. It was not, however, without events of great importance in the history of nations, and of paramount interest to us. Britain had already gone through two great revolutions, involving changes of the dominant race of its inhabitants.

Of the elements of old British society, preserved under the Romans, we learn very little from the Latin writers; and the British accounts have reached us in a form modern and corrupted. In the Lowlands, or large eastern part of Britain, the ancient language probably disappeared early, and has now left no traces. The rivers and mountains, indeed, those eternal features of nature, have preserved their primitive names; and we can count a few places, rare exceptions, still called as they were known to the adventurous merchant before the Roman conquest. We have the Isle of *Wight*, not much changed from that which the Romans Latinized into *Vecta* ; *Dover*, which they called *Dubris* ; *Kent* bore the same name two thousand years ago; and that ancient mart on the Thames, which the Romans tried to rechristen *Augusta*, has still preserved its more ancient name of *London*.

Chap. II.   Beyond the mountains, and generally on the western side of the island, this is different. Cornwall was called Bretland, or land of Britons, so late as the twelfth century, by the Norse; and until the middle of the sixteenth century, the primitive British or Logrian tongue was spoken there. In Man, it remained longer. In Wales, the Romans never had much footing, and there the British language has kept a stubborn hold. It was the same within time of record in Galloway; and I need not tell you, that beyond the Grampians, the native people preserve their native language.

Somewhat may perhaps be traced of the remains of British institutions as well as language; but it is a difficult and doubtful investigation, and I would only call your attention to that, which is said to be a vestige of ancient British custom, the law of Gavelkind, by which the sons or brothers inherit land equally, without distinction of seniority, of which there are still traces in Wales, in Kent, and in some parts of Northumberland.

B.C. 55-
A.D. 446.
The Romans were in Britain about five hundred years. They found it a thickly-peopled and fertile country. The natives of the better part of the island soon amalgamated with them, and enjoyed the protection and civilization that every where accompanied the Roman arms. Before they left it, there were forty-six military stations, and twenty-eight

cities of consequence, from Inverness and Perth, to that London, which Tacitus describes as a port famous for its number of merchants and extent of trade.[1] The military force required for the defence of the colony amounted, in general, to 20,000 foot and 1700 horse, and these were not birds of passage, like the troops in our colonies. The sixth legion remained at York as its head quarters for nearly three hundred years. The soil of the country all round is found full of their remains—from statues and altars, down to their domestic furniture, and pottery manufactured with their own stamp (Legio VI.) Its natural fertility and Roman cultivation, soon made Britain the granary of the northern provinces of the empire. The rich country required an immense organization of civilians, magistrates, and tax-gatherers. Its importance as a military station, and, perhaps, the pleasantness of the land, made it a favourite residence of several of the later emperors. Adrian and Severus, Geta and Caracalla, were amongst them; Constantine was born at York, and the Emperor Constantius Chlorus lived and died in Britain.

I do not know that there is anything that gives us a more startling insight into Roman life in Britain, than the villas which have been lately disinterred in

[1] Londinum copia negotiatorum et commeatuum maxime celebre.—*Tacit. An.* xiv. 33.

several parts of England. One of these, which I have fresh in my recollection, though I visited it many years ago, is in Oxfordshire, upon a haugh more than half surrounded by a little stream, the opposite bank of which, still covered with immemorial copse, defends it from the north and east. The walls can be perfectly traced, and show that the buildings, which never exceeded one storey high above ground, surrounded a small court open to the southern sun. It is for the fancy of the visitor to allot the different apartments, for a library, for banqueting-rooms, and family purposes. All of them were floored with tesselated pavements, of many colours and the most elegant designs, while some were spacious enough to have been employed for the exercises which formed so favourite a part of ancient life. One large room spoke its own history, from the furnace placed below, and innumerable flues marked only alternately with smoke, surrounding a bath large enough for swimming. The water was supplied through a leaden pipe, and, guided by its direction, we traced it to its source, some hundred yards off, in a spring deep and cold and pure as Blandusia. The master of the villa might hunt the boar and the wild bull in the forest which still surrounds that little valley; he might luxuriate beside the cool fountain, upon turf greener than ever adorned the banks of the Anio. Undoubtedly he was a person of taste and cultivation; and the number of similar rural retreats of the Romans through England, speaks a high degree of security and enjoyment, and of the blessings of civilization; especially when we consider, that with the Romans, country life was the exception, and their real home was in cities. We might argue as much from those stupendous roads, which every where intersect the Roman province, if it were not, that these might be chiefly required for maintaining the military communication through the country. The venerable Bede mentions the Roman towns, lighthouses, roads and bridges, as still existing in his time, or the beginning of the eighth century.

But far beyond all the rest for the civilization of Britain, the Roman occupation was the means of introducing into our country the Christian faith. The fostering care of Constantine was prominently felt in Britain. The old places of superstitious worship, whether Roman or British, were consecrated to the service of a purer faith. Out of Bangor, supposed to have been a place of Druidical worship, arose the most ancient of British churches and monasteries, while a temple of Apollo on the bank of the Thames served as the foundation of the Church, which afterwards became the Abbey Church of St. Peter of Westminster; and the Temple of Diana of London, gave place to St.

Paul's Cathedral. Three British bishops[1] attended the first council of Arles; and there is reason to believe that there were, even at that period, two other bishops in Britain, one of whom was in Wales and the other in Scotland. In like manner Britain sent three bishops to the council of Ariminum in 359.

The radical defect of Roman colonisation outweighed in the end all those advantages which Britain had derived from her government. She civilized, and perhaps instructed the poor Britons. She taught them to wear clothes instead of the skins of their sheep; refined and cultivated them with education and religion. But Rome withheld from her colonists altogether the employments, the institutions, the organization, which might have prepared them for acting with unity, when forced to act independently. The Roman Code, admirable as it is, knows no higher sanction than—*placet principi.* It was the policy of Rome, that the subject world should look to her as its centre and sole point of binding attraction, and when the evil days came, and she was obliged to gather in her armies for her own protection, there was no head to guide, no self-reliance, no experience or energy, in the deserted colony: liberty became helplessness; independence anarchy; and the

[1] Eborius of York, Restitutus of London, and Adelphius of Lincoln.

fabric fell at once to pieces before the onslaught of _{Chap. II.} the more vigorous barbarians.

The Romans had left Britain finally but little before the middle of the fifth century. That was the era of the famous message of the poor Britons to the Consul Aetius—" The barbarians drive us to the sea; the sea to the barbarians." In a century and a half _{A.D. 446.} afterwards, the polished language which had been for generations the common tongue, both of the settlers and of the natives, had entirely disappeared. Christianity was forgotten within all that had been the Roman province of Britain, and preserved a faint and struggling existence only in the fastnesses of Wales and Scotland. All the refinements and decencies of life, science, literature, and the arts, sunk at once before the energy and courage of a barbarous enemy. The Britons themselves sunk into a race of cultivators, little removed from hewers of wood and drawers of water, except the few who preserved their independence under the Welsh mountains, or in their aboriginal seats of Gaulish Brittany.

The people called Saxons, had become known in history as early as the second century. They then inhabited the islands at the mouth of the Elbe, and perhaps Holstein and Hadeln, from whence they infested the northern seas as pirates, and made themselves so formidable, that a high military officer of

Chap. II. the Roman empire was appointed for repressing them, and bore the title of "Count of the Saxon shore" in the end of the third century. Two other nations, similar in habits, and speaking dialects of the same tongue, were from the earliest time associated with them, and, indeed, pass continually under the common name of Saxons. These were the Angles, from the district of Angeln, now insignificant, but formerly of greater extent, and including Sleswic; and the Jutes, who occupied the northern part of that peninsula, whose coast and islands are so singularly adapted for the purposes of piracy.

I do not think it necessary to detain you to discuss the exact manner and time of the arrival of those new masters in Britain. The popular story of Vortigern, King of the Britons, begging for Saxon assistance, and the sudden and complete success of Hengist and Horsa, are now deservedly viewed with suspicion. The names of these leaders are not mentioned by any writer for nearly three centuries after their supposed era, in connection with the romantic story in which they are now made to figure so prominently; and there is reason to believe, that the Saxon pirates had been making attacks, and even settlements, along the eastern coast of Scotland and England, before Britain was left unprotected by the armies of Rome. After that, for certain, invasions were made rapidly and almost simultaneously by the piratical nations; and in a hundred and fifty years, all that had been Roman of our island had passed under the power of the new invaders. The gradual but constant progress made during that time, in the occupation of many parts of Britain by independent hordes of various races, looks less like a conquest than a progressive usurpation of the British territory.

The Jutes colonized Kent only, a county still remarkable for its peculiar customs, and for what, on a larger scale, might be called its *nationality*. It alone has a subdivision into six districts, called *Lathes*, a word unknown in the rest of England, and which appears to be connected with the *lething* of the Jutish law, in which it means a military expedition, or perhaps the district which might be summoned for it.

The great kingdom of Northumberland, and those of East Anglia and Mercia, that is, the whole of England north of the counties of Hertford, Northampton, and Warwick, was occupied by the Angles. If you examine the maps, or the admirable county histories of that great territory, you will find that the division of counties was into *Wapentakes*, and not into hundreds, and you will observe many of the names of towns beginning and ending in *kirk*, while *minster* is the southern word, and many ending in *by* (though this termination was given long afterwards by the Danes in Derby).

Chap. II.   The remainder of Roman Britain fell to the Saxons, who used the division of *Hundreds*, instead of the Anglian *Wapentakes*.

Such I believe to have been the general outline of the settlement of Britain, as gathered from the historians, to whom we owe the little information we have of that time—the laws and customs subsequently found in observance in each district—and the dialects of the three nations, as detected in the written and spoken language of the inhabitants. But I need hardly warn you against expecting precision in tracing the settlements of peoples so rude, so much intermingled from their piratical habits, and speaking a language so nearly identical. There is no doubt, moreover, that besides these leading tribes, others of the Teutonic peoples, and especially many Frisians, joined in the great adventure.

The only hero, whose deeds were memorable enough to be handed down on the side of the Britons, is King Arthur, whose gallant share in the last struggle of his countrymen has associated his name in the traditions of the country, from Cornwall to our own Strathmore. While the old lays of the bards of Wales and Brittany adopted him as their hero, it happened that the first romances of northern chivalry were built upon that foundation, and this accident has brought it about, that king Arthur and the Knights of his Round Table are celebrated in countries and languages to which his was a stranger, and have become the heroes, not of Britain, but of Christian chivalry.

The Saxons of the Continent, the Frisians and the Germanic races who settled in Britain, had no kings according to our sense of the word;[1] and it was the necessity of a leader in their invasions that induced them to submit to a commander, whom they called Heretoga—army leader—or Ealdorman—a word which has now assumed a more peaceful meaning. The chief military leader of the horde became in time the chief of the settled colony, and borrowed from his Germanic home the sacred appellation of *Son of the Nation*, which, in Saxon, became *Cyning*, now *King*. The king was elective within the range of certain noble families, and whatever preference there might be for sons of a deceased sovereign, the instances are innumerable in which the brothers, as more fit for the management of affairs, were chosen to the exclusion of sons—of which the great Alfred is an example; and the succession of the younger Ætheling, or king's son, is not unfrequent in preference to his elder brother. An affectation prevailed among the later Saxons, of copying the high-sounding titles of the emperors of the East and West, as *Augustus, Basileus*.[2]

---

[1] Bede, 5-10.
[2] So Edgar, King of Scots, styles himself on his seal—*Scotorum basileus*.

The Anglo-Saxon Queen (you are probably aware that *queen* means *wife*) was a person of great importance. She was to be chosen from a noble family, and was consecrated and crowned as solemnly as the king, and she was seated beside him in the hall at feasts.

A hereditary nobility is plainly to be traced, in the earlier times asserting its descent from Woden, and afterwards, contented with pushing its pedigree to the Military or the Sea-kings. These were the Æthelings. The leader of a tribe in primitive times was the man, the most venerable for age, and hence Ealdorman was the style of a chief of a great district. This office or dignity was bestowed by decree of the assembly of the people; but in effect and practice, became nearly hereditary. His duty was to lead the district in war, and to govern it in peace, and he had for his support, lands appertaining to the office, and a third of the fines and the profits of the courts, and of the other revenues of the king.

Next in rank were the Gesiths, or Thanes, and although these, like the Ealdormen, acquired their rank by service, there cannot be much doubt that it gradually became hereditary. Indeed the settled state of the country, and the increase of the Saxon population, and more than either, the influence of the Christian clergy, gradually led to the landed property becoming hereditary, and converted nobility by service, into nobility by birth.

Of those with no claim to nobility was the Saxon *churl*, or freeman, the native Briton (*Wealh*, literally a foreigner, a Welshman), who might be free and even might hold property; but was of inferior rank and value, according to that most curious system of discrimination, by which the injuries done to a man's person were estimated according to his rank.

The serf (*theow, esn*), was the lowest class in the Saxon society. They are supposed to have been the descendants of Roman slaves and of the native Britons. The most remarkable circumstance connected with them, is their unequal distribution and the smallness of their number. At the time of the census of Doomsday, their whole number was little more than twenty-five thousand. They were most numerous in the districts, where the British population maintained itself the longest. In Gloucestershire, for instance, there was one slave to every third freeman, and in Cornwall, Devon and Staffordshire, they were as one to five. In the Saxon States and in Kent, the serfs constituted a tenth of the population, and it is exceedingly remarkable, that in the shires of Lincoln, Huntingdon and Rutland, and in the great county of York, not a single slave is registered, and in the neighbouring counties, only a very small number, as in Nottingham, where they appear in the proportion of one to two hundred and fifteen.

The land at its first conquest, and perhaps for some short time afterwards, belonged to the people in common, and it was upon this theory that their system of land rights was founded. The *Folcland*, or public land, might, however, be occupied in common, or parcelled out to individuals. It could not be alienated in perpetuity, but only for a term or years, or for life, after which it returned to the public. *Bocland*, or charter-land, was such as was severed by an act of the government, that is, by the king, with the consent of his parliament or *witan*, from the public land, and so converted into an estate of perpetual inheritance. The former tenure was loaded with services and rents, from which the latter was free.

Many of the shires of England[1] were formed out of the petty kingdoms of the Anglo-Saxons; others from ancient bishoprics—which takes place in those shires that bear the name of their episcopal sees.[2] The shire was divided into *hundreds* or *wapentakes*, and those again into *tithings*, deriving their names from the original number of freemen who composed them. In each of these divisions, bound by an ascertained

---

[1] Kent, Sussex, Essex, Surrey, Norfolk, Suffolk, Devon, and Cambria.

[2] Durham, York, Lincoln, Chester, Worcester, Hereford, Oxford.

responsibility of the community and individuals to each other, there was a head man who assembled his district in courts, at stated times, for its common affairs and for trial of causes. In the mature Anglo-Saxon constitution, there was a meeting of the county court (a *gemot* of the *scir-witan*), twice in the year, in which the Ealdorman, afterwards called Earl, along with the Bishop, presided; and the Sheriff (*scir gerefa, vice comes*), was at first an assessor, and afterwards the presiding officer. The subordinate gemots met oftener.

The *witan* of the kingdom (the king's high court or parliament) consisted of the great men, whether ecclesiastics or laymen. Nothing of representation, strictly so called, is to be found in Saxon times.

As in none of the subordinate *gemots* could the head man determine anything but by the advice and with the assent of the assembly; so it was in the national assembly or parliament. The decision of public matters was in no case entrusted to individuals.

The feudal institutions had spread into England during the Anglo-Saxon period, and with them the institutions of chivalry. The *lean* lands or *lent* lands of the Saxons were evidently approaching to a sort of feudal tenure. Asser, the biographer of Alfred, speaks of *knights* and *vassals* in his time. There is something like the knightly girding with a sword, by Ælfred, upon Æthelstan, and an ancient Saxon oath of fealty, preserves the Saxon notion of vassal and superior.[1]

I have dwelt upon these details longer than they may appear to deserve, because we cannot but feel an interest in those from whom we inherit our Saxon blood and language; but yet more, because I think we can see, in these early English institutions, the causes why the Norman conquest did not abolish Anglo-Saxonism, as the Saxon possession obliterated everything of Roman Britain. There was something in these institutions of Saxon England themselves that was worth preserving; I think they secured a high degree of personal independence, with safety to the community. They inspired feelings of self-respect, and a sense of the obligations of men as members of society, that fitted them peculiarly in later times for a representative government. They produced that feeling of mutual responsibility and mutual confidence, and that binding together of

---

[1] "Thus shall a man swear fealty:—By the Lord, before whom this relic is holy, I will be to N. faithful and true, and love all that he loves, and shun all that he shuns, according to God's law, and according to the world's principles (*worold-gerysnum*), and never, by will nor by force, by word nor by work, do aught of what is loathful to him; on condition that he me keep as I am willing to deserve, and all that fulfil that our agreement was when I to him submitted and chose his will." The words of the original, of unknown antiquity, are rhythmical and alliterative.—*Thorpe's Ancient Laws and Institutes of England*, I. 178.

individuals and communities of the state, which I take to be the chief distinction of Britain. It is this firm coherence, joined to our admiration of that wonderful constitution under which we live, that makes shocks the most alarming pass without injury, and convulsions of public opinion which, in other countries, would shake the state and lead to revolution and blood, end with us in a dissolution of parliament, or a change of ministry.

I have said that the light of Christianity was extinguished in Roman Britain by the conquest of the Saxons. It may indeed have survived among the servile and degraded Britons, who consented to remain among the new lords of their country, and we know that it was preserved in Wales, as it was also in Ireland and Scotland; but the Saxons for more than a century after they had taken full possession of their English home, continued to worship Odin and Thor. When Augustine was sent from Rome by Pope Gregory the Great to preach the gospel to the Anglo-Saxons, he required the intervention of Franks as his interpreters. After he had converted Æthelbert of Kent, his people followed the king's example, and in one year more than 10,000 were baptized. Christianity as usual brought civilization in its train, and the first convert of the Saxon princes was the compiler of the earliest code of English laws, perhaps the earliest of those of

Chap. II. Northern Europe. In those days, conversions were made often by conquest, often by treaty and bargain. A defeated army acknowledged their gods the weaker, and received the religion of their conquerors, as they submitted to their tribute or levy. So, when a leader consented to be baptized, he led his whole nation with him to the font.

A.D. 717-633.

Edwin of Northumbria—known in our romantic ballads as the child of Elle, and who gave name to the Castle of Edinburgh—had been half converted, as we are told, partly by a miraculous interference in his favour, partly, no doubt, through the influence of a Christian wife. He gave his daughter to be baptized, when he was assured that his queen's life was saved in the hour of trial, through the prayers of the Christian Bishop Paulinus; and he promised to renounce his idols and serve Christ, if He would grant him the victory over his enemy Cwichelm, king of the West Saxons, who had tried to assassinate him. He obtained a great victory, and on his return he called a meeting of his friends and great council, and asked their opinion of the new faith. Bede, a venerable authority, details the conference;—Caefi, the high priest, declared that their old religion had no virtue or use; " for," said he, " not one of your subjects has been more zealous than me in the worship of our gods: and there are many who have received greater benefits and honours from you, and prosper more in all their undertakings; whereas, if our gods were of any power, they would rather help me, who have so zealously served them." The priest was satisfied with his own reasoning, and volunteered himself to profane the altars and shrines of the gods, with their enclosures. When the people saw him mount a horse and ride forward, armed for the purpose, Bede tells us that they thought him mad; but they very soon followed his example, and set fire to the place of heathen worship. Edwin was baptized with all his children. The nobles crowded for baptism, and Paulinus was employed in the king's dwelling for thirty-six days, from morning to evening, baptizing the people in the river Glen, the stream which gives name to Glendale. That was but a small part of the effects of the preaching of Paulinus, who was deservedly made the first Saxon Bishop at York, and received the pall of Archbishop from Pope Honorius.

It was necessary in such circumstances to bear with some non-conformity—some backslidings into the old worship, and the ways of their forefathers. And in this, truly, the Church was lenient enough. Gregory, to suit the habits of the Kentish neophytes, forbade the destruction of the old heathen temples, venerated by the people; even their accustomed sacrifices he wished to associate with some of the observances of the Church. But while Rome was tolerant of laxity in the practice of her neophytes, she never lost sight of her great policy of uniformity in all that touched the doctrines and observances of the Church. With this view, Augustine endeavoured to win over the Bishops of the ancient British Church, who differed from Rome in points that we may indeed think trifling, but which were of no small consequence, when they threatened to found a schism in the Christian Church. The Welsh Bishops met the Roman missionary at a tree which was long afterwards known as St. Augustine's oak, but without coming to any settlement of their disputes. At another conference, which was attended by seven British Bishops, and by the Abbot and several learned monks of Bangor, St. Augustine demanded compliance upon only three points:—

> To celebrate Easter at the proper season;
> To perform baptism after the manner of Rome;
> To join with the Roman missionaries in preaching Christianity to the Saxons.

The Britons refused compliance upon all those points, which were perhaps pressed somewhat overbearingly by the Pope's representative, apparently against the conciliating intention of Gregory himself. Augustine denounced against them the judgment of God, for refusing to aid in preaching the way of life to the Saxons, and it was not long after, when the Saxons fulfilled the prediction. "Those who pray against us," said they, "are our enemies, though unarmed;" and they put to death two hundred of the monks of Bangor.

While the recent memory of Saxon oppression led the Welsh Britons to refuse their aid for the conversion of the Saxons to Christianity, no such feeling prevented the Scotch Christians from devoting themselves to the Christianising of the North of England. But I shall have another opportunity of directing your attention to the preaching and success of the followers of St. Columba.

However introduced, Christianity came at length; and if you examine carefully the history of any nation, you will find that, besides higher blessings, it brought in its train three remarkable effects—a tendency to unite—an inclination for kingly governments—and a preference for hereditary institutions.

I cannot leave the subject of Christianity among the Anglo-Saxons, without adverting to the number of zealous missionaries whom the Anglo-Saxon Church sent forth, so soon after its own conversion. It seemed as if the Saxons of England thought they could in no way better show their affection to their German fatherland than by communicating to their kinsmen there, the blessing of a revelation which they themselves had so recently enjoyed. Wilbrod of Northumbria, and Winfred, better known by the name of Boniface of Devonshire, in

Chap. II. the early part of the eighth century, devoted themselves with the most untiring zeal to the instruction of the German peoples, and each lived to see churches cathedrals, and monasteries, taking the place of Pagan groves and temples; and whole nations, seeking for a succession of teachers from that country which was to them truly the island of saints.

A.D. 685-728.
The struggle between the Saxons and Danes brings us acquainted with two of the most memorable men that have stamped their names on English history—Alfred and Cnut. It is no wonder that Alfred should be the hero and idol of Anglo-Saxons. Their leader in the death struggle with the Danes, he had all the national sympathies on his side. He was the champion of Christianity against Heathenesse, as well as the defender of Saxons against their barbarian enemies—their saint as well as their hero. He was their king Arthur, only more fortunate. Neither is it wonderful that on such a hero, succeeding generations should have bestowed honours somewhat exaggerated. He is commonly called the Anglo-Saxon lawgiver; and he collected indeed the laws of former kings of the three principal states, which he governed; but he himself tells us, that he was cautious of inserting enactments of his own, as he was doubtful whether such would be approved by those that should come after him. The division

of the country into shires and hundreds, and the introduction of the system of frank pledge, or the system by which every man of a tithing was surety for every other, have been generally attributed to Alfred, apparently without foundation; but after making due discount for those overstatements, enough remains in Alfred to fill us with wonder and admiration. Occupied during the better part of his life in war against an invading enemy, he no sooner had breathing time than he turned himself to the great work of restoring and civilizing his country. His exertions were directed to all objects, and embraced every kind of improvement. He rebuilt the ruined towns; London itself, which, by the Danish conflicts, was become an uninhabitable pile of ruins, he cleared and rendered fair and habitable; he restored old roads and opened new ones; he encouraged agriculture, and in his own country dwellings, set an example of more convenient and more sightly buildings than the Anglo-Saxons had hitherto used. He reformed the art of ship-building, and provided a navy to cope with all the power of the Northmen. It sounds strange to us now, that he took the seamen for his new ships from the pirates, probably the Frisians, the best sailors of that time. While other Anglo-Saxon kings had taken advantage of the devastations of war, and appropriated to themselves the property of

CHAP. II. monasteries and churches destroyed by the Danes; Alfred followed a nobler policy, in restoring and re-endowing the establishments of religion, and in the utmost munificence and most dutiful service to the Church and Christian preachers. The laws, which he had collected and published, he was careful to enforce; and gave much of his time to hearing of causes and appeals in his own court. He was the enemy of oppression, and, as his biographer calls him, " the only friend of the poor." He maintained a more regular intercourse with Rome than his predecessors, and we must not forget that Rome was the centre of literature and the arts, as well as of religion. He invited learned men to his court, and endeavoured to restore some literature amongst his people, which had so decayed during the Danish war, that, at the time of his accession, very few south of the Humber, and none south of the Thames, knew Latin enough to translate an easy Latin work. You will observe that Asser, his biographer, to whom we owe this information, excepts Northumbria from the censure of such ignorance; and we may hope, that the cloisters of Wearmouth and Durham, where the venerable Bede had studied Lucretius and Homer 150 years before, still preserved some taste and love for letters.

Alfred, from his youth laboured under some unknown disease, and although he is praised for his vigour of body, and practised hunting to please his countrymen, his favourite pursuits were of another kind. He purchased privileges for the Saxon school at Rome, and he provided schools in Britain for education, both in Saxon and Latin, and not only for priests, but also for the young nobility, who he was anxious should learn to read and write; and especially that they should learn poems in their mother tongue by heart, before they were distracted by hunting and warlike exercises. I wish I could say with truth that Oxford was one of those schools established by Alfred. I think the evidence unsatisfactory; and, after all, even the honour of such a founder and of so high antiquity, would add but little to the dignity of that famous and venerable university. Alfred surrounded himself with men of learning, and devoted much of his own time to study. From his early youth he had delighted in reading and committing to memory the poems of his native language. He learned Latin when he was thirty-nine years old, and afterwards bestowed much of his time in making translations from Latin into Saxon. He translated Boethius on the Consolation of Philosophy, which, though now so little known, was perhaps the most popular book of the middle ages; and the pastoral letter of Pope Gregory, which must have been translated almost in the last year of

CHAP. II. his life. The History of the World, by Orosius, he not only translated, but prefixed to it a description of Germany and the north of Europe, compiled by himself from the narratives of the travellers Wulfstan and Ohthere. Many other works of translation are attributed to Alfred, but upon uncertain foundation, except, however, his Anglo-Saxon version of the history of the venerable Bede—a work which stands high, and almost alone, in the literature of the middle ages.

A.D. 901. Alfred died on the 28th of October 901, at the age of fifty-three. We love to trace in him the type of the Anglo-Saxon nature, refined by education, and exalted by religion, by adversity, and trial. His will has been preserved to us.[1]

[1] "On the death of Æthelred, some disputes arose regarding the succession, in consequence of which Alfred caused his father's will to be read before a witenagemot assembled at Langdene, pledging himself to bear no ill-will towards any one for speaking justly, and beseeching them not to fear declaring according to Folkright; so that no man might say that he had wronged his kin, either young or old.

. . . . .

"After this preamble, the king proceeds to the division of his property. To each of his sons he devises lands and five hundred pounds; to his wife, Ealhswith, and each of his three daughters, certain villages, and one hundred pounds; to Æthelm and Æthelwold, his nephews, and to Osferth, his kinsman, certain villages, and one hundred mancuses each;[1] to each of his Ealdormen one hundred mancuses; to Æthered, ealdorman, a sword of a hundred mancuses; to be divided among his

[1] The mancus was thirty pence.

In Cnut, whom our historians have named Canute we have the type of a different race. Acquiring the crown by fraud, and securing it by plentiful murders, he yet ruled a people, jealous of him as a foreigner and an enemy, so strenuously, but with such fairness, as to make them happier than they had been lately under their native sovereigns. He was a remarkable instance of a barbarian (for such he was in all respects),—without education, without religion—apprehending by the grasp of his own intellect the conduct that was fittest for his situation when wielding the sceptres of three kingdoms. The savage sometimes shone out in him

followers, two hundred pounds; to the archbishop and three bishops, one hundred mancuses each. Lastly, two hundred pounds for himself and his father, and those friends for whose souls they had both made intercession, to be thus divided: fifty pounds to as many mass priests, fifty to as many poor ministers of God, fifty to the poor, and fifty to the church in which he should rest.

"Alfred adds—'And I will that those to whom I have bequeathed my bócland, dispose of it not out of my kin after their death, but that it go to my nearest relative, except any of them have children, and then it is more agreeable to me that it go to those born on the male side, as long as any of them shall be worthy of it. My grandfather bequeathed his lands on the spear-side, not on the spindle-side; therefore, if I have given what he acquired to any of the female side, let my kinsmen make compensation; and if they will have it during the life of the party, be it so; if otherwise, let it remain during their days as we have bequeathed it.' He then desires his relations and heirs not to oppress any of his people, whether bond or free, nor aggrieve them by exactions of money or otherwise; but that they may serve whatever lord they will."—*Thorpe's Lappenberg*, II. 81.

Chap. II. unmitigated. After his defeat on the river Helga, where he owed his life to his brother-in-law Ulf Jarl, he retreated to Roskilde to spend his Christmas, but out of humour for the festivities of the season. On Christmas eve, Ulf gave a great entertainment, and the brothers-in-law began to play chess. Cnut was inattentive, and lost a knight; but refused to give it up. Ulf rose from the table, and in making for the door, threw down the board. "Ho! coward Ulf! are you running away?" cried the king. "Not so far or so fast as you would have run," said Ulf, "when I rescued you at the Helga, where the Swedes were cudgelling you." Cnut went to bed; but next morning he gave orders to a servant,—"Go and stab Ulf." The man returned and told him that the Jarl had fled to the church of St. Lucius. But what was the protection of the church to the savage Cnut? He called to a Norwegian, named Ivar Huida: "Go, stab the Jarl dead." Ivar went, found Ulf in the choir, and ran him through with his sword. To his widowed sister Cnut paid a blood-fine of two provinces.

Though thus ferocious, Cnut was a stern administrator of the laws; and for enforcing them, used to journey through his English states, attended by his councillors and scribes. He has left us a large body of laws for the regulation and protection of the

Church and clergy, and he distributed with impartiality their several rights to the Saxons and Danes. We cannot attribute to him much true religious feeling, and he was exempt from all superstition; but he had a just sense of the interest of his people, and therefore he protected religion, and favoured and enriched the clergy. He preferred England to his Danish dominions, and the English people learned to look upon the stern Dane as their friend and good king.

After his journey to Rome, he sent a letter to his English subjects, which has been preserved, and some part of which is very remarkable. It was sent by the hands of Living, the abbot of Tavistock, afterwards the bishop of Crediton.[1]

---

[1] "Cnut, king of all England and Denmark, and of part of Sweden, to Æthelnoth, the metropolitan, and Ælfric of York, and to all bishops and primates, and to the whole nation of the English, both noble and ignoble, wishes health. I make known to you that I have lately been to Rome, to pray for the redemption of my sins, and for the prosperity of the kingdoms and peoples subject to my rule. This journey I had long ago vowed to God, though, through affairs of state and other impediments, I had hitherto been unable to perform it; but I now humbly return thanks to God Almighty for having in my life granted me to yearn after the blessed Apostles Peter and Paul, and every sacred place within and without the city of Rome which I could learn of, and, according to my desire, personally to venerate and adore. And this I have executed chiefly because I had learned from wise men that the holy Apostle Peter had received from the Lord the great power of binding and loosing, and was key-bearer of the celestial kingdom; and I therefore deemed it extremely useful to desire his patronage before God.

CHAP. II. The invasion of the Danes, however productive of suffering, and often threatening ruin to the very existence of the English nation, did not eventually produce much change upon the established institutions. As soon as the Danish freebooter had acquired an interest in the soil, and settled his family in the fields or towns of England, he con-

> Be it now known to you that there was a great assembly of nobles at the Easter celebration with the Lord Pope John and the Emperor Conrad, to wit, all the princes of the nations from Mount Gargano to the nearest sea, who all received me honourably, and honoured me with rich gifts. But I have been chiefly honoured by the Emperor, with divers magnificent presents, as well in golden and silver vases, as in mantles and vestments exceedingly precious."
>
> . . . . .
>
> "I then complained to the Lord Pope, and said that it greatly displeased me, that, from my archbishops such immense sums of money were exacted when, according to usage, they visited the apostolic see to receive the pall; and it was agreed that thenceforth such exactions should not be made. And all that I have demanded for the benefit of my people from the Lord Pope, from the Emperor, from king Rudolf, and from the other princes through whose territories our way lies to Rome, they have freely granted."
>
> . . . . .
>
> "Now, then, be it known to you that I have vowed, as a suppliant from henceforth, to justify in all things my whole life to God, and to rule the kingdoms and peoples subjected to me justly and piously, to maintain equal justice among all; and if through the intemperance of my youth, or through negligence I have done aught hitherto contrary to what is just, I intend with the aid of God to amend all."
>
> . . . . .
>
> "I therefore wish it to be made known to you, that returning by the same way that I departed, I am going to Denmark for the purpose of settling with the Counsel of all the Danes, firm and lasting peace with those nations which, had it been in their power, would have deprived us of our life and kingdoms."
>
> . . . . .
>
> "I therefore conjure all my bishops and ealdormen, by the

formed readily to the usages and laws of a people of kindred origin and manners, and almost common language. "Scarcely," says an old chronicler, "was there one village in England in which the Danes were not mixed with the English." The same author gravely relates "that the Danes bequeathed to England as a legacy . . . their custom of drinking fair." I fear the Saxons were willing and apt pupils.

I must not indulge myself by dwelling longer on the English portion of British history—a history full of interest in itself—crowded with romantic incident, and where the details are gathered from those simple unsuspected sources, the most fascinating reading, those contemporary chronicles of which France and England are so rich, and we so poor. The study would be fascinating from the mere dramatic interest, the bold and truthful outlines of individual character, the scenes

fealty which they owe to me and to God, so to order that before I come to England, the debts of all which we owe according to the old law be paid; to wit, plough-alms, and a tithe of animals brought forth during the year, and the pence which ye owe to St. Peter at Rome, both from the cities and villages; and in the middle of August, a tithe of fruits, and at the feast of St. Martin the first fruits of things sown, to the church of the parish in which each one dwells, which is in English called coricsceat. If when I come, these and others are not paid, he who is in fault shall be punished by the royal power severely, and without any remission. Farewell."—*Lappenberg*, II. 212.

Chap. II. full of high passion, and all the materials of deep tragedy. But to us Britons, to us Scotchmen, bound now for ever to the fortunes of mighty England, bearing with her the burden, sharing with Englishmen their noble birthright—each event, each apparently insignificant accident, assumes an importance beyond the rise and fall of empires, if it can be traced as the remote cause of any of the steps of progress, any of the peculiarities of our revered constitution.

I might perhaps have an excuse for dwelling at greater length on the Norman conquest—an event that very speedily affected the institutions of Scotland, though producing no change in its dynasty—but I feel that I must press forward to that which I have prescribed to myself, as my proper and peculiar object.

When William of Normandy had proclaimed his crusade against England, and prevailed with the Pope (or rather with Hildebrand, the scheming prelate who then ruled the Roman councils as effectually as when he afterwards consented to wear the tiara as Pope Gregory the VII.) to bless his banner; there was no dearth of allies and assistants. Every man had heard of the riches of England; its cities crowded with trade; its fields covered with corn and sheep and cattle; its lordly castles and fat monasteries. Every needy adventurer who hoped to make his fortune by his sword; every younger brother who aspired to wed a wealthy Saxon heiress—all came to his summons and all were welcomed, provided they were tall men of their hands—good men at arms—"*proceri corpore, præstantes robore.*" One churchman, Remi de Feschamp, who had raised twenty men-at-arms and provided a ship for the expedition, had a promise of an English bishoprick, and obtained it.[1] Among the crowd of adventurers, we are interested in two youths, Brian and Allan, two of the sons of Eudes, Governor, or as we should say *Tutor*, during the minority of his nephew the Count of Bretagne. They were called by their own people, in their own Celtic tongue, *Mac-tiern*—the sons of the chief. We can conceive the feelings with which those youths embarked on the high enterprise, to recover their ancient birthright in England, and to take vengeance on the Saxons, who had expelled their forefathers.

It would exceed my limits to enter upon the inquiry as to the cause of the success of the Normans in England, and why the country, which had struggled so stubbornly against defeat and disunion in the Danish invasions, seemed to peril its existence now on the issue of one battle, and having

[1] Bishopric of Lincoln.

lost it, to submit slavishly to a mere handful of invaders. The intrigues of Rome had some effect, and yet more, the Norman feeling, so unhappily spread through the English clergy since the time of the Confessor.

When the rashness of the gallant Harald had thrown away his kingdom and his life, and made a handful of Norman cavaliers lords of broad England, most of the phenomena were renewed which had rendered their occupation of Normandy so remarkable. They had, in the century and a half of their occupation of France, acquired a new language; and the Norman-French they had so lightly adopted, was for a time the only tongue for a gentleman, while Saxon was the mark of the Franklin and Churl. They had brought with them the newest customs of feudalism, and found the Norman tenures well fitted for oppressing the native occupants of the soil. They brought their laws of the game, their cruel forest law. They imported all that they had learned in their short sojourn in France. But they were scarcely well embued with those French institutions. They had not elaborated laws to suit their own position. Their customs of chivalry were merely caught by contagion. Their language they had not cultivated. No chronicler or poet had yet sung of the French Normans, or given stability or precision to their dialect. All this contrasted remarkably with the situation of their new subjects. The Anglo-Saxon language had been long cultivated in prose and poetry, and was endeared to the people, from having been written by their great Alfred and by the fathers of their Church, before any other vernacular tongue of Europe had been studied by the learned. Their laws, too, had been methodised, and gave a definite protection to the person and property; and their institutions were eminently those of free men. For centuries afterwards, when Englishmen, roused by oppression, shouted a general claim of right, it was, that they might be governed by the laws of Alfred and of Edward the Confessor. There was an earnestness in the people that gave a zeal to their nationality before which the novel customs of the Normans could not long stand. As had happened to the Normans before, and as had happened in similar cases since the days of the Roman conquest of Greece, the cultivated and written language prevailed over the rude and unwritten, and the institutions of the civilised subjects modified and refined the customs of the barbarous conquerors.

I confess that even these causes do not quite account for the rapid recovery by the English of their rights and privileges under their new masters. With all the haughty Norman oppression which our

Chap. II. English chroniclers so condemn, there was plainly no attempt at extermination, nor even an effort to degrade the old occupants into a servile condition. That is proved even by the number of the Norman chiefs, who made their fortunes by marrying Saxon heiresses. Perhaps the conquerors at length felt some sympathy with their kinsmen of the old Teutonic race. Perhaps they found it dangerous to press to extremity, a gallant, a numerous, and united people.

CHAPTER III.

Perhaps it does not require much apology when I request your attention to that part of European policy, which was developed in our own country. I cannot think that even among strangers, the history of Scotland could be regarded as uninteresting. We know that it is not the mere size, or population, nor the actual power of a nation, that gives it a prominent place in the history of mankind, since the little provinces and single cities of Greece have made an impression on the history of the world, which nothing else can rival, and which time cannot efface.

An English writer—an English lady—speaking of her own country, has challenged a comparison even with the ancients :—" Nor is it only valour and generosity that renowne this nation. In arts wee have advanced equall to our neighbors, and in these that are most excellent, exceeded them. The world hath not yielded men more famous in navigation, nor ships better built or furnisht. Agriculture is as ingeniously practised. The English archery were the terror of Christendom, and their clothes the ornament. But these low things bounded not their

CHAP. III. great spirits. In all ages, it hath yielded men as famous in all kinds of learning as Greece or Italy can boast of."[1]

I venture to claim a part of the same character for Scotland. If it has been denied to our country to create and perfect art, and to preserve immortal thoughts in language as immortal, we have yet been allowed to treasure up some associations with our bygone events, which have commanded a sympathy far beyond our political influence or the spread of our language. Our poor and narrow country has developed principles and feelings that know no limits of time or space; and our history and literature are regarded, if I am not mistaken, with a heartier sympathy over the civilised world, than those of many countries of the greatest political importance.

A.D. 1093.

We have no extant Scotch writing, so early as the reign of Malcolm Canmore, who died in the year 1093. That the art of writing was known and practised among us to a small extent before, we cannot doubt; but it was probably used only for books connected with the Church, its forms and service. At least there is no evidence of the existence, so early as that reign, of any charter, record, Charters. or chronicle. The oldest Scotch writing extant, is a charter by King Duncan (not " The gracious

[1] Mrs. Lucy Hutchinson.

Duncan," murdered by Macbeth, but his grandson, who reigned in 1095), granted to the monks of St. Cuthbert of Durham. It is kept in the treasury of Durham, and is in perfect preservation. The rude pinning of a seal to it has raised some suspicion with regard to its genuineness; but I think without foundation. The appending of the seal is apparently a modern and clumsy attempt to add a sort of authentication, which the charter did not want. It is executed in the Anglo-Saxon manner, by the granter and the several witnesses affixing their crosses, and in most Anglo-Saxon charters, seals were not used. We have several charters still preserved of Edgar, the brother and successor of Duncan, who reigned till 1106, and who uses a seal after the Norman fashion, on which he takes the barbaric style of *Basileus*. From his time, that is, from the beginning of the twelfth century, we have charters of all the Scotch kings, in an unbroken series, as well as of numerous subjects, and derive from them more information for public and domestic history, than is at all generally known.

There is still preserved a poor fragment of a Scotch chronicle, which appears to have been written about the year 1165. It is a single leaf, now inserted in the MS. of the chronicle of Melros, in the Cottonian library. The rest of that venerable chronicle, written in the thirteenth century, in the Abbey of Melrose, is the most ancient Scotch writing

CHAP. III. of the nature of continuous history that is now extant. A few other fragments of chronicles of that century perhaps, but being for the most part bare lists of the Scotch and Pictish kings, are now deposited in the royal library at Paris. When used by Camden and other historians, they were in the library of Cecil, Lord Burleigh.

Laws. Of collections of the laws of Scotland, the oldest is one which has been lately restored to this country, from the public library at Berne. It is a fine and careful MS., written about 1270; and, what adds greatly to its interest, containing an English law treatise and English styles, as well as some of the most ancient laws of Scotland, particularly David I.'s venerable code of Burgh laws; and last of all, the ancient laws of the Marches, concerted by a grand assize of the borderers of the two kingdoms in 1249. This singular mixture of the laws of two countries (which might have served as the materials for the mysterious fabrication of a so-called Scotch code) excites our curiosity as to the owner of the book; but the only clue we find to guide us is a memorandum scribbled on the last leaf, of an account of sheep taken from John, the shepherd of Malkariston, on Sunday next before the feast of St. Andrew, in the year 1306, when the flock is counted in ewes, dynmonts, and hogs. Next in interest to the Berne MS., is a book of Scotch laws, chiefly Burghal, which was picked up in a book-stall in Ayr in 1824, and its previous history cannot be traced. It is a fine MS., of the age of Robert I., or at least of the early half of the fourteenth century. After that period, there is no want of MS. collections of our laws; but all of the character of private and unauthentic compilations.

State papers, properly so called, few, but of great importance, begin in the reign of Alexander III., or the latter half of the thirteenth century; and there are still preserved imperfect records of parliamentary proceedings, from the age of Robert Bruce downwards.

These are all the materials of the civil history of Scotland which we still possess, previous to the work of John Barbour, of which I shall have occasion to speak hereafter. Soon after his time, Andrew Wyntoun, prior of Loch Leven, wrote his rhyming chronicle, and John Fordun laid the foundation of Scotch history, in his Scoti-Chronicon. These two writers were engaged upon their works at the same time, about the latter years of the fourteenth century; but neither seems to have been aware of the other's undertaking.

Looking at the kingdom of Scotland, then, at the beginning of the twelfth century, as the very earliest period for which we have any historical materials, the dominions of the Scotch king consisted of several states recently amalgamated. The Scots, properly so called, a people who seem to have come from Ireland as early as the fourth century, when they become known by name as the terror of the degenerate Romanized Britons, had their original seat on the west coast, and to the north of the Firth of Clyde. The Caledonians or Picts, whom Tacitus, and a better authority, the venerable Bede, describe as differing in their size, their red hair,[1] and in their language, from the Scots, possessed in the eighth century, and down to the end of it, all the Eastern Lowlands of modern Scotland, including Lothian; but the last probably only for a short period. At the end of that century, they possessed also Galloway and the Orkney islands.

In the middle of the ninth century, these two nations were joined under Kenneth MacAlpine, and from that time the proper kingdom of the Scots extended from sea to sea, across Scotland; but it was confined on the south by the powerful kingdom of Northumbria, which extended to the Forth; and soon afterwards, on the north, the northern sea-kings, who had long ravaged the coasts, made good a settlement, which for two centuries, extended their power over the Orkney and Shetland islands, the Hebrides, and the northern peninsula of Scotland, reaching to the Moray Firth. The kingdom of the Scots continued in the line of Kenneth for many

---

[1] Rutilae comae, magni artus Germanicam originem asseverant. —*Agric.* II.

generations, though not succeeding according to the modern and feudal notions of inheritance. One of his descendants, Kenneth, the son of Malcolm, succeeded in wresting from Edgar of England the northern district of the province of Northumberland, which then began to be known by the name of Lothian. One of the fragments of chronicles, formerly mentioned, relates, that in the time of Indulfus, a king a few years earlier than Kenneth, Edinburgh (*oppidum Eden*) was given up to the Scots. I cannot but think that this was a part of the same transaction by which the English Saxons solemnly conceded to the Scots the northern district of Northumberland; and it is remarkable that the earliest historical fact precisely recorded in the chronicles of both countries, should relate to the accession of this rich province which Scotland has never since abandoned, and the city which was destined to become the capital of the kingdom.

To exhaust the map of Scotland, it is necessary to allude to the district on the south of Clyde; but I shall not at present open up the much vexed question of the kingdoms of Strath-Clyde and Cumbria. Of the ancient British kingdom, having Dumbarton for its capital, we know chiefly from notices of the Northmen, who for centuries reaped their harvest of plunder along the shores of the Clyde. Whether this kingdom were the same with that of Cumbria, or whether Cumbria included with modern Cumberland the whole or part of the south-western peninsula of Scotland, I shall not stop to examine; but it is necessary to mention the fact, that Malcolm I. of Scotland obtained from Edmund of England, a formal recognition of his rights to the kingdom of Cumbria, which evidently consisted, in part at least, of modern Cumberland, and it became from that time the usual appanage of the Tanist, presumptive heir or prince of Scotland.

Chap. III.

A.D. 946.

The red hair and large limbs which Tacitus has bestowed on the inhabitants of Caledonia, and from which he argued a Germanic descent, have naturally enough led some of our historians to seek for a Teutonic origin for the Picts, whom they hold to be the same with the Caledonians; and the contest between them and their Celtic opponents has raged loud and fierce, with more of passion than one would at first sight imagine could be excited by such a subject. If you remember the animated discussion in the dining-parlour of Monkbarns, between Mr. Oldbuck and Sir Arthur Wardour, which was stopped at last by the baronet choking upon the hard names of the list of Pictish kings; you learn that the controversy rests upon the narrowest possible foundation— upon the etymology of a single word, found in Bede,[1]

[1] Bede, in describing the Roman wall, draws it from a place "qui sermone Pictorum *Peanfahel* appellatur"—to Dumbarton.

and which is said to be the only ascertained remnant of the ancient Pictish language. I would not wish to interpose, even as a mediator, in such a quarrel.

Long before the period of ascertained history in Scotland, all marks of two distinct aboriginal races had disappeared. The language of the hereditary natives of Scotland, from the Mull of Galloway to the Moray Firth, was a Celtic speech, which remained in Galloway until the fifteenth or sixteenth century, and which is still spoken over the Highlands. We cannot doubt that another tongue was spoken in the sea-ports and along the level shores of the eastern coast. If we consider what was going on along the eastern coast of England, from the time of the Romans and for centuries afterwards, we must be satisfied that the tribes who so eagerly sought for settlements along her coasts, were not likely to be limited by the Firths of Forth or Tay; and there are plain marks in the appearance and language of the people, and some indications in the names of places and families, of a Teutonic and sea-borne colonizing, along our eastern sea-bord from Tweed to Burghead.

Still, I think, it cannot be questioned that the language of Scotland,—king, court, and people, Highland and Lowland, except a narrow strip of sea coast,—in the reign of Malcolm Canmore, was

Chap. III. Celtic or Gaelic. When the sainted Margaret, speaking the language of Saxon England, wished to convince the Scotch clergy of their error with regard to the times of Easter and Lent, her husband, Malcolm Canmore, was obliged to translate the discourses of the queen, even for the clergy, into Gaelic.

Even under Malcolm Canmore, there are sufficient proofs of a tendency in the rulers of Scotland towards southern manners and civilization. Malcolm recovered his father's kingdom, and slew Macbeth by the aid of Edward the son of Edmund Ironside, along with Siward, the giant Earl of Northumberland. Soon afterwards, he married the daughter of Edward, the last of the kingly line of the Anglo-Saxon monarchs, who exercised great influence over him, and made his court the object of all the affection and sympathy of the Saxons of England, after the death of Edward the Confessor. How many a poor follower of the Ætheling from Hungary, how many a Northumbrian thane and churl, would find a reward and resting place in the castles and glens that had belonged to the faction of Macbeth! But if *Malcolm* had motives for an English feeling, these were much increased in his family. Henry I. of England, upon his accession to the throne, feeling his doubtful title, and opposed by all the Normans, threw himself upon the favour of the Saxon population, and found no way better than to choose his wife from the line of their ancient kings. He married Maud, the daughter of Malcolm and Margaret of Scotland, who was so long and so affectionately remembered in England by the title, which was even inscribed upon her monument at Winchester, " Mold the god quen."¹ She had much cause to use her influence with her oppressive husband, as a chronicler tells us she did,—" Mold the god quen gaf him conseile to luf his folc."² The English connection was kept up by Alexander I., son of Malcolm Canmore, marrying a daughter of Henry I. of England. But the young David, the most distinguished of his race, was especially Anglicized. He was brought up in his youth at the court of his sister, the queen of England, and the seal which he used before his accession to the throne, sets forth his titles simply as " Earl David, brother of the queen of the English." He had some difficulty in obtaining possession of his appanage of Cumberland from his brother, king Alexander, and succeeded at last through his influence with Robert the Bruce and the great Norman barons, who afterwards boasted that the terror of their name had gained it for him without bloodshed. Thus we see that when he came to the throne, he had many bonds of attachment to England, even independent of his marriage with Maud, the co-heiress of Northumberland and Huntingdon.

¹ Angl. Sac., I. 277.   ² Robert of Brunne, p. 98.

Chap. III.   Long before this time, the high officers of state, the attendants of the court, were of the southern strangers. The witnesses to the charter of Duncan, besides the king's brothers, Malcolm and Edgar, are Accard, Ulf, Hermer, Ælfric, Hemming, Teodbald, Vinget, Earnulf, and Grenton the scribe, apparently all Saxon or Danish.

A charter of his brother Edgar, free from all suspicion of forgery, gives the following witnesses: Ælfwyn, Oter, and Thor the long, and Aelfric the steward, and Algar the priest, and Osbern the priest, and Cnut Carl, and Ogga and Lesing, and Swein son of Ulfkill, and Ligulf of Bamburgh, and Uhtred, Eilav's son, and Uniæt hwite and Tigerne,—in all which list we do not find a name, unless perhaps the last, which the most zealous Celt can claim for a countryman.

The tide of English favourites and courtiers had now begun, and although we have no records during that time of their acquiring lands, that is probably for the simple reason, that there are no records of the acquisition of lands by laymen earlier than the reign of David. In that interval, the progress they had made is remarkable. The great family descended from the Earls of Northumberland, which afterwards took its name from its castle of Dunbar, had already obtained immense grants in the Merse and Teviotdale. The De Umphravills, the De Morvills and

Somervills; the Lindsays, the Avenels, the Bruces, the Balliols, the Cumins, the De Sulis, the De Vescis, the great family of Fitzalan, hereditary Stewards, had possession of immense territories in the south of Scotland, upon which they were rapidly settling their families, and the martial retainers to whom they owed so much of their consequence.

These were all Normans, and for the most part brought their territorial names from their castles in Normandy. But there were not wanting settlers, whose names speak their Saxon and Danish blood. Such were Alwin fitz Arkil, the progenitor of the race of Lennox; Swain and Thor, the ancestors of the Ruthvens; Oggu and Leising; Osolf, Maccus, the original of the Maxwells; Orm, Leving and Dodin, who have given names to Ormiston, Levingston, and Dodingston; Elfin, Edulf and Edmund, whose names remain in Elphinston, Edilston, and Edmunston; and many others, who had not yet given into the new fashion of surnames. Some had grants of forfeited lands or of the ancient demesne of the crown; some married heiresses; all obtained charters, and held their lands according to the most approved feudal form of England and Normandy; and in turn, their followers got grants from them, subject to the same conditions of service and profitable casualties.

David himself, attached as we have seen by many

ties to England, held for the greater part of his reign the Earldom of Northumberland, and made his favourite and frequent residence at Newcastle upon Tyne. He thus in a manner united once more the whole northern section of the ancient kingdom of Northumbria. Ruling Lothian as king, and Northumberland as earl, he had power and leisure during the distractions of the reign of Stephen, to introduce into his territories order and civilization, which were unknown in southern England. "In those days," says an old English chronicle, "England was foul with many sores; for the king was powerless and the law was weak. But the northern region, which had come into the power of David king of Scots, as far as the river Tees, enjoyed peace through his diligent care."[1]

When David had been deprived of Northumberland, and endeavoured to recover it by force of arms, he led with him a motley army of his subjects; and their depredations soon roused the resistance of his old companions in arms, the Barons of Yorkshire and Northumberland. They gathered round the Standard of the Bishopric, few in number, but confident in the ascendancy of the gentle Norman blood. When some of the hastily-raised force were showing signs of panic, old Walter Espec, the leader of the English barons, climbed up on the waggon of the

[1] Newbr. and Brompt.

Standard and made a speech. He told the barons, that if they had as much experience as himself, he would willingly be silent and take his sleep; "or I should play at dice or chess, or if these games were unsuitable for my age, I would study legends and church histories, or after my own manner would listen to some bard, relating the high deeds of our forefathers." He pointed out the unreasonableness of their fear of the enemy, however numerous—" Why should we despair of victory, when victory has been given by the Most High as an inheritance to our race? Did not our forefathers with a few soldiers invade the greatest part of Gaul, and wipe out from it the nation and the very name of Gaul? How often have they routed the armies of the Franks! How often beaten, few against a multitude, the forces of Cenomania, Anjou, and Aquitaine! Verily our fathers and we, have in brief space, subdued and brought under our laws, this island, which of old the victorious Julius scarcely conquered in many years, and with the slaughter of multitudes of his troops. . . . Who but our Normans have subdued Apulia, Sicily, and Calabria? . . . Who would not laugh then rather than fear, when against such warriors comes this vile Scot with his naked breech! To our lances, our swords, our arrows, they present a naked hide; for they use a calf-skin for a shield, animated by an unreasonable contempt of death, rather than by true courage. Why should that unwieldy length of spears, which we see so far off, frighten us? The wood is brittle, the point blunted as it strikes. It is destroyed when it clashes on our armour, scarcely enduring a single blow. Receive the thrust upon your staff, and the Scot will stand unarmed before you." . . . He then tells of the goodness of their cause, fighting for their king, their country, their church, and their hearths, and relates the horrible barbarities perpetrated by the enemy, especially by the Galwegians. The chronicler puts in Espec's mouth a speech of the greatest spirit throughout, concluding with an oath, that this day he would either overcome the Scots or be killed by the Scots.

On the other side, the king of Scots called together his earls and nobles to consult on the order of battle. The majority were of opinion that the men-at-arms and the archers should lead the van. The Galwegians opposed this, and said that it was their right to form the first line, and to attack first. The others resisted the placing of unarmed men in front, and the king leant to that side. The historian makes the Galwegians remonstrate—"Why are you so much afraid, oh king! of these iron coats? . . . What the better were the Normans of their mail at the field of Clitherow? Did not these unarmed men oblige them to throw away their coats of mail, their shields and helmets? . . . We gained the victory over the mailed warriors at Clitherow, and, to-day, you will see us lay low those boasters with our lances, taking courage for our shield."

The king still resisting, Malis Earl of Strathern, representing the ancient Scotch nobility, addressed him in a rage;—"Why is it that you follow the wishes of the Frenchmen? Not one of them, with all his arms, shall be more forward in battle this day than myself." Alan de Percy, a Norman, took offence at these expressions. "These are proud words, but for your life, you shall not make them good this day." The king interposed to prevent a quarrel, and yielded to the demand of the Galwegians.

The king's son, Henry, commanded the second line of men-at-arms and archers, with the men of Cumbria and Teviotdale. The prince is painted in glowing colours — unrivalled for beauty, courage, modesty. With him was Eustace Fitz-John, lord of Alnwic, one of the great nobles of England, a favourite of the late king Henry I., a man of the greatest skill and prudence in civil affairs, who had retired from the English court, being offended that, contrary to the custom of his country, he had been seized in the king's court, and obliged to restore the castles which king Henry had committed to his charge.

The third brigade was composed of the men of Lothian, with the Isles-men and the Lavernans (a

Chap. III. name which seems corrupt). In the fourth line, were the Scots or men of proper Scotland, and the Moray men; and as the king was there among them, he had a band of English and French men-at-arms for his body-guard.

When the armies were just joining battle, and the priests on either side in their white robes, with crosses and relics of saints, were shriving the soldiers, Robert de Brus, an aged baron of great possessions, grave in his demeanour, of few words, who spoke with a certain dignity and weight, stepped forward. He was a subject of England, but from his youth had been attached to the king of Scotland, and had been admitted to his greatest confidence and friendship. He then, a man of veteran service and great experience, seeing with his natural sagacity the danger that threatened the king, and prompted by his long friendship, asked leave from his comrades, and went to the king to dissuade him from fighting, or, according to the custom of his country, to take his leave and retire; for he was bound to the king, not only by his friendship, but by the bond of fealty. He told him to consider against whom he was about to fight, against English and Normans, in whom he had always found good counsel and ready aid and willing service. "How long is it," he asked, "that you have found so much faith in Scots, as to give up the English and Norman side, and take theirs instead? . . . Think by whose assistance your brother Duncan routed the army of the usurping Donald. Who restored your more than brother Edgar to his kingdom? Who but our Normans? Remember only last year, when you called for our help against Malcolm, the heir of his father's hatred and rebellion. How cheerfully and readily this very Walter Espec and many other English nobles came to your assistance at Carlisle. . . . Whatever hatred the Scotch have against us, it is all on your account; for whom we have so often fought against them, repressed their rebellions, and subdued them to your will."

The whole speech is affectedly rhetorical, and unsuitable to the character given to the speaker; but I cannot refrain from giving the concluding sentence.

He tells the king that despair had given them courage, and that he had no doubt of victory. "Hence," said he, "is my grief, hence my tears, that I shall see the death or the flight of my sweetest lord, my most loving friend, my old companion, in whose friendship I have grown grey, whose munificence I have experienced in gifts of all kinds, and grants of many lands and estates; and I grieve the more, when I remember the days when we played together as children, and the deeds of arms and perils that we have encountered, and the pleasant sport that we have enjoyed together, with our hawks and hounds." The king was moved to tears by the baron's friendly remonstrance; but evil counsellors interrupted their concord, and Bruce, renouncing his fealty *(patrio more)*, returned to his own party.

The result of the battle is well known. The Galwegians rushed on with their three yells, but were beaten back by the English men-at-arms, and the archers, which had even then become a terrible arm of English war; and their flight occasioned the confusion and defeat of the rest of the army. Only the king's brigade stood firm, and formed, with its royal standard of the dragon (so says our author), a rallying point for the fugitives, and presented a formidable body in retreat.

I have given these details from the contemporary chronicler, Abbot Ailred, because they seem to me, not only to exhibit the fortune of that famous battle, but to give us a vivid glance of the situation of David, between his native subjects and the Norman and Saxon strangers.

Part of the great design of David, for the civilization of his subjects, was effected in planting everywhere those southern settlers, carrying with them the refinement and high feeling of Christian chivalry. Another channel, through which the great reformer prepared to attack the barbarism of

EARLY CHRISTIANITY—SAINT NINIAN—COLUMBA.

his native people, was through the Church; and this leads me to speak of the ancient Scotch Church. I wish I had ability and time to do justice to the subject.

We have reason to believe that Palladius was the first who preached the gospel in Scotland, in the fifth century. We are told by the venerable Bede—you will notice that he lived and wrote about the year 700, and spent his life in the district of England, nearest to the Scotch border—that the Southern Picts—those seated to the south of the mountains—reported that they had received their Christianity from Ninian, who came from Rome in the fifth or sixth century, founded the See of Whithern (in Latin, *Candida Casa*), called so from a church which he built there, *of stone*, a practice unusual among the Britons. But this is only a preface of Bede to his history of the conversion of the northern Picts by St. Columba. He tells us, that Columba, a priest and abbot, came from Ireland to Britain, to preach the gospel to the northern Picts, those who are separated by steep and dreadful mountains from their southern provinces, and obtained as a site for his monastery the island of Hii, " which," says Bede, " is not large, but only about five families, according to the calculation of the English." Columba, by his preaching and example, converted that people to the faith of Christ, and after thirty-

Sent to Scotland, A.D. 431.

A.D. 673-735.

Corrected date, A.D. 563.

CHAP. III. two years spent in his British ministry, he was buried there. "Of his life and preaching," says Bede, "there are said to be some accounts written by his disciples; but," he continues, "whatever he may have been, we know this of him for certain, that he left successors of great continence, and remarkable for their love of God and regular institution." Bede was reserved in his praise of the founder of that church which dared to celebrate Easter at an uncanonical season. He seems only to have *heard* of the lives of St. Columba, written by his disciples, Adomnan and Cumin. They are still preserved, and are now accessible to every student of history. They manifest the simplicity and credulity of a rude age; but it is impossible to charge them with any intention to deceive. From them, we learn the mode of life adopted in Iona. But it is not only what they have written—that was not an age of writing—it is from what they have done, that we learn the effects of the preaching of St. Columba and his disciples.

I do not know anything in the history of Christian Europe, that, if rightly considered, is more interesting than the island of Iona in the sixth century. Columba obtained a gift of the island from Conal, a king of the Scots, who then held the western shore of Scotland, and settled A.D. 563. his followers there. The handful of Christian priests, who built their humble thatched church on that little island, could look out on one side on a boundless and tempestuous sea, on the other, on the mountains inhabited by Pagan savages. They might be carried in thought and in prayer to other regions of the earth and beyond it; but to the visual eye there was no support, no sympathy around. There was nothing of pomp to fascinate, nothing to tempt ambition. Praise and the approbation of man were shut out. We must not call them monks, those devoted men; at least those of us who think monk another name for a selfish, lazy fellow. But in truth, as each age of this globe is said to have its peculiar growth of plants and animals, every age of the world of man develops the institutions and forms that suit its progress. Religious men and preachers of the truth do not now retire into desert islands and weary heaven with prayer; but neither are whole nations won over now to the true faith by the preaching of a poor missionary, himself claiming no inspiration. The life of those monks of Iona was divided between prayer, reading or hearing the Scriptures, and works of needful labour, either of agriculture or fishing. Those qualified were employed in teaching the young, and in the important work of writing the books required for the service of the Church. Columba himself was a great penman, and some fine copies of the Psalter and Gos-

Chap. III. pels in Ireland are still attributed to his hand, on better evidence than might be expected. He and his immediate followers, undoubtedly practised celibacy, and enforced penance and the most rigid asceticism. Without discussing the use of such mortification of the body, to the zealot who practises it, it has always been and always will be, a great engine for swaying a simple and uninformed people. They associate such self-denial with the absence of all the passions to which they feel themselves most addicted, and soon come to think the preacher, who can so subdue his human nature, as something raised above humanity.

Education soon became the great object to which the successors of St. Columba devoted themselves. Hither resorted the young from all the adjacent continents, from Scotland, from Ireland and England, and even from Scandinavia, to acquire the learning and study the discipline of the Columban church. From hence, for centuries, went forth priests and bishops to convert and instruct, to ordain, and to found similar establishments; and hither, as to a holy refuge, more than one, when their course of duty was run, retired to be at rest, and to lay their bones beside the blessed Columba.

The Columbites sent continual preachers among the rude people of the opposite continent. In the midst of war and plunder, they made their way through the fastnesses of that difficult land, converted the northern Picts, and penetrated Scotland from sea to sea. That was too near and too easy a task. The desire for new dangers and yet greater hardships, joined to some mystical love of retirement, led some of their number to dare the northern seas, in their boats of skins, and carry the cross into the extreme islands of the Orkneys, Shetland and Färoe. The Norsemen called these missionaries *Papae;* and many of the islands, on which they found some preacher from Iona, still bear the names of *Papey* and *Papeyar.* Even Iceland was not too remote or inhospitable. We do not know the daring and zealous man who carried Christianity thither. He is said to have been Aurlig, a Norwegian educated in the Hebrides. But we know that the first Christian church in Iceland, which was at Esinberg, was dedicated to St. Columba. The little colony of Columbites in Iceland sunk, perhaps, under the severity of the climate. Long afterwards, when the Norwegians went first thither, they found no traces of civilization, but the crosses, bells and books in the Irish ritual, of the monks of Iona.[1]

A.D. 870.

---

[1] *Arii scheda de Islandia, F. Joannis.* The first constitutions by which Christianity was established in Iceland, are extremely curious, and partake even more than Pope Gregory's policy in Kent, of the nature of a compromise between Christi-

Chap. III.

But nearer to us, and more interesting, is the conversion of Northumbria by the monks of Hy. In one of those commotions to which the petty kingdoms of the heptarchy of England were from their nature liable, Oswald, a pagan prince of the royal blood of Northumbria, was obliged to seek refuge in the court of the king of Scots, somewhere on our Argyllshire coast; and there, by the preaching of the Columbites, was converted to the Christian faith. Soon afterwards he succeeded to his kingdom, and having, in his wars with Kedwel, king of Cumbria, fought and conquered under the banner of the Cross, he vowed to establish Christianity in Bernicia, the northern province of his kingdom. For this purpose he solicited, and obtained one of the Columban family of Iona. He was not fortunate in the first

unity and Paganism. After the assembly in which they had been voted, our historian tells us, all the people were signed with the cross immediately, and some baptized; but many refused baptism, on account of the coldness of the water, for which a remedy was found in the hot springs of the island. These proceedings, however, were long after the preaching of the Columbites of Iona. I must not omit to mention, that in the conversion of those northern peoples, there was something which throws a doubt upon their zeal for Christianity, whilst it shows at the same time perhaps, how lightly they held by the superstitions of their fathers. As soon as Christianity was preached among them, they seem to have turned an eager eye to the revenues of the new church, which arose at first from the offerings of the faithful, and afterwards, from tithes and other sources. The nobles, in many cases, became ecclesiastics, priests and even bishops, and retained both their civil and ecclesiastical dignities. They built churches, reserving the usufruct to themselves, and giving the property in heritage to their heirs.

selection. The monk Corman was disgusted with the rude Northumbrians, and soon returned to the shelter of his island cloister. But his place was taken by one more fitted for the task. Ædan was consecrated bishop, and was the first successful teacher of the faith in Northumberland. His taste in the site of his church was remarkable. With all Northumbria to choose, he built it and the humble dwellings of his followers, on the little island of Lindisfarne, destined to be the Iona of the eastern coast. The island is in sight of the castle of Bamburgh, where the kings of Northumbria had not long before fixed their dwelling. The church and cloisters were a merely temporary edifice, and in that lowly structure, Ædan and his brethren daily taught the assembled multitudes. Bede says, "It was a beautiful spectacle, when the bishop was preaching, and was not quite understood, from his imperfect English, and the king, who had learned Scotch in his exile, acted as his interpreter." With such assistance, Christianity spread fast. Churches were built in populous places; monasteries were endowed by the zealous king; and in each of these a school was established for qualifying a regular succession of ministers. Ædan and his monks conducted the education of twelve English youths, two of whom we are able to trace in after life; for Æta became successively Abbot of Melrose and Bishop of Lindisfarne, and Cedde became the Bishop of Mercia, and afterwards the patron saint of Lichfield—the popular St. Chad.

Bede, who did not approve Ædan's tenets in regard to Easter, may be trusted as free from prepossession in favour of the monks of Lindisfarne. "Among other rules of life," says that venerable authority, "he left the most wholesome example to his clergy of abstinence and continence; he taught nothing that he did not practise; he sought nothing, loved nothing, cared for nothing, of this world; whatever was bestowed upon him by kings or nobles, he loved to give to the poor. It was his custom to travel everywhere, in towns and through the country, not on horseback, but on foot, unless necessity compelled, that he might, wherever he went, invite rich and poor to the faith if they were unconverted, or comfort them if already Christians, and excite them to alms and good works by his preaching and his example. His daily work, and that of all who were with him, clerks or laics, travelling or stationary, was reading the Scriptures and repeating the Psalms. On the rare occasions, when he went to the king's banquet, he sat down with a single clerk or two, and hurried over his meal that he might go out with his attendants to read or to pray. Following his example, the religious men and women of that time practised fasting on the fourth and sixth days of the week to the ninth hour, except the remission of the fifty days of Easter. He never spared the offences of the rich, for honour or fear of any man, but corrected them with sharp reproof. He never made gifts to the great, except only their food if he received them as his guests, but rather employed what he received from them for the use of the poor, or for the redemption of those who were sold into slavery unjustly. Many slaves whom he had redeemed became his disciples, and he instructed them and gave some of them church ordination, even up to the rank of a priest. Ædan died on the 31st August 651, in the seventeenth year of his episcopacy, and was buried in the cemetery of his little church of Lindisfarne."

He was succeeded in his bishopric by Finan, by Colman, by Æta, all monks of Iona, or educated in their school, and finally by Cuthbert, the shepherd boy of Lauderdale, brought up in the discipline of St. Columba at Melrose. The history of Cuthbert's earthly ministry, and of the wandering of his poor bones, when the monks, driven out of the island by the Danes, carried his body along with them, seeking a place of rest, is exceedingly picturesque and interesting; but I believe that it is pretty generally known. I will only say a word on the subject of his canonizing. At the end of the seventh century, when all the Saxon sees had canonized bishops of

Chap. III. their own, and boasted of their patronage, it became necessary for the honour of the cathedral church of Lindisfarne to do the like. But Lindisfarne was peculiarly circumstanced. Its first four bishops were Columbites, and heterodox in the matter of the observance of Easter, as well as in the shape of the tonsure; and Æta, the fifth, had been called from the island see to the bishopric of Hexham, where he soon after died, in the odour of sanctity, and became the tutelar saint of that see. Cuthbert, therefore, was the first bishop of Lindisfarne, out of whom a patron saint could fairly be made. Upon the important subjects of Easter and the tonsure, though brought up in the opinions of the Church of Scotland, he had conformed to the Romish observance. This was plainly the reason of his being preferred over Ædan, the founder of the see.

From Lindisfarne flowed the christianizing of the midland English or Mercians, and of the east Saxons, the inhabitants of modern Essex.

Bede tells us that such was the reverence for St. Columba, that the whole province, and even the bishops within it, were subject to the authority of the Abbots of Hy.

From the settlement of St. Columba to the ruin of his monastery, two hundred years afterwards, by the invasions of the Danes, it would be possible to collect a tolerably complete list of the succession of the abbots. Iona had gone on, not perhaps with all its original humility; for kings and nobles sent their sons to be educated there, and the persecuted prince of Northumbria found a secure refuge among its monks; but still zealous and active, propagating the faith by its missionaries, and forming the centre of respect and reverence for a great part of Christendom. In the middle of that period lived Adomnan and Cumin, to whom we owe our chief information regarding Columba and his family of Hy. But their progress in the great work for which they were established is to be gathered from still better sources. The names of places are little liable to change; and churches over all Scotland, in the recesses of the mountains and in the open valleys, dedicated to the early disciples of St. Columba, and still bearing their names, though now forgotten by the people, mark the extent of their preaching, and the attachment of their followers.

From the circumstances of the Church and the time, the distinction had not yet arisen between the secular clergy and the regular monastic orders. In a pagan or lately converted country, I need not say there were no churches or church districts. Iona was the college, whence poured out streams of zealous missionaries, who founded chapels and oratories where they could obtain means and a body of hearers; and although sometimes looking to Iona

Chap. III. as their support and place of rest, yet they often lived and died amongst their converts. Upon their rude foundations, in after times, rose the baptismal churches and the parish divisions of Scotland—the oldest of our existing institutions. Many of these—I believe I may say hundreds—can still be connected with their dedication to the preachers who first taught there the faith and doctrines they had received from St. Columba.

As the district of their ministry extended, it became necessary to found other houses for preserving the discipline and the education of the clergy. Other primeval religious orders no doubt participated in the work of organising a system of national instruction; but the order of the Culdees has left more traces of its establishments than any other, and they have had the undeserved fortune of being claimed as Protestants by the zealous opponents of Rome.

The first of these Culdee houses was Abernethy, a place of mysterious and unknown antiquity. Its foundation is placed as high as the middle of the fifth century, in the time when St. Columba was still alive. Fordun describes it as the principal seat of royalty and Episcopacy of the kingdom of the Picts, and gives three successions of bishops there when its bishop was as yet the only one in Scotland. The translation of the Pictish see from Abernethy to St. Andrews, soon after the union of the Picts and Scots, may have introduced the Culdees into St. Andrews, where they flourished so long.

Of the first foundation of St. Andrews, which is said to have taken place about the year 825, we have no details; but some of the earliest records of its church are connected with its Culdees, who then formed the chapter of the bishop.

The Church tradition, and indeed somewhat better evidence, ascribes the first foundation of the church of Dunkeld to St. Columba himself; but its re-founding and dedication to St. Columba seem to have taken place about the middle of the ninth century. From that period, at least, the Culdees were established there; and we know that they were the chapter of the bishopric until they were outed by King David, in the beginning of his reign.

The church of Dunblane was in a different situation from the other bishoprics of Scotland. That diocese was dependent upon the great Earls of Stratherne; and among other indications, some of which we have already seen, that Malis Earl of Stratherne did not come willingly into the new notions of David I., it may perhaps be counted one, that the Culdees continued to act as the chapter of that cathedral for a century after they had been outed at St. Andrews and Dunkeld.

Chap. III.   The same, however, happened in the church of Brechin, where the Culdees of the chapter appear acting with the bishop, and engaged in all the transactions of the time, down to the middle of the thirteenth century.

We have many other Culdee establishments, not connected with bishops' sees and cathedrals, as at Muthil, in Perthshire; the island of St. Servanus, in Loch Leven—a house that has left us a catalogue of its little library before the middle of the twelfth century—and Monymusk in Mar.

In the ninth century came the hordes of Northmen to ravage the coasts of Western Europe. Scotland in general suffered less from those pirates than the fertile plains of England; but it fared ill with her coasts and islands. Their island site and sanctity were no protection for the family of Columba against the heathen Vikingr, any more than Lindisfarne could defend the bones of St. Cuthbert. The Irish annals record, in quick succession, "the ravaging of Icolumkill," "the Hebrides laid waste by the Danes," "Icolumkill burnt by the Gentiles," "the family of Y slain by the Gentiles." That light was put out which had shed religion and civilization over Britain, and the harassed successors of Columba found uncertain shelter in the monasteries of Ireland. Then comes a period of thick darkness, and when

A.D. 794.
A.D. 798.
A.D. 801-2.
A.D. 806.

we again become acquainted with Iona (in the reign of William the Lion), it is the seat of a convent of Cluniac monks of unknown foundation; and the memory of St. Columba and his family is gone. Chap. III.
a.d. 1214.

Whatever may have been their original institution and discipline, the Culdees, in the time of David I., lived in a manner that must have been inconsistent with any monastic or collegiate discipline. They were generally married, which brought about the appropriation of the common property by the individual members of the house; and not less certainly led to a hereditary succession in the office of the priesthood, than which no greater mischief can befall a church and country. We are not to be surprised, then, that David, the friend of religion and civilization, endeavoured first to reform those irregular monks, and afterwards, finding them irreclaimable, everywhere superseded them, by the introduction of the strict monastic orders brought from France and England. For the most part, the canons regular of St. Augustine took the place of the Culdees. They became the chapters of St. Andrews, Dunkeld, and Brechin, and obtained possession of the property of many of the rural houses of Culdees. One of David's charters concerning them, is short and characteristic:—" I give to the canons of St. Andrews the island of Loch Leven, that they may there institute their
a.d. 1124-1153.

Chap. III. order of canons; and the Culdees, who shall be found there, if they please to live regularly, let them remain in peace under the canons; but if any of them resist this rule, I will and command that he be turned out of the island." It is said by his biographer, Ælred, that David found three bishoprics in Scotland and left nine. Several of these were restorations of Episcopal churches, fallen into decay and neglect, through the dreadful convulsions of the government and society in Scotland. In Glasgow, for instance, there was an old tradition, still fresh in memory, of a church founded by St. Kentigern in the middle of the sixth century, and endowed with ample possessions by the munificence of the early converts. In such a case, David appointed an assize, or great jury of the country to enquire what possessions of right belonged to the see of Glasgow, and the return of that inquest, the earliest title of the property of the Church, is still preserved to us. Much of this property, thus reclaimed to the Church, was then undoubtedly without lawful owner, from the changes of dynasty, and the continual forfeitures of the unsuccessful party.

This was still more the case in the wild Northern districts, where whole provinces had stood in arms against their sovereign, in favour of some claimant of the Crown, under the old Celtic custom of succession, and unwilling to be ruled by an innovating Norman. Whether the lands thus given or restored to the Church, were also waste and uncultivated, it is not now so easy to say. We know little of the cultivation of the soil, till it had got into the hands of those industrious agriculturists, the monks; but if there was upon them the usual agricultural population, they made no bad exchange, in being subjected to the unchanging and peaceful sway of the Church, instead of the fluctuating and lawless lay lords of the soil.

Many of the monasteries, which are said to owe their foundation to David, were restorations of decayed houses of the Culdees. Such was Melrose, which still preserved much of its old sanctity in the estimation of the people, though ruined and impoverished. Upon these the king bestowed partly the old possessions of the house, partly the estates forfeited by rebels, and in some few instances, portions of the demesne lands and property of the Crown. Even if he had given more of such property, I do not know that he would have deserved the character which his successor gave him, of "Ane soir sanct for the Crown." However it may have become the fashion in later times to censure or ridicule this sudden and magnificent endowment of a church, the poor natives of

Chap. III. Scotland of the twelfth century had no cause to regret it. Before, they had nothing of the freedom of savage life, none of the picturesqueness of feudal society. For ages, they had enjoyed no settled government. Crushed by oppression, without security of life or property, knowing nothing of the law but its heavy gripe, alternately plundering and plundered; neglecting agriculture, and suffering the penalty of famine and disease; the churches venerated by their forefathers had gone to ruin, and religion was for the most part degraded and despised. At such a time, it was undoubtedly one great step in improvement to throw a vast mass of property into the hands of that class, whose duty and interest alike inculcated peace, and who had influence and power to command it. Repose was the one thing most wanted, and the people found it under the protection of the crozier.

The donations of Crown lands to monasteries were not altogether uncompensated; the greater abbeys were for many ages the dwellings of the court, in its frequent progresses; and in this way, they paid a return for the royal munificence. But if a sovereign is to look to something more than mere revenue from royal lands, it may be doubted whether they could be turned at that time, more to the benefit of the country, than in the administration of the religious houses.

That it was not merely as a priest-ridden king, CHAP. III. that David augmented the power and possessions of the Church, we may judge from the equal attention which he bestowed upon the law. I shall have another opportunity of directing your attention to the law reforms of David. It is perhaps improper to use these words, for he was the *founder* of the law, still more than of the Church in Scotland. We cannot get beyond him. We owe to him all the civil institutions and structure of our present society. When any legislators of a later age wished to stamp their institutions with a name of authority, they founded them upon the laws and statutes of the good king David: and this was not a mere image magnified in the distance; I shall be able to show you hereafter, enough of the actual laws and institutions of David, to justify that impression. His life has been written by a companion and friend, and it is remarkable, that this has happened with three of the four great monarchs, whom I have had occasion to notice, as builders of the great fabric of civilization—Charlemagne, Alfred, and David. The others had a wider field; but none of them has left a character of greater usefulness, or more endearing than David. His biographer, Ælred, writes of him with a hearty and fervent affection, that makes us overlook the affecta-

Chap. III. tion of his style. With one or two of his simple traits of character, I must conclude:—

"I have seen him," says the Abbot, "with his foot in the stirrup, going to hunt, at the prayer of a poor petitioner, leave his horse, return into the hall, give up his purpose for the day, and kindly and patiently hear the cause."

"He often used to sit at the door of the palace, hear the causes of the poor and old, who were warned upon certain days, as he came into each district."

"If it happened that a priest or a soldier, or a monk, rich or poor, foreigner or native, merchant or rustic, had audience of him, he conversed so condescendingly, and gave such attention to the affairs of each, that each thought he cared only for him, and so all went away happy and satisfied."

The improvement David effected, even in his own time, in the prosperity of his country, is described in the most absurd style of his panegyrist; but we can make allowance for his partiality and magniloquence, and we must not exclude the testimony of an eye-witness—"The land, which was uncultivated and barren, he has made productive and fertile. Thou Scotland, formerly the beggar from other countries, bore on thy own hard clod nothing but famine to thy inhabitants; now, softer and more fertile than other lands, thou relievest the wants of neighbouring countries from thy abundance. He it was who adorned thee with castles and cities, who filled thy ports with foreign merchandise, and brought the riches of other nations to mix with thy own. It was he who changed thy shaggy cloaks for costly robes, and covered thy former nakedness with fine linen and purple; he, who reformed thy barbarous manners with Christian religion, and taught thy priests a more becoming life!"

CHAPTER IV.

<small>Chap. IV.</small> THERE is a curious glimpse of national prosperity in Scotland, in the reign of one whom we are almost bound to believe a usurper and bloody tyrant. Our <small>A.D. 1039-1056.</small> old chronicles all agree, that the reign of Macbeth, of seventeen years' duration, was a time of great abundance and strict administration of justice. Old Winton tells us that—

> "All his time was great plenty,
> Abounding both on land and sea.
> He was in justice right lawful,
> And til his lieges all, awful."

But that period of national prosperity and fabulous wealth is but a bright spot in a dark picture. The defeat and death of Macbeth were the commencement of great troubles to Scotland, which became the scene of constant disputed successions and civil wars—the deadly war of hostile races, which continued with little intermission till the accession of David; and all we know of the domestic history at the commencement of his reign, shows a state of things such as we should expect to follow a long period of disastrous foreign war and civil commotions. The reign of David is the beginning of a new policy, vigorously and consistently enforced; and its effects upon the country are to be traced in nearly two centuries of steady and progressive prosperity, contrasting equally with the century that had passed, and with the dreadful distress that followed, during the wars of the succession and the long war of independence.

I will endeavour to show you such light as our records furnish, upon the state of the different classes of society during that time.

Of David himself I have already spoken. I hope that you consider him not as the mere monk or priest-ridden king. His life seems to have been one of constant action and activity. Besides the movements, which we learn from the public or historic events of his reign, his private charters show a continual change of residence. I cannot trace him indeed so much in the north, which was probably the stronghold of the opposite and Celtic faction. But in the southern provinces his court was constantly in motion. He was attached to Dunfermline, as the favoured foundation of his parents. He lived a great deal at Stirling, from whose battlements he could look down upon his own abbey of Cambuskenneth, and the little chapel of Saint Serf, the confessor of Culross, amidst as fair a scene as ever churchman cultivated, or monarch ruled over.

Chap. IV. It is remarkable how many of the favourite residences of our ancient kings are distinguished for their natural beauty. David frequently resided at Scone and Perth, in the midst of that rich champaign, watered by the majestic Tay, and bounded by its noble amphitheatre of mountains; and at our own Edinburgh, perhaps the most striking situation in which a city was ever built. We find David and his son Henry, and his whole court, at Berwick, Roxburgh, Traquair and Elbottle; at Glasgow and Cadyhow and Strath-Irewin, at Abernethy and Banff. The bounds of civilization were extending in the reign of his grandson William, and we have charters marking that king's frequent residence at Selkirk, Melrose, Traquair, Roxburgh, Lanark, Rutherglen; at Stirling, Linlithgow, Clackmannan, Edinburgh, Haddington; at Dunfermline, St. Andrews and Kinghorn; at Forfar, Aberdeen, Elgin, Forres, Nairn, Inverness.

Before the reign of David, we meet with no great officers of the Crown, but a chancellor to look to the rights of the Crown and royal charters; a constable, and a justiciar. In David's reign, such was the progress of feudalism and hereditary institutions, the offices of great steward and high constable had become hereditary in the families of Stewart and De Morevil. The office of marischal was probably introduced also in his reign. The great chamberlain, as the name implies, had the general control of the treasury; but his functions, both administrative and judicial, had more particular reference to the affairs of the burghs, a considerable source of revenue, and the defined constitution of which is one of the remarkable features of this reign.

When we first have information on the matter, in the reign of Alexander III., the annual salary of the Chancellor of Scotland was £100, and about the same period, we have the earliest notice of the Chamberlain's fee, which long continued to be £200 per annum.

A.D. 1249-1275.

These great officers, with their attendants and followers, with numerous churchmen, the men of letters of the day, and the ordinary crowd of nobles and courtiers, formed a large body in attendance upon the king; and their support (some part of which was extorted from the country, under the names of *kain* and *conveth*, *priscæ et cariagia*, imposts not altogether abolished till a much later period) was felt so heavy a burden, that it afforded an additional motive for their frequent changes of residence.

The chief support of the king's household, undoubtedly, was from the demesne lands of the Crown, furnishing the necessaries of life in kind, and a considerable revenue in rents or *ferme*. The *mails* of the royal burghs might come under the same head. To these were added, perhaps as early as the reign of David, the feudal casualties of ward, relief, marriage, and nonentry—payments arising to the sovereign as superior of lands held immediately of the Crown. We must not allow too much for the customs and duties of merchandise, although I shall have occasion to show you that these were more productive than is generally imagined. Another source of income, and not the least in importance, was from the fines and escheats of the king's courts, which seem to have been chiefly converted into money. In a single year, in the reign of Alexander III., the chamberlain accounted for the receipt of £5313 in money.

In the chamberlain's column of expenditure that year, we have the following articles:—" Servants' wages, four score pounds. Gifts by the king, six score pounds. King's messengers (probably heralds or ambassadors), £150. Pay to soldiers, £180. Ten pounds to Luke de Gizors for harness for the king. Eight score and eighteen hogsheads of wine, £439. The king's expenses at play, the moderate sum of £16 : 2 : 9. To Alexander the Queen's clerk, for the expenses of the Queen, £795. The expenses of the household, £2224. Silk stuffs, furs, spices, preserves, or sweetmeats, and other small expenses, £410."

We find a considerable expense for repairing and maintaining the royal castles, and for victualling and paying their garrisons. In the year 1264, the year of the Norwegian invasion and of the battle of Largs, the accounts of the Sheriff of Ayr contain a note of the expenses of the master gunner,[1] with his two watchmen and porter in the king's castle of Ayr; the expense of repairing the castle itself; a payment of messengers, who thrice went as spies on the king of Norway; wages to the watchers of the king's ships for twenty-three weeks; three dozen of bow-staves; and the price of oatmeal, wheat, cows, salt, and wine for the garrison; and there is a payment of fourteen shillings and eight pence for cleaning of the king's own arms.

When the king moved in peace, he was accompanied by his hawks and hounds, and their train of attendants. Forfar and Glammis were ancient demesnes of the Crown. In the time of Alexander III., Edward de Montealto, sheriff of Forfar, stated as part of the expenses for the year 1263, eight and a half chalders of corn, consumed by William de Hamyl during his stay at Forfar with the king's falcons for twenty-nine weeks; four chalders for the food of seven puppies and their dam; twenty-four chalders for the king's horses, and four and a half chalders for the wild boars, *porci silvestres*. Are we

[1] Balistarius.

to conclude from this last, that the native wild boar of the Caledonian forest had become extinct or scarce in the valley of Strathmore, and that a supply was reared for sport?

There is a payment allowed also, at the king's castle of Forfar, for a gardener, which always marks a certain degree of civilization. When Augustin, the king's tailor, required to purchase cloth and furs for the king's use, he repaired to the fair of Dundee; and thither also went the king's wain, drawn by oxen, to bring home the casks of wine of Gascony for his majesty's summer drink. The meat, then, as for ages afterwards in Scotland, was eaten fresh only during the season of pasture. When that was over, which was about the feast of Martinmas, the good man killed his mart, which was salted by for winter use; and the king fared no otherwise.

He had fish, however, in abundance, salmon, lamprey, and the royal sturgeon, then, as now probably, valued for its rarity. The western lochs furnished herring, which were, even at that early period, an important article for the support of the people; and the king's household accounts notice the consumption of myriads of eels, furnished by the inland lakes. The lake of Cluny, in Stormonth, in particular, produced a large quantity of this fish, which is now hardly used by the people in Scotland. When hard pressed, the court had recourse to grosser viands. So late as the reigns of the Jameses, the clerk of the kitchen sometimes notes among the contents of the royal larder, with other strange food, *dimidium phocæ*—a side of seal. We do not find purchases of vegetables. They were probably reared round the castle. We find the *hortus olerum* an appendage of our better dwellings from the earliest records; and some kinds of " kail " have been used in Scotland by all classes, as far back as we have any knowledge of.

In 1263, the sheriff of Stirling was employed in repairing the ancient park, and in constructing a new park there for Alexander III., and was allowed in his accounts an outlay on that head of £80. Twenty years later, when the king was dead, there was an allowance for two park-keepers, and one hunter of wolves at Stirling; and for the expenses of four hundred perches of palisade round the new park; and for mowing and carrying hay and litter for the use of the fallow-deer in winter.

I do not think it is generally known that Alexander III. and his queen, the daughter of the lordly De Coucy, chose Jedburgh and its lovely valley as a favourite residence. After the death of that king, John Cumin rendered his account as bailiff of the king's manor of Jedworth, in which he charges himself with 66s. 8d. as the rent of the new park which used to be the place of the queen's

Chap. IV. stud (*equicium reginæ*), 26s. 8d. for the sales of dead wood; and states his outlay for mowing 66 acres of meadow, and for winning and carrying it for forage for the castle. *Item*, for nine hundred perches of ditch and hedge (*fosse et haye*), constructed about both the wood and the meadows of Jedworth, 116s. 6d. I think I cannot be mistaken in translating these words ditch and hedge, and if so, you have by far the earliest instance of such a fence on record. I suppose the wood so enclosed may have been the bank of Fernyhurst, still a bank of magnificent oaks, and the meadows those fairy fields by the side of Jed, which form one of the most beautiful and peculiarly Scotch scenes I have ever seen.

I think these details, however individually trifling, give us a useful insight into the real home life of royalty in the thirteenth century; but its state and grandeur are better gathered from the habits of the nobles, who thought it not unworthy of them to follow the court of the Scotch monarch. Many of those great lords had estates, that for extent, and even for value, would make a modern principality, and were attended in war and peace by trains of knightly followers as noble as themselves.

The earls of the great earldom of Stratherne were of the old native race; but conforming to the manners of the times, and connecting themselves with all the highest families of the Norman chivalry. It was, in later times, the only palatinate in Scotland, and the family, even in the twelfth century, were not without something of royal style and pretension. They seem to have founded and endowed a bishopric of their own, and they were for centuries, patrons and superiors of the bishops of Dunblane, who were sometimes called bishops of Stratherne. Earl Malis made a muni- *A.D. 1200.* ficent endowment to the abbey of Inchaffray, to commemorate worthily the place of sepulture of his eldest son, which he had also chosen for his own. Under the protection of that great house grew up the knightly stocks from which the present great families of Perthshire are descended; two branches of the wide spreading De Moravias, of whom the Dukes of Athole are the Perthshire chiefs, the various families of Drummonds, and many others.

The Bruces, already great proprietors in Yorkshire, acquired the magnificent valley of Annandale by the gift of David, whom they had served so well; and their followers whom they settled there, took so firm a hold of the soil, that it became a remark, ages afterwards, that all the lairds of Annandale bore the arms of Bruce.

The Stewarts, amongst the other Norman nobles, whom David paid for their services with territorial

Chap. IV. grants, had all that which is still called the "barony" of Renfrew, equivalent to the whole shire of that name; immense territories in Ayrshire; with the barony of Innerwik, Hassenden and other great estates in the Merse and Teviotdale. They held these lands, and the stewardry of Scotland, for performing the service of a certain number of knights, and at one time, in the reign of William the Lion, we learn from charters, that some of the knights, who actually performed that service for the Stewarts were two brothers, called indifferently Falconer or De Halkerston, taking their surname at one time from their office and again from the lands attached to it, a Montgomery, an Avenel, and a Roland. These and their other followers had manors and estates, held by military service, which can be still traced with great accuracy, and from the dependant knights and squires of the Stewarts have descended the best gentry of the western shires, the noble houses of Eglintoun, Cathcart, Cochrane, Boyle, and many a name, like that of Avenel, remembered only in tradition, or embalmed by one who could control and direct even the current of popular tradition.

Of the service of those nobles and their followers in war, it is not very necessary for me to speak; for there was nothing peculiar to Scotland in tactics before the days of Robert Bruce. The knight and noble rode armed in mail, always of foreign manufacture, from Flanders or Italy. Without denying them the proud feeling of doing battle for their country and defending their homes against an invader, it must be confessed, that those knightly soldiers were often animated by baser motives. They looked to the camp as their profession, bound to maintain them. The spoils of the rich fields of England; the miserable peasant, swept off with the marauding army; above all, the ransom of some higher or more wealthy captive, were willingly weighed in the scale against their own risk and probable loss in battle. But it would be unjust to deny them the lighter feelings of the gallant warrior. The pride of strength and courage, the enjoyment even of danger, the fierce delight in the whirl and shout of battle, were the highest enjoyments of a high nature, not yet schooled to anything of intellectual or refined pleasure.

Kindred to the passion for war, was the passion for the chase. The Norman knights brought it with them from Normandy and England, and it could not fail to take root in a country which nature seems to have formed for the hunter. When the family of Avenel granted the territory of Eskdale to the monks of Melrose, they reserved to themselves the right of game, specifying hart and hind, boar and roe, the eyries of falcons and tercels. The monks were excluded from hunting, or allowing others to hunt with hounds or nets, from setting traps, except only for the wolves, and from taking the eyries of hawks. Even the trees in which hawks usually built, were to be held sacred, and those in which they had built one year, were on no account to be felled, till it should be found whether they were about to build there the next year or no. The early grants, by the Stewarts, to the same abbey, of their great territories in Ayrshire, expressed the same reservation. The monks had a right of pasture within the forest, but were prohibited from hunting and taking hawks—"Hoc enim illorum ordini non convenit."

We have some interesting notices of forest matters in the Chartulary of Paisley. Among their munificent gifts to that abbey, the Stewarts reserved to themselves the manor long known by the name of Blackhall, with its park and forest. Blackhall itself was evidently a hunting residence of the Stewarts, even before the foundation of the abbey. At its foundation, Walter Fitzalan gave to the monks a dwelling upon the rock, where his hall was founded, together with the tithe of all his hunting, and all the skins of deer taken in the forest of Fereneze, and pasture for their cattle and swine through all his forest of Paisley. The succeeding Stewarts, in addition to that extensive and wild range of forest, established a more exclusive tract for game, which they called their park, on the west bank of the river Espedare. The monks and their servants required a license to pass through the forest, with their wains, horses, or oxen, for the carriage of their necessaries, and by the customary roads and tracks of the country; they were allowed to pass armed like other travellers, and to take with them their grey-hounds and other dogs. But if they passed through the park or preserved forest, they must lead their hounds in the leash, and unstring their bows.

There are several interesting notices of the attention paid by the kings and great lords of Scotland, during the thirteenth century, to the breeding of horses. Roger Avenel, the lord of Eskdale, had a stud in that valley. Patrick, Earl of Dunbar, in preparation for his departure to the Holy Land, sold to the monks of Melrose his stud of brood mares in Lauderdale, for the considerable sum of one hundred merks sterling. Alexander III. had several establishments for rearing horses, to be used in hunting, doubtless, as well as in war. The king himself lost his life in a rash midnight ride.

In our hasty glance at the elements of society in old Scotland, we must not pass over the Church and its clergy.

The oblations and offerings to the altar and the priest were as old as the introduction of Christianity;

but the first enforcement of tithes—the first division of parishes, or the appropriation of definite districts to a baptismal church—cannot be placed higher in Scotland than the age of David I. To him we are indebted for the very foundation and framework of our national establishment and parochial divisions. Under his care, the more distant districts of Moray and Galloway were brought to pay the dues exacted by the Church, as they had been long paid in the civilized dioceses of St. Andrews and Dunkeld. Every lord's manor became a parish, and the Church divided the respect of the people with the Castle. Of the early independent secular clergy we know but little. They were frequently of the family of the patron; and it is to be remarked how seldom, in the earlier times of record, a secular clergyman was distinguished in any way, or rose to the higher offices of the Church, which were all filled by the Regulars. At a very early period—as early, indeed, as our records reach—it had become the custom for the patrons of churches, with the consent of the bishop, to confer them in property upon the great monasteries and religious houses of Regulars. Thus Paisley had its thirty parish churches; Holyrood, twenty-seven; Melrose and Kelso, each as many; and to such an extent did this prevail, that in some districts two-thirds of the parish churches were in the hands of the monks. This was probably the greatest evil of monachism, though but an accident. The duties of the distant rural parish, whether performed by a monk of the convent or by a vicar dependent upon it and paid with a grudging and grinding parsimony, were always made subservient to the interests of the monastery. The incumbent was looked to as the steward for ingathering the profits of the parish—that is, his own vicarial part—the small tithes, the altar offerings, the Pasque presents, the funeral and baptismal dues; and the convent concerned itself but little as to the manner in which he discharged his duties amongst the poor people committed to his charge. Amongst the innumerable disputes recorded between convents and their rural vicars, I believe there is not one that turns upon any question as to how the cure of souls was performed.

It is difficult, at the present day, to consider the monastic institutions apart from the change of religion which overthrew them. I fear that it is almost as rare now as in the heat and zeal of the Reformation, to find the freedom from passion and prejudice, necessary for forming a correct estimate of the good and evil of the convent. I wish to consider the institution only as it was exemplified in Scotland, after the great spread of monasteries during the time of king David and his grandsons; and we have abundant materials for testing its operation. I think it is a mistake to suppose that any great body of men, professing a common object, and that a high and sacred one, are ever wholly insincere. I apprehend another mistake consists in our misapprehending the duties which the monks themselves professed to consider the objects of a monastic life. If we were to consider the monks in Scotland, as charged with the instruction and religious discipline of the people, we should at once pronounce them inefficient, and all but useless; but if it be held that that duty did not lie upon them, but chiefly, at least, upon the secular clergy, we begin to view the monastery with more favour. We regard the monks as a set of religious men, freed from domestic and worldly ties, whose time ought to be devoted, first, to divine exercises and contemplation, and afterwards, to the duties of their society, to the duties imposed upon them by their relations as neighbours and as great landholders. All the monasteries were zealous agriculturists and gardeners, at a time when we have no proof that the lay lord knew anything of the soil beyond consuming its fruits. They were good neighbours and kind landlords, so that the kindly tenant of the church was considered the most favoured of agriculturists. Their charity and hospitality have been acknowledged by their enemies. Above all, they were by their profession and situation addicted to peace. Surrounded by warlike nobles, unarmed themselves, they had nothing to gain by war, and it is not easy to over-estimate the advantage to a half-civilized country, of a great and influential class, determined supporters of peace and order.

The learning of the Scotch Convent may not have been carried to a high pitch; but such learning as there was, was always found there. An abbot of Melrose, visiting the dependent house of Home Cultram, laid down rules for the indefatigable reading of sacred literature, and founded his rule upon the quaint and probably proverbial gingle, "*claustrum sine literatura, vivi hominis est sepultura.*" They cultivated and promoted such education as was then known. Kelso had schools in the town of Roxburgh, in the time of William the Lion, and Dunfermline had endowed schools in the city of Perth, at least as early; and they furnished instruction within the monastery, to a higher class than those who benefited by their burghal schools. In the thirteenth century, the widowed lady of Molle, a great proprietor in the Merse, resigned to Kelso a part of her dowry lands, on condition that the monks should maintain her son among the scholars of the best rank in their monastery. This education consisted a good deal in the studies preparatory for the Church. There were schools for teaching singing and chanting in the different cathedral cities, and the term " sang-school" is not yet forgotten in the north, where the choral school has often been the ground-work of our burgh grammar schools. The education, even of the chorister, required a knowledge of reading, not a very valuable acquisition for the laity when books were so scarce; and to this was added instruction in the principles of grammar, and the beginning of classical learning. But surely I need not impress upon you, that in a good school the amount of knowledge acquired is not to be measured by the extent of learning; and that any possible amount of knowledge and learning are as nothing, compared with the industrial training, the moral discipline which these are chiefly useful to convey, but which may be acquired without them.

That some of the arts, moreover, were cultivated within the abbey walls, we may conclude without much extrinsic evidence. The great interest of the monk was for the honour of his monastery; and everything that tended to its grandeur and embellishment was a praiseworthy service. The erection of one of our great abbeys was often a work of centuries, and during all that time, its members were in the midst of the work of the most exquisite artists in every department, and assisted with their own hands. That could not fail to raise the taste and cultivate the minds of the inmates of the cloister. It would be a grievous mistake to suppose, that the effect was merely that of living and working in an artist's shop. The fine arts— the high imaginative and intellectual arts of architure, painting and sculpture—were not yet separated from the other ornamental hand-works. They were carried on together, and all tended to elevate and refine those who lived among them. But, indeed, the interest and honour of the convent, the honest rivalry with neighbouring houses, and other orders; above all, the zeal for religion, which was honoured by their efforts, the strong desire to render its rites magnificent, and to set forth in a worthy manner the worship of the Deity; all these gave to the works of the old monks a principle and a feeling above what modern art must ever hope to reach.

It was a common practice to obtain by gifts to the Church, a participation in the prayers of the convent, and permission to rank as a brother of the order; and the Church records of that time, present us with innumerable instances of men, who had lived in the throng of life, brave warriors and wise statesmen, sick of the world, or willing to prepare for another, retiring to the quiet and contemplation of the cloister. These things are inconsistent with any general opinion of vice, sloth, or irreligion in the monasteries; and, in truth, such imputations were not cast upon them for a long time afterwards.

We may be satisfied, then, that the monastery

was fit for its time. It kept alive the flickering light of literature. It gathered together and protected the spirits too delicate for a rough season. It reared up a barrier against oppression, and taught the strong to respect the meek and gentle. The monastery was the sphere of mind, when all around was material and gross.

There is preserved a curious Rental of the great abbacy of Kelso, of the end of the thirteenth century, which gives us some insight into the rural affairs of the monks. At that time and probably always, they held a great part of their ample lands and baronies in their own hands, and cultivated them by their villeins from their several Granges.

The Grange itself, the chief house of each of the abbey baronies, must have been a spacious farmsteading. In it were gathered the cattle, implements, and stores needed for the cultivation of their demesne lands or mains; their corn and produce, the serfs or carls who cultivated it, and their women and families. A monk or lay brother of the abbey superintended the whole.

Adjoining the Grange was a mill, with all its pertinents and appearance and reality of comfort, and a hamlet occupied by the cottars, sometimes from thirty to forty families in number. The situation of these was far above the class now known by that name. Under the monks of Kelso, each cottar occupied from one to nine acres of land, along with his cottage. Their rents varied from one to six shillings yearly, with services not exceeding nine days' labour. The tenants of twenty-one cottages at Clarilaw, having each three acres of land, *minus* a rood, and pasture for two cows, paid each two bolls of meal yearly, and were bound to shear the whole corn of the abbey Grange at Newton.

Beyond the hamlet or cottar town, were scattered in small groups, the farm steadings of the *husbandi* or husbandmen, the next class of the rural population. Each of these held of the abbey a definite quantity of land, called a husbandland. Each tenant of a husbandland kept two oxen; and six united their oxen to work the common plough. The Scotch plough of the thirteenth century was a ponderous machine, drawn, when the team was complete, by twelve oxen. The husbandland was estimated long ago in the Merse, as twenty-six acres, " where scythe and plough may gang." The husbandmen were bound to keep good neighbourhood, the first point of which consisted in contributing sufficient oxen and service to the common plough.

As a fair specimen of the rents at which these tenants sat, we may take the barony of Bowden, which, I believe, is now the property of the Duke of Roxburghe.

The monks had twenty-eight husbandlands

there, each of which paid 6s. 8d. of money rent; but to this were added considerable services in harvest and sheep-shearing, in carrying peats and carting wool, and fetching the abbot's commodities from Berwick. These stipulations are exceedingly precise, fixing even the service, in which the husbandman was to have his food from the abbey, and where he was to maintain himself.

In the whole catalogue, no service is imposed on women except harvest work, and I believe agriculturists will agree that we have a still more decided proof of advancing civilization in the fact, that at the period of the rental, the whole *services* were in the process of being commuted for money.

Above the class of husbandmen was that of the yeoman or bonnet-laird, as he is now called in primitive parts of Scotland. Such an one was that Hosbernus, whom Abbot John of Kelso styles " *Homo noster*,"—" our man,"—and who got a half plough of land in heritage and perpetuity in Middleham, and became the liege vassal of the abbey, paying a *reddendo* of eight shillings, and giving certain services in ploughing time and harvest. He no doubt paid for his hereditary right to the lands, and felt himself much above the husbandmen whose title was precarious.

Still higher in the scale were the great Church vassals, who held a place only second to the baronage and freeholders of the Crown. These generally had their lands free of all service, and paid only a nominal quit-rent.

I have said that of the inhabitants of the *Grange*, the lowest in the scale was the *carl, bond, serf*, or *villein*, who was transferred like the land on which he laboured, and who might be caught and brought back if he attempted to escape, like a stray ox or sheep. Their legal name of *nativus*, or *neyf*, which I have not found but in Britain, seems to point to their origin in the native race, the original possessors of the soil. Earl Waldev of Dunbar, in a deed of four lines, made over a whole tribe to the Abbot of Kelso:—" I give and confirm to the abbot and monks of Kelso, Halden and his brother William, and all their children and all their descendants."[1] Another later benefactor of the abbey, after conveying lands in Gordun (by a boundary so plain, that it must be still easily traced at the distance of five centuries), throws into the bargain two crofts, occupied by Adam of the Hog, and William son of Lethe, " and Adam of the Hog himself, my native, with all his following," with pasture in the mains for forty beasts, with all their followers of one year, etc.; and then he warrants to the abbey, " the said lands, meadows, *men*, and pastures." Richard de

A.D. 1170.

A.D. 1280.

---

[1] " Sequaces eorum," as we speak now of a mare and her follower.—*Register of Kelso*, p. 98.

Chap. IV. Morvil, the constable, sold to Henry St. Clair, Edmund, the son of Bonda, and Gillemichel his brother, and their sons and daughters, and all their progeny, for the sum of three merks; but on this condition, that if they leave St. Clair by his consent, they shall not pass to the lordship of any other lord, nor to any other lord or land than De Morvil. In the Register of Dunfermline are numerous "genealogies," or stud-books, for enabling the lord to trace and reclaim his stock of serfs by descent. It is observable that most of them are of Celtic names.

We learn something of the price of the serf from the efforts which were made by the Church for his manumission. Their own people were evidently in
A.D. 1290. progress of emancipation at the period of the rental I have been quoting from. The stipulation of a certain amount of service implies that the rest was free. But when the Church wished to emancipate the slaves of others, it was necessary first to purchase them. Adam de Prendergest sold to the Almoner of Coldingham Stephen Fitz Waldev, with his following and goods.[1] In 1247, Patrick de Prendergest, burgess of Berwick, bought the freedom of Renaldus a slave, with his whole following, for twenty merks sterling. This is a remarkable transaction; for Patrick, the burgess, had formerly been a slave, or at least a native, and obtained his liberty through

[1] Servum meum et ejus sequelam et catalla.

the house of Coldingham; but what is more curious, Reynald, who was thus emancipated for a sum of money, is styled in the charter *prepositus*, meaning, no doubt, alderman or bailie of the town of Berwick; and that accounts for the greatness of his price; for about the same time, the Abbey of Coldingham purchased the freedom of Joseph, the son of Elwald, and all his posterity, for the price of three merks; of Roger Fitz Walter and all his posterity for two merks: and Eustace of Newbigging sold to the Prior of Coldingham the freedom of William of Newbigging, and Brunhild his wife, and Walter and Mabil their children, and all their issue, for the sum of fifteen shillings. These are instances of purchased emancipation.

Two entries in the ancient Register of Dunfermline, seem to me to mark the progress from servitude to freedom very *graphically*.

In 1320, on the feast of St. Peter *ad vincula*, an inquest was held in the chapel of Logy concerning the liberties which the Abbot of Dunfermline's men of Tweeddale claimed from the Abbot. First, they sought to have a bailiff, appointed by the abbot, of their own race, who should repledge them from more oppressive lay courts to the Abbot's court. To that the assize of inquest made answer, that such bailiff should be given them, not of fee, but of usage. Their second demand was, that if any one of their race verge to poverty, or fall into helpless old age, he shall have support from the monastery. To this the jury replied, that the abbey was not bound to this as of right, but from affection, because they were its men. The third article was, that if any of their race slay a man, or commit any other crime for which he must seek the immunity of holy church, if he come to Dunfermline for that immunity, he shall be sustained as long as he stays there, at the expense of the monastery. The jury declared that the abbey would do so to a stranger, much more to a man of their own, and of the race of the claimants. Lastly, they claimed, that if any of their race commit homicide, and incur a fine therefor, the Abbot and convent shall be bound to contribute twelve merks toward payment of the fine. To which the jury made answer, that they never heard such a thing all the days of their lives —*nunquam tale quid omnibus diebus vite sue audierunt.*[1]

Twenty years later, Alexander, Abbot of Dunfermline and his convent, declare by a formal charter, that Marcormi and Edmund and Michael his son and heir, and the brothers and sisters of the said Michael and Mervyn and Gyllemycael and Malmuren and Gyllecriste and Gylmahagu, and all their progeny, are our free men, and are in our peace and the peace of the Church, with all their posterity, whom king David gave to our church, along with Crebarryn (Carberry), in perpetual alms; they

[1] Register of Dunfermline, 354.

only paying to us yearly, an ox of two years old, or four shillings.

It was in such transactions, as I have before mentioned, we perceive the chief opening for escape from villeinage. It is manifest, that the cottar who was able to stipulate regarding the amount of his service, was far advanced towards entire freedom.

The Church was one great means of emancipation. But the free institutions of burghs not only afforded the machinery, but supplied the spirit and motive for it. Men perhaps also found by experience, what political economists have proved in their science, that slave labour is not cheaper than that of the free workman. At any rate, the curse of hereditary servitude, for which " the air of Britain was too pure," died out among us, without any special enactment. The last case I have met with, of proceedings under the formerly well-known brief for recovering fugitive slaves, was in the court of the Sheriff of Banffshire in 1364.

Great attention was bestowed upon agriculture from the earliest period of our records. The same corn was grown as is now used. Wheat was grown even in Morayshire in the thirteenth century. We find everywhere strict rules for the protection of growing corn and hay meadows, which were rendered more necessary by the existence of a custom, formally sanctioned under Alexander III., who

Chap. IV. declared it was of use, by ancient custom and the common law throughout Scotland, that travellers, passing through the country, might quarter for one night on any barony, and there pasture their beasts—saving only growing corns and hay meadow. Roads appear to have been frequent, and though some are called the green road, *viridis via*, and by other names indicating rather a track for cattle, others, bearing the style of " high way," *alta via*, " the king's road," *via regia—via regalis*, and still more, the caulsey or *calceia*, must have been of more careful construction, and some of them fit for wheel carriages. We find agricultural carriages of various names and descriptions, during the thirteenth century—*plaustrum—quadriga—charete—carecta—biga*—used not only for harvest and for carriage of peats from the moss, but for carrying the wool of the monastery to the seaport, and bringing in exchange, salt, coals, and sea-borne commodities. The abbey of Kelso had a road for waggons, to Berwick on the one hand, and across the moorland to its cell of Lesmahagow in Clydesdale. A right of way was frequently bargained for and even purchased at a considerable price.[1]

On the estates of the monasteries, water-mills and wind-mills were used for grinding corn in the thirteenth century and previously, though the rude

---

[1] The road leading south from Inverness is called *via Scoticana* in a charter of 1376.

process of the hand-mill kept its ground in some districts of Scotland to a recent period. In the reign of Alexander II., the monks of Melrose purchased the right of straighting a stream that bounded their lands of Bele in East-Lothian, on account of the frequent injury done by its inundations to the hay-meadows and growing corns of the Abbey.

The Monasteries of Teviotdale had necessarily a great extent of pasture land; and the minute and careful arrangement of folds on their mountain pastures for sheep, and byres for cattle, and of the lodges or temporary dwellings for their keepers and attendants, shows that they paid the greatest attention to this part of their extensive farming. But the immense number and variety of agricultural transactions, the frequent transference of lands, the disputes and settlements regarding marches, the precision and evident care of leases, the very occurrence, so frequently, of the names of field divisions, and of the boundaries between farms, settled by King David in person — show an enlightened attention and interest in agricultural affairs, that seem to have spread from the monastery and reached the whole population during that period of national peace and good government, which was so rudely terminated by the war of the Succession.

CHAPTER V.

Chap. V. THERE is no more important mistake in history than when we speak of the extermination of a people by an invading enemy. Such extermination, probably, never takes place, certainly not where the conquered people is the civilised, the invaders the barbarians. I do not mean to controvert the slow retreat and gradual disappearance of an inferior race before a more energetic one. That is passing under our own eyes, wherever the white man of Europe comes into lengthened opposition to the red man of America, or the aborigines, I may say, of any other clime. But the intentional and total extermination of a powerful and civilised people is contrary to all reason, and the nearer each alleged instance comes to our own examination, the more easy do we find it to disprove it. Undoubtedly no such general and violent destruction took place when the Roman empire fell before the invading barbarians. Neither the old people nor their institutions were altogether rooted out. The provincial cities of Europe were already ground down with intolerable taxes to Rome. The barbarians could get no more. They could not reconcile themselves to a town life, and they left the inhabitants to live according to their old customs, only transferring the payment of taxes to their new masters. The result was, that in most of the great cities of France and Germany, the institutions for town police and local management remained on the old footing. They had their *curia* or council, chosen by the citizens, which administered the affairs of the community. Such of the cities as enjoyed the *jus Italicum* had magistrates, with civil and criminal jurisdiction, also chosen by themselves. I would not have you to believe that there was a real independence in those old Roman cities. They had never known it under the Roman sway, and still less could they expect to enjoy it under new masters, regardless of their laws. The magistrates were apparently controlled and thwarted by the state government, and subjected to all indignities. But still the germ remained of self-government, and throve not the worse, that in most of the conquering tribes it met a similar principle. By it, peace was promoted and union, and some degree of security ensured for person and property. The convenience of the system caused it to spread among the new towns, which rose round bishops' cathedrals and the castles of princes; and when, at a later time, it became a state policy to defend the people and an infant commerce against an insolent nobility, the framework was there ready, and the community, long bound together by such ties, and confiding in its chosen leaders, required nothing but the protection of the Prince and the law to make it capable of defending itself. Accordingly, when we get at what are called the charters of erection or incorporation of any of the more ancient towns, we find them to indicate a pre-existing body, enjoying some definite constitution or government.

The first country of modern Europe, in which the old municipal institutions were called into new life and activity, was Spain; but there, the revival of privileged towns was for a peculiar purpose, and the cities were invested with freedom and property, on condition of defending their country against the Moorish enemy. The Fuero, or original charter of a Spanish community, was properly a compact, by which the king or lord granted a town and adjacent district to the burgesses, with various privileges, and especially that of choosing magistrates and a common council.

Of this kind, Leon had a charter in 1020, and Barcelona in 1025. In both of these, there is evidence of a municipal constitution and council already in use.

Henry V., Emperor of Germany, was the first emancipator of the German cities from the tyranny of their bishops and princes. With a more questionable policy, he encouraged and incorporated bodies of men, of the same craft and occupation, as we should say, the *trades* of the towns—thus sanctioning their separation from the mercantile or high burgher class, with whom they ought to have been rather encouraged to unite. We do not find in his charters, nor those of his successors, any grant of the right of electing counsellors and magistrates; but in fifty years after his time, all the cities of Germany had counsellors of their own choice, and before the end of the thirteenth century, the free cities of Germany were acknowledged sovereign and independent, and sent deputies to the national diet, along with the electors and princes.

About the middle of the thirteenth century, the free towns of Lubeck and Hamburgh entered into a league for mutual defence and protection of trade. Other towns soon joined their confederacy, and in a short time, eighty of the most considerable cities, along the shores of the Baltic, from the mouth of the Rhine to the gulf of Finland, had united into that famous confederacy, which is still remembered by the name of the Hanse league. Like many burghal usages, such combinations must have been floating over Europe for centuries before. We find a similar fellowship, on a small scale, in our own country, known by the same name of Hanse, in the reign of David I., one hundred years before the great Baltic association came into being. The great Hanse was divided into four classes, of which Lubeck, Cologne, Brunswick, and Dantzick, were the heads, and Lubeck was the centre of the association. It had four foreign staples, London, Bruges, Novogorod and Bergen, in Norway. The Hanse league, so powerful for good or evil, exercised the lawyers in discussions upon its legality, but went on, nevertheless, in prosperity and power, while bound together by its delegates, meeting for its proper and legitimate purposes of trade. It was only when its vast influence seemed to offer an inducement to scheming princes to use it for political power, that the Hanseatic cities gradually fell asunder, and, after the sixteenth century, left only the name of their mighty union.

When Mr. Hallam wrote his history of the middle ages, he was inclined to deny that the burghs of England had any municipal administration by magistrates of their own choice; but he admits that the possession of corporate property implies an elective government for its administration, and there is now abundant evidence collected, of burghal property in England before the Conquest. Mr. Hallam himself, indeed, has been shaken in his opinion, by the express terms of numerous charters which he had overlooked. I am sure that a fair examination of the subject will convince any student that such towns as London, York, Lincoln, and Winchester, full as they were of wealth and enterprise, managed their common affairs, their police and internal economy, before the Conquest. It is only to my mind difficult to fix a time at which they did not do so.

Those centuries I have chosen to illustrate, seem to me peculiarly interesting for Scotland, not merely full of remarkable events, but big with promise and foreshadowing of mighty change. It is as if the elements of society, bound up in the frost of ages, had been at once relaxed and set in motion. There is great clashing and confusion, but as the tide subsides, you may observe rising through it the rude shapes of institutions now familiar and endeared to us.

Whilst David I. was introducing a new and chivalrous aristocracy, and reforming and extending the Church, he did not neglect the third class of society. The rise of free towns, with privilege of trade, and the ascertained right to govern themselves by their own laws, is perhaps always and everywhere the most important step in national advancement. But it requires us to imagine a country like Scotland in the beginning of the twelfth century, only recovering from an age of anarchy, to appreciate the effect of that statute of the laws of the burghs, which declares that "Gif ony mannis thryll, barounis or knychtis, cummys to burgh and byis a borowage, and dwellis in his borowage a twelfmoneth and a day, foroutyn challenge of his lorde or of his bailye, he sall be ever mare fre as a burges within that kingis burgh, and joyse the fredome of that burgh."[1]

This code of Scotch burghal regulations, though collected in the reign of David, and sanctioned by him, was the result of experience of the towns of England and Scotland. I lately found, in the Record Office of the Tower at London, a memorandum of the laws and burgh usages of Newcastle in the time of Henry I., written in a hand as old as the reign of Henry II. It consists of eighteen chapters, almost consecutively, of the well-known burgh laws of Scotland. There was indeed a sufficient connection between Scotland and Northumberland, whilst both were under the rule of David, to render it very probable that the framer of a body of Scotch burgh laws should adopt the customs used at Newcastle; and there are even traces of a more extensive correspondence between the Anglo-Saxon and Scotch burghs. The charters of Winchester, granted by Henry I., which soon became the favourite models of burgh charters of England, were themselves only the embodying in special grants, of privileges and liberties enjoyed before by the city itself, or known

[1] Cap. 15.

and enjoyed before and time out of mind by the towns of England, though defeated and thwarted by adverse circumstances. It is curious how close a resemblance those charters of Winchester bear to the privileges of Scotch burghs, conferred by king David. Everything shows us that there was at that time a general movement in favour of the privileges of towns; and no feelings of hostility yet interfered to prevent the inhabitants of lowland Scotland and of England, kindred in blood, language, and manners, from adopting together the steps of a system, which opposed to the oppressive power of the armed feudal lords the union of numbers in each town, and the combination and mutual support of the trading communities of the whole island.

The important, indeed the vital, point of the Scotch burgh laws, was that regarding the election of their magistrates. In other countries this was long withheld or grudgingly bestowed—

"At the fyrst mute, next eftir the feste of St. Mychael, the aldirman and the bailycis sal be chosyn, thruch the consaile of the gud men of the toune, the quhilk aw to be lele and of gud fame. And thei sal suer fewte till the lord the king, and to the burges of the toune. And thai sal suer to keep the customys of the toune, and at they sal nocht halde lauch on ony man or woman, for wrath, na for haterit, na for drede, or for luve of ony man,

Chap. V. bot thruch ordinans, consaile and dome of gud men of the toune. Alswa, thai sal suer that nother for radnes, na for luve, na for haterit, na for cosynage, na for tynsale of their silver, thai sal nocht spare to do richt till all men."[1]

The election of councillors of Berwick is prescribed in the code of Statutes of the Gild, showing at least the custom of the thirteenth century. There were to be twenty-four good men, of the best and discreetest and most trustworthy of the town, elected for this purpose, along with the mayor and four bailies.[2]

Who the electors of magistrates truly were—the "probi homines villæ, fideles et bonæ famæ"—has been made a subject of controversy; but, as it cannot be imagined that a right or franchise of this nature could possibly depend on any other than plain or tangible criteria, there seems to be no good reason for supposing that the epithets in question

[1] Cap. 70.
[2] *Constitucio facta de Gubernacione communitatis Berwici.*

37. Statuimus insuper per commune consilium quod communia de Berwico gubernentur per xxiiij probos homines de melioribus et discretioribus ac fidedignioribus eiusdem Burgi ad hoc electos vna cum maiori et quatuor prepositis. Et quandocunque predicti xxiiij homines fuerint citati ad commune negocium tangendum qui non venerit ad citacionem sibi factam ultra noctem dabit duos solidos ad Gildam.

Constitucio de electione maioris et prepositorum.

38. Item statuimus quod maior et prepositi eligentur per visum et consideracionem tocius communitatis. Et si aliqua

had any other meaning or effect than as descriptive of the class of proper burgesses, in contradistinction to the unprivileged inhabitants of the district. Such appears, accordingly, to be the import of the oldest record of a burgh election now extant, that of Aberdeen for the year 1398:—" Die lunæ proximo post festum beati Michaelis archangeli, anno domini milesimo tricentesimo nonagesimo octavo. Quo die Willelmus de Camera pater, cum consensu et assensu totius communitatis dicti burgi electus est in officium Aldermanni, et Robertus filius David Simon de Benyn Johannes Scherar ac magister Willielmus Dicson electi sunt in officium ballivorum." To the term " the whole community," here used, no other sense can well be assigned than that of the entire body of regular burgesses; any other interpretation would seem to be entirely arbitrary.

controversia fuerit in electione maioris uel prepositorum fiat tunc electio eorum per sacramenta xxiiij proborum hominum predicti Burgi electorum ad eligendum unam personam ad dictam communitatem regendam.

Constitucio de congregatione communitatis pro communi negocio.

47. Item ordinatum fuit die Sabbati proximo post festum Sancte Trinitatis anno Domini M° CC° octogesimo quarto quod quandocunque Aldirmanus et Ferthyngmanni propter commune negocium tractandum voluerint confratres Gilde congregari, campana per vices pulsata in Berfredo scilicet primo, secundo, et tercio, debet per intervalla pulsari. Et quicunque confrater Gilde hoc audierit et ad locum congregationis possit accedere et noluerit venire antequam a pulsacione cessatur sit in misericordia xii denariorum.—*Statuta Gilde.*

Satisfied with having sanctioned these invaluable privileges to the whole, David does not seem to have granted what we should call charters of incorporation or erection, to the individual burghs. Lawyers choose to presume, that what are now called "corporations by prescription," must have had royal charters, now lost or destroyed. But the facts seem to run against that presumption of law. It is scarcely credible that all the charters of erection should have been destroyed or lost, while so many closely following them in antiquity have been preserved. In one instance, that of Ayr, we still have what appears to have been the first charter that was granted to it; and yet it is nothing of the nature of a deed of incorporation or erection. It would appear then, that towns and trading communities existed among us as early as we can pretend to speculate upon our history—carrying on the little commerce of the country, through the impediments of lawlessness and insecurity of property, and the oppressions and exactions of the government that ought to have protected them; and that the burghal reformation of David consisted in throwing around these the protection of the law, and encouraging them to elect for themselves managers of their common affairs; and magistrates to administer justice among them and to lead them in defending themselves against aggression.

Berwick was the seat of the principal trade on the coast of Scotland, and its burgesses were particularly active and zealous in establishing their privileges. When Bishop John of St. Andrews was desirous of erecting a burgh at his episcopal see, the king granted him the site, and transferred to the new burgh the services of Mainard, as its provost, a Fleming and a burgess of Berwick, where he had learned the burgh usages and the duties of his office. Such was the beginning of the city of St. Andrews as a trading burgh.

Our own ancient city, or rather its castle (deriving its name, from being the burg or fortress of Edwin of Northumbria), very early became a frequent and favourite residence of our kings, when Lothian had been ceded to Scotland. St. Margaret resided there, during the fatal expedition of her husband Malcolm into England, and died there. Her son David had a dwelling on the rock, and a garden on the bank, between it and the church of St. Cuthbert. The town which grew up under the protection of the castle, in the midst of the royal demesne, was naturally an object of royal favour, and David I. granted to its burgesses, not only exemptions and freedoms within their walls, but an exclusive right of trade and manufacture over a district extending from Colbrandspeth or Edgebucklin brae on the east, to the water of Avon

Succeeded A.D. 617.

Chap. V. on the west, corresponding to what was afterwards the Sheriffdom of "Edinburgh principal." So considerable was the trade of Edinburgh, after Berwick was lost to Scotland, that in the middle of the fourteenth century, the customs paid from it, were about one half of the sum raised from the whole customs of Scotland.

Other burghs of David's erection were not destined to take so high a position. He erected his demesne village of Rutherglen into a royal burgh, with the exclusive privilege of trade over an extensive district, the limits of which cannot now be fixed with certainty. It certainly included Glasgow, however; and when soon afterwards, the bishop
A.D. 1175-8 obtained the privilege of trade for his little city, this gave Rutherglen, the king's burgh, an opportunity of tyrannizing over it, which it exercised in levying toll and petty custom up to the gates of Glasgow.

The oldest charter of Rutherglen preserved is one of William the Lion, which confirms all the customs and rights the burgh had from David; but is chiefly remarkable for specifying the boundaries of its extensive jurisdiction. It denounces any who shall withhold the tolls or other customs, which belonged to the town in the time of David; and the king concludes in these words, "I strictly command, that no one bring anything to sell within these bounds, except it have been first at the burgh of Rotherglen." You must not imagine Rutherglen always so insignificant as it is now. Its ferme or rent paid to the Crown was considerable. After some pretty large assignations, made from them by successive kings, for various purposes in the Cathedral of Glasgow, the burgh still paid of ferme to the Crown in 1331, £15, while Linlithgow paid £10, Edinburgh £32, and Berwick £46. Rutherglen might have decayed at any rate; but we find a sufficient cause of its dwindling into its original state of a rural village, in the overshadowing of the neighbouring city of Glasgow.

The beautiful situation of Perth must have early attracted attention. Its fertile soil, its central position at the opening of so many passes into the inland and upland country, and at the highest navigable point of its noble river—with its fishings, which were of great value before we had learnt to decoy fish out of the Firth and the open sea—were such as our ancestors ever chose for a town. It may have been, as it is very confidently asserted by antiquaries, one of the Roman cities of Britain; and we may indulge in the imagination of the Roman soldiers comparing the Tay to the Tiber (which from them was a compliment!) and fixing their dwellings on its banks. It is certainly a place of very high antiquity. No record or chronicler alludes

Chap. V. to its origin. It is probably, in some shape, as old as any sort of civilized society among us. The commencement of its trading privileges dates from David I., who had a house in the town, and called it his burgh; and who seems to have granted to it the exclusive privilege of trade within the whole county of Perth.

The earliest charter of Perth preserved, is one of William the Lion, which I notice more particularly, because it appears to have served for a style and copy in later burgh constitutions. It commences with a prohibition against any stranger merchant (*mercator extraneus*), buying or selling anywhere within the sheriffdom, except at the burgh—"but," says the king, "let the stranger merchant come with his wares to my burgh of Perth, and there sell them and invest his money." The foreign merchant is also prohibited from cutting his cloth for retail in the burgh, except from Ascension Day to the feast of St. Peter ad Vincula; between which terms they were allowed to cut their cloths for sale, and buy and sell their cloths and wares as freely as the burgesses. This long period, from ten days after Easter to the 1st of August, allowed for strangers retailing, was a great relaxation of the privileges of exclusive trade. A singular privilege follows. No *tavern (taberna)* is to be allowed in any place within the sheriffdom of Perth, except where a person of knightly degree is lord of that place, and lives in it; and then only one tavern. This was plainly to secure for the burgesses the monopoly of retailing drink over the whole county, if that could be effected by a royal charter. The king grants to the burgesses the right of having their merchant guild, excluding fullers and weavers (*fullones et telarii*). This curious exclusion of artizans, not generally ranked as merchants, I do not pretend to explain. We may conjecture that the trades employed in the making of cloths had risen to greater wealth than the other craftsmen, and had pretended to an equality and participation of the privileges of the merchant guild, which it required the royal authority to repress. The charter next prohibits any one from making cloth, dyed or shorn, within the sheriffdom, except a burgess and gild brother, paying his share of the town burdens and royal aids; and any cloth found contrary to that prohibition, is to be dealt with according to the custom that existed in the time of king David. The king prohibits strangers from buying or selling hides or wool, anywhere but in the burgh.

We learn from this charter both the favourite monopolies which formed the distinction of those early burghs, and something of the trade and manufactures that were then carried on among us.

Chap. V. I shall have occasion to speak of these last more fully hereafter.

Aberdeen owed its origin to the Church, but the village which grew up at the mouth of the Don round the bishop's cathedral, was soon overtopped by the offset which had been attracted by the better harbour and the fishings of the river Dee. The first of the extant charters of Aberdeen informs us of the existence of that league among the northern burghs of Scotland, taking its name from the German *Hanse*, and, like its great namesake in after times, doubtless a combination for mutual defence and counsel. The charter is very short:— "William, by the grace of God, king of Scots, to all good men of his whole land, greeting: Be it known that I have granted, and by this charter, confirm to my burgesses of Aberdeen, and to all my burgesses of Moray, and all my burgesses dwelling on the north part of the Munth, their free *Anse*, to be held where they choose, and when they choose, as freely as their ancestors had their Anse in the time of my grandfather king David. Wherefore I prohibit any from vexing or disturbing them while holding the same, under pain of my full forfeiture." This document, while it serves to indicate that the individuals in whose favour it was conceived could not have been united into a single burghal community in the present meaning of the terms, may be regarded as proving, that among the traders of the country, there had been formed a federal connection, and that to the north of the Grampian mountains there existed a set of *hanse towns*, whose alliance, and whose common privileges and immunities had been recognised and protected at least as early as the reign of king David I. The only other charter of William, preserved in the city archives, grants to the burgesses of Aberdeen in terms, the privileges granted to Perth by William.

Aberdeen benefited, no doubt, by being the port of the bishop's see. But its harbour, on an inhospitable coast, and the produce of its mountain pastures and its river, drew to it, at a very early period, an extensive foreign trade, which placed it immediately after Edinburgh and Berwick in the scale of commerce.

The archives of the burgh of Inverness are rich in burghal history. In them is preserved a charter of William the Lion, granting to " his burgesses of Moray," the common privilege against suffering distraint for the debts of others. The same king granted to the burgesses of Inverness specifically, exemption from toll and custom over all Scotland; the exclusive privilege of trade in the burgh and county; and conferred upon them, in property, the Burgh Haugh. The burgesses were taken bound, on the other hand, to construct and maintain constantly in good repair, a fosse and palisade, which the king was to make round the town.

The next charter to this burgh, also by king William, is more remarkable. It grants to the burgesses exemption from wager of battle. They were no longer to be obliged to do battle at the appeal of any one, but might support their cause by oath. This, however, was not the oath of witnesses knowing the truth, but the oath of compurgators, swearing their belief that the cause was good. The charter, as a farther boon, reduced the necessary number of compurgators for the burgesses of Moray by one half, and the amount of their forfeit, that is apparently of the king's amercement, to the half of that of other burgesses.

The remaining charter of William, to Inverness, gives a right of a weekly market, and assures the "king's peace" to those frequenting it. It grants to the burgesses all the laws and customs which the burgesses of the other burghs possess, and concedes in terms, the privileges of exclusive trade within the county I have already mentioned as granted to Perth.

I fear to exhaust your patience with these details of charters, but I must still direct your attention to one of considerable interest locally, and also to the legal antiquary. In the year 1197, King William had built a castle on the river Ayr, and had encouraged the settlement of a town or burgh, where probably a village had long existed. About ten years after, he granted a charter to Ayr. In it the king sets forth that he has made a burgh (*burgum fecisse*) at his new castle upon Are, and has granted to the burgh and its burgesses all the liberties and free consuetudes which his other burghs and burgesses through his kingdom enjoy. He then grants to the resident burgesses exemption from toll or petty custom everywhere, as in other burgh charters. He grants a territory by named boundaries now not easy to ascertain. Each burgess holding a full toft, is to have a right to six acres, which he may clear of wood, the reddendo for the toft and six acres, twelve pence. Toll and other customs due to the burgh are to be levied at certain places named, apparently on the outward boundaries of the territory granted.

Upon this charter, which is evidently the first charter of the burgh, the most learned of our constitutional lawyers has remarked, That in it, as in all others of the same early date, there are evidently no words of incorporation—such, at least, as would now be deemed requisite; and the obvious inference seems to be, either that the mere denomination of *burgus* in a royal grant was held sufficiently to import the immediate creation of a corporate character in the inhabitants, or, as seems more probable, that such artificial unions, instead of being the sudden product of royal prerogative, were the slow and natural growth of circumstances and situation. It is in accordance with this supposition, that the original right and character of burgess appear to have depended on the actual possession of real property within the burgh. In this charter the meaning seems to be, that all those are to be burgesses of Ayr, and entitled to the peculiar privileges thereby conferred, "who shall come to inhabit the burgh and shall be there abiding." And in some of the earliest charters to other burghs royal, similar declarations are contained, from which it seems just to infer, not merely that a freeman was bound to acquire property within the burgh, but that such acquisition constituted the prime, if not the sole qualification, and entitled him to those privileges and immunities, which constituted the peculiar advantages of burghership.[1]

While the sovereign was raising the third estate by the security and privileges of his burghs, the great lords of the Church, desirous to participate in the advantages of trade which attended them, obtained privileges of the same nature for the towns and villages that sprung up round their cathedrals and abbeys.

I have already mentioned the origin of St.

[1] Thomas Thomson, Introd. to Scotch Burgh Reports, p. 11.

Andrews. Each of the episcopal sees, and many of the great monasteries, in like manner obtained foundations and rights of trading for their dependent villages. Some of these never rose much beyond their original condition. Dunkeld, Dumblane, Rosmarkie, Dornoch, continued the dependent rural villages which their old masters had made them. Arbroath and Paisley, the one by a small foreign trade, the other by manufacture, rose a little in importance. But amongst these, Glasgow stands the chief. The charter of King William, which gave to the Bishop the privilege of having a burgh at Glasgow, with a market on Thursday, was granted between the years 1175 and 1178. We smile at the present day to think of the oppression which the bishop's burgh of barony long suffered from the royal burgh of Rutherglen. Even after 1450, when the bishop had obtained a jurisdiction of regality, and Glasgow rose a step in the scale, it had to maintain a struggle against the king's burghs of Renfrew and Dumbarton, which sought to monopolise the trade of the river, as Rutherglen did to circumscribe the city to landward. Though represented in Parliament so early as 1576, and emancipated at the Reformation from subjection to the bishop, who formerly controlled the election of its magistrates, the city did not become legally a royal burgh, till the charter of Charles I., con-

Chap. V. firmed in parliament 1636. It was not even for some time after that Glasgow began to put forth its hidden strength and capacity for improvement. Since the beginning of last century, its progress in manufacture and trade, in wealth and splendour, has been rapid beyond any parallel.

Unity of interest naturally produced union among the burghs of Scotland. We have already seen a hanse or league established among those north of the Grampians, including Aberdeen, as early as the reign of David I. The southern burghs had a yet more definite and solemn combination. As early almost as we have any knowledge of the constitution of burghs, the greater burghs of the south seem to have held assemblies in which the great Chamberlain of the kingdom presided. From thence is supposed to have emanated the collection of the laws of the burghs in the time of David. In the thirteenth century they were called the court or parliament of the four burghs, Edinburgh, Berwick, Roxburgh and Stirling. In 1368, when Berwick and Roxburgh had fallen into the power of the English, Lanark and Linlithgow were substituted for them. This burgher parliament acted as councillors to the Chamberlain in judging of burgh causes appealed from his *air* or circuit, and also made laws and regulations for trade and burgh affairs. Haddington appears to have been their established place of meeting, but it necessarily varied; and in 1454 it was fixed by royal charter at Edinburgh. Before that time "the court of the four burghs" had extended its constitution, and summoned to its meetings commissioners from all the burghs royal south of Spey. In the course of the following century the ancient burgher court or parliament had merged in the Convention of Burghs, of which it is not necessary to speak. I believe it still exists.

<small>Chap. V.
A.D. 1405.</small>

Besides this parliamentary process for consultation, the burghs of Scotland advised with each other upon any question or difficulty that occurred in their administration; and, having ascertained the prevailing custom in the several towns, they unhesitatingly adopted that as law. Some of these evidences of fraternity appear to me of singular interest. At a very early period it appears that a doubt arose as to the right of alienating real property on deathbed. The burgesses of Perth, Lanark, Edinburgh, and Aberdeen, took an interest in the question, and reported the custom of their burghs to be against such alienation, whether the lands were of inheritance or of "conquest," and the customary law being thus ascertained, it forthwith appears upon the statute book, running, "consuetudo burgorum est."[1]

[1] The consultation, queries, and answers, are preserved in

CHAP. V.   In other cases of difficulty the Scotch burghs wished to learn the practice of the burghs of England; and in two of these the response of the burgh of Newcastle appears to have settled the doubt, for the precise words of that answer form the law as it stands recorded among the laws of the burghs of Scotland.[1]

Travellers have been so occupied with the natural beauties of Scotland that they have paid too little attention to the beauty of our towns. Their

---

the old law MSS. The law, as founded on their usage, runs thus :—

A seke Burges may nochtanaly.

It is for to wyt that the custom of the Burgh is that na man lyande in bedde of dedde ony landis the quhilk he has heritably in burgh na yhete other the quhilk he purchest in his hele fra the verray ayre may analy or till ony other geyff or sell but gif it war sua that he war sua gretly constreignit throu nede that it behovit hym algatis do for nede has na law And that his ayre walde nocht or for poverte is nocht of poner his faderis nede to stanche or his dett to pay redyly.—*Leges Burgorum*, c. 101.

[1] *Of ane Burges ejected furth of his Possession.*

This is the assise of the New Castell that gif ony man of ony burgh war in the possession of ony land quhether it be rychtwysely or wrangwisly & sua cummys ane othir in sayand that he is veray ayre of that ilk lande and hym out puttis that was in possession of his awn authoritie and withouten dome. Quharfor it is askit at us Burges of the New Castell quhether he that was first in possession sal recover his sesing befor that he answer till him that put him out. To that than answer we that he that was first in possession rychtwisly or unrychtwisly sall all tym first recouer his possession, and efter that gif he tyn his possession in forme of law & dome that he is halden to doo. And he that puttis him out be his awn proper authority and will sall remayne in the kingis amerciament.—*Leg. Burg.*, c. 99.

sites are generally surprisingly fine ; I do not speak only of those most known and celebrated—Perth, Edinburgh, Inverness—but of all our rural capitals. The excellence of their building materials has, I suppose, induced the citizens to lay them out on a spacious plan. There is at once an airiness and a solidity, and in many of them an approach to grandeur, which we seek in vain in the provincial towns of other countries. Our old burgesses loved to copy the steep roofs and tall gables of their Flemish allies in trade; and the towns they have built in imitation of them, stand better on the banks of our rivers and firths, and backed by our mountains, than even the fine old cities of decayed splendour on the shores of the Zuyder Zee, or the Great Canal. Setting aside Glasgow as something too large to deal with as one of a class, our Scotch burghs seems to me the natural, healthy and happy growth of an industrious and steadily progressive country. The privileges, necessary at first perhaps for their existence, and so beneficial to the country, they have gradually abandoned, as they appeared to obstruct an extending commerce. Their citizens have always worthily filled the important place and functions of a third estate. In early times, I mean when the old Church was no longer efficient, they were the zealous supporters and encouragers of a liberal education. When there was less mixture of

Chap. V. ranks than at present, and more gross immorality, they were free from many of the temptations and many of the vices of the rural gentry. Not extremely given to busy themselves in public affairs, they yet took a reasonable interest, a patriotic concern in the affairs of the country, so far as the perversion of their ancient free constitution (now restored) gave them power. Above all, their steady industry and active enterprise—quite removed from the mad speculations that now surround us—their honest frugality, and simple primitive manners, not rarely united with some accomplishment and learning [1]—formed a class of men that I should be sorry to think was altogether extinct.

[1] Many of the old citizen-merchants of Edinburgh had studied at the University, and appear in the lists of graduates.

CHAPTER VI.

It requires no evidence to convince us that there existed a system of law in Scotland, before the great revolution in the dynasty and institutions of the country that followed the death of Macbeth. Wherever society exists, life and the person must be protected. Wherever there is property, there must be rules for its preservation and transmission. Accordingly, in the most ancient vestiges of the written law of Scotland, we find references to a still earlier common law, *Assiza terræ*—the law of the land—*lex Scotiæ*—evidently of definite provisions and received authority.

It has been very confidently asserted that in Scotland we have not, and never had any *Common Law*. To answer that monstrous proposition, I need only call your attention to the law of primogeniture. It is certainly no act of Parliament, or ancient ordinance before Parliamentary times, or adoption from the Roman code, to which we owe this foundation of our heritable rights. What excludes sisters from the succession in heritage, whilst they have it in moveables? What gave *representation* in land from the earliest times, whilst we have only last year adopted it in personal succession? Certainly no written law that can be pointed out in our statute book.

If the assertion had been that there was nothing, or but little of local and peculiar in our common law, it might be assented to with less difficulty. I believe Scotland, at the different eras of her history, used the laws of the people cognate to her then dominant race. Whilst under a Celtic sway, her laws were those which have received a certain shape and definiteness, from their longer use and greater cultivation in Ireland; and her customs (the most important part of law) were those maintained in the wilds of Galloway, as long as the Celtic language prevailed there; and which are only now disappearing among the patriarchal tribes of the Highlands. You will not expect me to prove this proposition, which is in itself so likely that it seems to throw the burden of proof upon the controverter of it. The only facts we have, capable of historical record, to prove the existence of a peculiar Celtic law in Scotland, are connected with the institutions of succession and marriage.

The law of succession was according to the law which is called, in Ireland at least, the law of Tanistry—a system which depended upon a descent from a common ancestor, but which selected the man come to years fit for war and council, instead of the infant son or grandson of the last chief, to manage the affairs of the tribe, and who was recognised as the successor, under the name of Tanist, even during the life of the chief. To take one instance, from the ancient history of Moray, a district which long continued to pay respect to its ancestral Maormors. Maolbride is the first known Maormor; he left a son Malcolm, but the office or dignity did not descend upon him, but went to Finlay the brother of Maolbride. After Finlay's death, Malcolm at length succeeded to his father's place; he was succeeded in turn by his brother Gilcongain. Gilcongain was succeeded by Macbeth, the son of Finlay; and after Macbeth had lost his local dignity and his crown with his life, he was succeeded in the maormorship by Lulach, the son of Gilcongain; the maormorship thus passing, in as many generations, to the brother, nephew, brother, nephew, and cousin-german.[1]

In the competition for the crown of Scotland

---

[1] Here is the pedigree and the order of succession:—

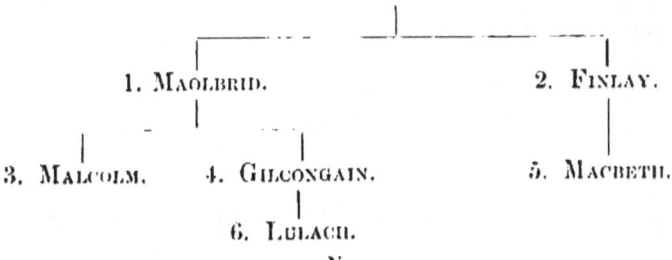

CHAP. VI. between Bruce and Balliol, where no art of the most dexterous advocate was omitted, Bruce pleaded that, as nearer in degree, he should exclude the representative of the elder line; and to illustrate this, he alleged that anciently, in the succession to the kingdom of Scotland, the brother was wont to be preferred to the son of the deceased king; and he cited a number of instances in which this took place. Balliol, while he denied the inference, did not question the truth of the examples; but he alleged that the son, and not the brother, was the nearest in degree. Lord Hailes remarks upon this argument,—" Here Balliol attempted to answer Bruce's argument without understanding it. Bruce supposed an ancestor to be the common stock, and the degrees to be the persons descending from that stock. Hence the king's brother stood in one degree nearer the common stock than the king's son."

I have said that the law of marriage was viewed as one of the peculiarities of the Celtic race, but there is nothing more likely to mislead us in a subject necessarily of much obscurity than to found upon the loose practice of a half savage people, a theory of a definite system of law. The system of hand-fasting, we may judge from its very name, was not peculiar to the Highlands at the time when we know it in operation, and we have no evidence or approach to proof that it or any other peculiar customs of marriage were recognised in Celtic Scotland after the introduction of Christianity had given one rule of marriage and legitimacy to the whole Christian world (unless we are obliged to except England).

When the Anglicising policy of the descendants of Malcolm Canmore had everywhere throughout Scotland thrust aside the ancient race, the institutions and laws of Saxon England rapidly spread over our country. There are some indications, however, that on the whole these were not much opposed to the old usages of the old people. Let it be remembered that that was a peaceful revolution, at least not effected by open war or conquest. If there had been any fundamental change introduced in the rights or laws of the people, it must have given rise, if not to disputes, at least to a general expression of resentment amongst the parties suffering by the change (for all changes of law produce suffering to some party), but in the recorded transactions and chronicles of that time we do not find a trace of any violent or general alteration of law, except in the matter of succession, which I have already alluded to; a change which ought in fact to be treated as part of the great feudal system then introduced, and spreading rapidly over all Britain.

At the earliest period, then, of which we have

CHAP. VI. information of an authentic kind, the laws and institutions of Scotland did not differ materially from those of the other northern nations of Europe. Even that vestige of an earlier age which I have pointed to, the preference of the brother to the son in succession, amongst the patriarchal clans, was, as I have already shown you, of frequent occurrence in Saxon England, and we cannot doubt that it must have taken place amongst all rude peoples, where the law was not yet strong enough to support a young and untried heir.

The system of the estimation or valuation of persons according to their class, and in connection with it, the adoption of pecuniary penalties and compensation for crimes, prevailed with us as with the other northern nations. We find a price or value set upon every one according to his degree, and different amounts of injury taxed with minute and affected precision.

In a fragment which I conceive to be the oldest written portion of the laws of Scotland, and which was known and proscribed as barbarous by Edward I. in 1305, we have some details of this system. The chapter is called " *The Laws of the Brets and Scots.*" Unfortunately, our earliest version of it is in Norman French. The system of compensation prescribed in it, commences at the top of society. The estimation, or *appraising* as we should say in vulgar parlance, of the king of Scots, was a thousand cows, or three thousand of the coin called *ores*, each of which was equal to sixteen pennies. The king's son, or an earl, was estimated at seven score cows and ten. An earl's son, or a thane, at a hundred cows. The son of a thane, at sixty-six cows and two-thirds. The nephew of a thane, or an ogettheyrn was estimated at forty-four cows, and $21\frac{2}{3}d$ —and, says the law, all lower in the parentage are to be considered as villeins—translated in the Latin version "*rustici*," and in the Scotch, "*carlis ;*" the estimate of a villein was sixteen cows. The estimate of a married woman is less by a third part than that of her husband. If unmarried, it is equal to that of her brother.

The compensation prescribed for drawing blood is graduated with equal minuteness :—" The blude of the hede of ane erl or of a kingis sone is ix ky. Item the blude of the sone of ane erl or of a thayn is vi ky. Item the blude of the sone of a thayn is iii ky. Item the blude of the nevo of a thayn is twa ky and twapert a kow. Item the blude of a carl, a kow."

I have not troubled you with the ancient Scotch terms applicable to these laws of compensation. Some of them are more or less intelligible to the Celtic scholar; but I cannot venture to speak of etymologies from that language, of which I am entirely ignorant. There is no reason to doubt, from the similarity of the laws, that the terms *Cro, galnis,* and *enach,* are nearly equivalent to the *Wērs, wites,* and *Bots,* of the old English law.

Among laws deriving their remote origin from a society where the lands were not individual property, but held in common, we should seek in vain for any early provisions concerning the inheritance or the transmission of land. Transactions and contracts were also unknown, or so simple that they had not yet required the attention of the lawgiver. Hence the preponderance in those early codes, of laws regarding crimes, over those more subtle distinctions which the complicated relations of commerce demand. Our oldest laws are full of provisions regarding the proof and punishment of theft and murder. The murderer taken red-hand (*layun-darg* in Gaelic), or the thief caught with the *fang* or *bak-berand* or *hand-habend,* was "justified," we may believe, without any unnecessary and inconvenient delays of process. It was where the matter was not quite so plain; where an accusation was brought and denied, that the peculiarities, as we consider them, of the old law appear. If we may trust to the eras of our published laws, it would seem that in the reign of David I., a man accused of theft might clear himself, either by doing battle, or by the purgation of twelve leal men.[1]

You will observe that there is nothing here said of the evidence of witnesses on either side. By our old law, indeed, little use was made of that kind of evidence. If the accused denied, he did not call witnesses cognisant of the facts; but was bound to find compurgators to swear for him, that they believed him guiltless—men of the vicinage, and knowing the character of the parties accusing and accused.

The number of compurgators, which varied from one to thirty, seems to have been determined by the nature of the crime and the characters both of the accuser and the accused. When goods were stolen from the poor and weak, who had no help of man, but were under the king's protection, if one man swore upon the holy altar, as the use was in Scotland, and before worthy witnesses, that he knew the thief, and named him, the individual so accused was bound to restore the goods if he could not establish his innocence.

If it could be proved by two "leil" men that an individual had violated the king's peace in gyrth,

---

[1] Gif ony appelis ony man in the Kingis court or in ony othir court of thyft it sall be in the lykyng of hym as beis appelyt, quhether he wil bataile or to tak purgacioun of xii leil men with clengying of a hyrdman.

he was at once punished according to the nature of his crime.

In William's reign, if a man habit and repute a thief was pursued by the suit of one barony and could find no borch, he was hanged.

Twenty-four leil men were necessary to " clenge a man anent the king," and if he was "appealed" of felony or of life or limb, the compurgators must be found in the sheriffdom where the crime was perpetrated. If a priest was adduced in warrant for theft, and declared that the thing challenged was reared by himself, he was bound to prove that by the oaths of *three* worthy men approved by the lords of the town. A lord, from whose prison a thief had escaped, was obliged to clear himself of being accessory to the theft's escape by twenty-seven men and three thanes.

In the case of burgesses the law of acquittance was a little different. If a burgess was prosecuted by the provost for breaking of assize, and in complaints between an uplandman and a burgess that might be settled by oath, the law prescribed " clenging by six hand." If a burgess was challenged for theft by an uplandman, or if he was challenged to do battle after the age of fighting, he was to clenge him by the oath of twelve of the neighbourhood.

A man accused of theft might choose purgation

of twelve leil men with clenging of a "hyrdman," or to do battle.

When there was as yet no trust reposed in the evidence of witnesses, if the accused or the defender failed in bringing his sufficient band of compurgators, his last resource was in the "judicium Dei," where the theory of the law trusted to the direct intervention of the Deity to decide the rights of parties. The first and most usual mode of this appeal was the judicial combat, or wager of battle; and solemn laws and rules were made for its mode of procedure; and courts and reverend churchmen and judges and monarchs sat to witness the combat, where the strong man overcame the weak; and still forced themselves to believe that God decided the cause.

In the earliest of our laws, restrictions were introduced in the application of trial by battle. Churchmen were specially exempted from it, which had not always been the case; and men above sixty might decline the combat. Burgesses had privileges with regard to it. The burgesses of king's burghs might claim combat against those of burghs dependent on subjects, but could not in their turn be obliged to grant them the combat. Knights and free tenants might do battle by proxy. Those of foul kin were bound to fight in person.

After the judgment was pronounced ordaining

Chap. VI. trial by battle, or by the other ordeals of fire or water, it was no longer open to compound the cause for a penalty; and any lord of a court lending himself to such a transaction forfeited his court.

During the judicial combat the strictest silence was preserved. The judges of Galloway enacted, that he who should speak in the place where battle was waged, after silence was proclaimed, should forfeit ten cows to the king; and that if any one should interfere with his hand, even to the extent of making a signal, he should be in the king's "merciament of lyf and lym."

Among the common privileges and prerogatives of jurisdiction granted to the greater monasteries, was a right of trial by fire and water. The earliest charter of the abbey of Scone by Alexander I. (and we have few earlier in Scotland), confers such a jurisdiction, and I believe the place in which the actual ordeal was held, was the little island in Tay, which lies midway between the abbey and the bridge of Perth. We find nowhere the details of the application of the ordeal of hot iron in Scotland. It was considered as somewhat the more honourable of the two; and by the laws of England, parties declining combat by reason of age or maiming, were to purge themselves by hot iron, if free men, and by the ordeal of water, if of servile rank. This last among other barbarities was revived when, to the disgrace of humanity and of an age that called itself Chap. VI. civilized, our courts of justice were occupied with the discovery and punishment of witches. I do not know if the results then are to be taken as any test of the old system of trial and torture. In many instances the poor wretches, persecuted to madness, not only admitted the whole of the charge against them, but went beyond what the imaginations of their accusers could conceive, and disclosed hellish mysteries and impossible horrors as taking place in their own presence or in their own persons.

David I. saw the abuses to which such a system of trial was liable, and, in one instance, he provided that his own judge should always be present in the court of the Abbot of Dunfermline, to see that justice was duly administered. It is extremely probable that he passed a general law to the same effect, though it has not been preserved to us. In 1180 a statute of William the Lion enacted, that "na baron have leyff to hald court of lyf and lym, as of jugement of bataile or of watir, or of het yrn, bot gif the scheriff or his serjand be thereat, to see gif justice be truly kepit thar, as it aw to be."

But all ordeals were falling into disrepute at the earliest time when we can mark our law in operation. A statute of King William enacted, that if one were accused by a certain number of persons of repute, he should underlie the ordeal of water; but if, in addition to those accusers, three witnesses could be found to speak to the fact, he was not to undergo the ordeal, either of fire or water, "but hastily to be hangit."[1]

In 1230 a statute of Alexander II. was passed which has been twisted ingeniously in some of our old law manuscripts, to import an entire abolition of the ordeals of fire and water.[2]

The title given to this law in the Ayr MS. is, "Deletio legis fosse et ferri et institutio visneti," and it supports that title by a curious misreading of the law. The statute of Alexander only gave the accused the choice of putting himself upon an assize, and declared, that one who has already been acquitted

---

[1] Quha sa ever efter lentyrn nixt efter the deliverans of oure Lord the King be chalangit of thyft or that he has gevin thyft-bote and that may be tayntit on hym be the greyff of the towne and thre othir lele men he sale be tane and underly the law of wattir. And gif forsuth anent the samyn thar may be witnessing of thre lele men of eld togidder with the forsaid witness thruch na batal sal he pas na to wattir na yet to yrn bot hastily he sal be hangit. Alsua leffuil it is to na man to take redempcion for thyft efter dome gevyn of wattir or of batal.—*Assize R. Willelmi*, A.D. 1181.

[2] The King Alysandir has statut that gif ony man chalangis ony othir man of thyft or of reyflake & the defendour wil put him on a gud & leil assise & the assise sal mak him clene quhit sal he be & the followar sal be in the amercyment of the King or of the Erl or of the baron gif it be of thyft. And gif the defendour be foul thar sal be done on hym rychtuis dome. And it is to wyt that fra this tym furth thar sal be no ingement done (on him) thruch dykpot na yrn.—*Statuta R. Alexandri II.*, A.D. 1230.

by an assize shall not for the same offence be required to undergo the ordeals. *When* judgment by assize or jury was introduced we cannot tell, nor when the custom of ordeal was abolished. The laws I have quoted to you seem to mark it in a state of transition. In certain civil causes of the greatest importance, the proof, even in the time of David, was by an assize of twelve good men (*assisa bonæ patriæ*). That took place in pleadings under brieves of mortancestry and novel discisin.[1] At least as early, the Church courts of Scotland were in the use of taking and recording in writing the evidence of witnesses; and assizes of sworn men were used as the rude machinery for trying other civil causes. It would set at defiance all our notions of the sense of men, and the value of experience, if any country, having in some points admitted proof by witnesses, could long have adhered to a settlement of questions the most important to mankind, by the ordeals of fire or water, or still more to that law which really declared the strong hand to be always in the right.

---

[1] It is statut that breiffis of Mortancestre & new dyssesing neirr mair sal be impleydit be challange of the party askand bot allanerly be an assyse of the gud cuntre & nane othir ways, and na challangis lyis thar to for quhi tha xii the quhilkis ar chosyn of the gud men of the cuntre till an assise sal say allanerly thar entent and thar veredyk eftir the poyntis and the artikyllis of bayth the breiffis and eftir that as that assyse pronouncis in veredyk rycht sa that dome sal be geyflin to the partiis.—*Assize R. David*, 35.

Chap. VI.   The penalties of theft were not with us so heavy as in England; but the compounding of theft or protection of a thief were very carefully guarded against. By the ancient law of Berthynsak, summary procedure was established with a thief caught with his burden, such as a sheep or a calf, but you will observe there was there no capital punishment.[1]

Another statute of undoubted antiquity, although its precise date cannot be fixed, prescribes the gradations of punishment for different degrees of theft.[2]

If a thief took refuge in "*Gyrth*," or sanctuary, he could lose neither life nor limb, but enjoyed the

---

[1] Of byrthynsak that is to say of the thyft of a calf or of a ram or how mekil as a man may ber on his bak thar is no court to be haldyn bot he that is lord of the land quhar the theyff is tane on swilk maner sall haf the scheip or the calf to the forfalt.

And the theiff aw to be weil dungen or hys er to be schorn. And that to be done thar sal be gotten twa lele men.

Na man aw to be hingit for les price than for twa scheip of the quhilkis ilkane is worth xvi d.—*Assize R. Willelmi.*

[2] Giff ony be tane with the laff of a halpenny in brugh he aw throu the toun to be dungyn. And fra a halpenny vorth to iiij. penijs he aw to be mare sairly dungyn. And for a payr of shone of iiij. penijs he aw to be put on the cuk stull and eftir that led to the hed of the toune, & thar he sal forsuer the toune.

And fra iiij. penijs til viij. penijs & a ferthing he sal be put upon the cuk stull and eftir that led to the hed of the toune and thar he at tuk hym aw to cut his eyr of. And fra viij. penijs and a ferthing to xvi. penijs and an obolus he sal be set upone the cuk stull and eftir that led to the hed of the toune and ther he at tuk hym aw to cut his othir ear of. And efter that gif he be tane with viij penijs and a ferding he that takis him sal hing him. Item for xxxij penijs. j obolus he that takis a man may hing him.—*Fragmenta Collecta* 42.

king's peace. Nevertheless, he was bound to restore as much as he stole; to make amends to the king according to the law, and to swear on the holy relics or the book of the Evangel, " that fra that time furthwartis, never mair he sal do reyflake na thyft."

While, as I mentioned, a value was set upon every man, and by that rule, a fine could be imposed for injury done to his person, and much more for his slaughter,—at the same time, undoubtedly the legal and strict punishment of murder was death. We cannot discover from the imperfect relics of our ancient code of customary law, how this seeming inconsistency was reconciled. It is at least exceedingly probable that it lay with the kindred and friends of the murdered man to abstain from prosecuting to the utmost those accused of his death, where their feelings of indignation and vengeance could be solaced with a pecuniary compensation. The law had not yet pervaded all society; and public justice was scarcely separated in men's minds from private revenge.

It was not the estimation of the person alone that, by those old laws, ruled the amount of the penalty for slaughter. That, indeed, was the assythment paid to the kindred of the slaughtered man, but another penalty was due if the peace of the king or other lord had been violated by the shedding of his blood. The person guilty of the slaughter of a man within a place where the king's peace was proclaimed, forfeited nine score cows. The manslayer within the peace of an earl or king's son, incurred a forfeit of four score and ten cows; and so progressively in the lower degrees of rank.

It was no doubt with a laudable intention that the sovereign, in the profuse distribution of rights of jurisdiction to subjects in Scotland, reserved what were long called the four pleas of the Crown — murder, rape, fire-raising, and robbery. It was intended that at least those great crimes and their punishment should be removed in some degree from private influence. At a later time, and under a different system of penalties, it became a point of economical policy to preserve for the impoverished Crown a jurisdiction which afforded so large an income, by the fines and escheats of the justiciar's court.

There was only one province of the Scotch king's dominions that we find asserting peculiar customary laws. We know little of the early history of the district now called Galloway. It had scarcely come under the confirmed dominion of the kings of Scotland in the reign of Malcolm Canmore. We have seen the rude insubordination of its people, under his son David at the Battle of the Standard. The native lords were still too powerful for the distant authority of the sovereign. William the Lion had a code of laws for its government (*assisa mea de Galweia*), and judges for administering them. They met at several places, and we have still records of a few of their decisions, some of which are remarkable.[1] Among other places, the judges of Galloway are found at Lanark prescribing rules to the Mairs of the province regarding the mode of collecting the King's *kane*.

For long after that time, Galloway continued to be governed according to its own peculiar laws. In the reign of Robert Bruce, its people had not yet acquired, nor perhaps desired, the right of trial by jury, but practised the mode of purgation and acquittance according to their ancient laws—those very laws of the Brets and Scots which Edward in vain endeavoured to abolish. As late as 1385, Archibald Douglas, lord of Galloway, while undertaking in Parliament to further the execution of justice within his territory, protested for the liberty of the law of Galloway in all points.

A.D. 1306-1329.

---

[1] At Dumfries it was ingit be the iugis of Galoway that gif ony Galoway man be convickyt ouder be batal or be ony other way of the kingis pece brokin the king sal haf of hym xij^{xx} ky and iii gatharionis or for ilk gatharion ix ky the quhilk ar in numer xxx and vij.

Na Galoway man aw to haf visnet but gif he refuse the law of Galoway and ask visnet.

Item thar the samyn day be the samyn iuges it was ingit that gif ony in the palice quhar that batal is wagit quhair pece sulde be haldin hapins for to spek outan thaim that ar to keip the palice the king sal haf of hym x ky in forfalt. And gif ony man puttis his hand to or makys a takyn with his hand he sal be in the kingis merciament of lyf and lym.—*Assize R. Willelmi.*

Chap. VI.   At a time when the punishment of crime, and the compensation even for accidental damage, depended on the feelings or caprice of individuals, it was the highest humanity to interpose between the wretch fleeing from vengeance and justice, and his pursuer armed with the powers of the law, but stimulated by private motives. And here the Church raised its arm in mercy. It had, indeed, from the earliest time of Christianity, been held sacrilege to violate a church with bloodshed; but it was a subsequent invention to proclaim for it a right of sanctuary; to declare that persons fleeing to the Church, or to certain boundaries surrounding it, should for a time at least, and under certain conditions, be safe from all persecution. Much doubt has been expressed regarding the constitution and privileges of the church sanctuaries of Scotland. Without going into the very curious Teutonic antiquities of the subject, or speculating upon the times when among our forefathers, as in Judæa of old, places of refuge were anxiously provided "that the slayer may flee thither which killeth any person unawares"—"that the manslayer die not until he stand before the congregation in judgment"—I would observe, that by the canon, and the more ancient ecclesiastical law, all churches were held to afford protection to criminals for a limited period, sufficient to admit of a composition of the offence, or, at any rate, to give time for the first heat of resentment to pass over before the injured party could seek redress. In several English churches there was a stone seat beside the altar, where those fleeing to the peace of the Church were held guarded by all its sanctity. One of these still remains at Beverley, another at Hexham. To violate the protection of the *frith-stol*— the seat of peace, or of the *fertre*—the shrine of relics, behind the altar, was not, like other offences, to be compensated by a pecuniary penalty: it was *bōt-leas*, beyond compensation.¹

That the Church thus protected fugitives among ourselves, we learn from the ancient canons of the Scotican councils; where, among the list of misdeeds against which the Church enjoined excommunication, after the laying of violent hands upon parents and priests, is denounced "the open taking of

---

¹ There is an English notice of a breach of sanctuary and its punishment by ecclesiastical authority in 1312. The bishop of Durham heard with dismay that certain children of evil had incurred excommunication by withdrawing from the church of the Carmelites of Newcastle, some who had fled thither imploring church protection for the safety of their lives; and afterwards, when the guilty person is discovered, namely, Nicholas le Porter—he is sentenced to appear bare-headed and bare-foot, wearing only a linen robe, at the door of the church of St. Nicholas of Newcastle, every Sunday for a whole year, and there to be publicly scourged (*fustigatus*) by the curate, in presence of the assembled congregation, and from thence scourged to the church of the Carmelites, all the way confessing his fault. Moreover, he is to have the same penance at the church of St. Nicholas and the cathedral church of Durham, on three days of Whitsun week.

thieves out of the protection of the Church." But, though all were equally sacred by the canon, it would seem that the superior sanctity of some churches, from the relics presented there, or the reverence of their patron saints, afforded a surer asylum, and thus attracted fugitives to their shrines rather than to the altars of common parish churches. We must not be surprised that in rough times even Holy Mother Church was not always able to afford protection to her suppliants against the avenger of *red-hand;* and it was to strengthen her authority, and to support what in the circumstances of society was a salutary refuge against rash vengeance, that the Sovereign at times granted his sanction to particular ecclesiastical asylums.

The most celebrated, and probably the most ancient of these sanctuaries, was that of the church of Wedale, a parish which is now called by the name of its village, "the Stow." There is a very ancient tradition, that King Arthur brought with him from Jerusalem an image of the Virgin, " fragments of which," says a writer in the eleventh century, " are still preserved at Wedale in great veneration." About the beginning of his reign, King William issued a precept to the ministers of the church of Wedale, and to the guardians of its " peace," enjoining them " not to detain the men of the Abbot of Kelso who had taken refuge there, nor their goods, inasmuch as the Abbot was willing to do to them, and for them, all reason and justice."

In the year 1144, David I. granted the Church of Lesmahago as a cell to Kelso, and by the same charter conferred upon it the secular privilege of sanctuary in these terms—" Whoso, for escaping peril of life or limb, flees to the said cell, or comes within the four crosses that stand around it; of reverence to God and St. Machutus, I grant him ' my firm peace.' " To incur the censure and vengeance of the Church was sufficiently formidable; but to break "the king's peace" brought with it something of more definite punishment. It was not the mere mysterious divinity that doth hedge a king: "The king's peace" was a privilege which attached to the sovereign's court and castle, but which he could confer on other places and persons, and which at once raised greatly the penalty of misdeeds committed in regard to them. By our most ancient law, the penalty of raising the hand to strike within the king's girth was four cows to the king, and one to him whom the offender would have struck; and, as I have already mentioned, for slaying a man "in the peace of our lord the king," the forfeit was nine score cows to the king, besides the assythment or composition to the kin of him slain " after the assise of the land."

Chap. VI.	In granting the same privilege to Inverlethan, Malcolm IV. ordains, "that the said church, in which my son's body rested the first night after his decease, shall have a right of sanctuary in all its territory, as fully as Wedale or Tyningham; and that none dare to violate its peace 'and mine,' on pain of forfeiture of life and limb." Of the sanctuary of Tyningham, thus mentioned as of almost equal celebrity with Wedale, we have but little further information.

The Scotch law of sanctuary or girth was early ascertained with much precision, and carefully guarded from the danger of encouraging crime by affording an easy immunity to fugitives. In later times, and during a period of intolerable misrule, among other temporary enactments for the suppression of homicide, the Parliament of Scotland enacted that whoever took the protection of the Church for homicide should be required to come out and undergo an assize, that it might be found whether it was committed of "forethought felony," or in "chaudemelle;" in case it should be found of chaudemelle, he was to be restored to the sanctuary, and the sheriff was directed "to give him security to that effect before requiring him to leave it."

CHAPTER VII.

There is something melancholy in considering the constitution of an ancient and independent kingdom, when it has been absorbed in a greater. School our minds to it as we will, sum up all the benefits of the Union, and dwell with all truth upon the ancient miseries of war between the sister nations, and the degrading and demoralizing of the later provincial government of our end of the island, no Scotchman can look back without some sadness to the independence of his country so dearly won, and of which we still idly cherish the memory.

A different feeling at first weighs upon the historical inquirer. The origin of our constitution, our ancient parliamentary usages, can no longer be appealed to as precedents, or quoted authoritatively as rules of practice. They are in this view mere matter of antiquarian curiosity, or to be used only as illustrations by analogy. The machinery of our system of government is of a different origin, and has reference to the history of another people. But when we look deeper, we come to regard those ancient foundations of our political system as a part, and an important one, of that which has formed our national habits and character, which separate us so widely from the rest of the world, and distinguish us somewhat even from England.

In a feudal kingdom the constitution of legislation and government is intimately connected with the tenures of estates, and we therefore look with much interest to the earliest specimens of charters or title-deeds of lands.

I mentioned before that Scotland has no charters nor writings of any description so early as the reign of Malcolm Canmore. In the reigns of his sons who preceded David I., we have a few grants to religious houses, but none to individuals or laymen. These first appear in the reign of David, but very few of that reign have been preserved to our time.

It may perhaps be too rash to conclude that there were no written titles of land at an earlier period of Scotch history, but, at any rate, we must abandon all discussion or speculation as to their form and character.

When we first become acquainted with the charters or writs by which estates and lands were held and conveyed in Scotland, they exceedingly resemble, I may say they entirely coincide with those of a parallel date in England. They consist of a grant by the king, or some lord of the soil, to an individual and his heirs of certain lands described, and they specify a *reddendo*, or a certain amount of military service. There is nothing to distinguish these early charters from those of Norman England, or, indeed, of any strictly feudal kingdom. They are distinguished from modern conveyancing by nothing so much as their brevity. Take first one of the very few extant charters of David I. to a layman:— A.D. 1124-1153.

"David, by the grace of God King of Scots, to all his barons and his men and friends, French and English, greeting: Know that I have given and granted to Robert de Brus, Estrahanent (Strath Annan) and all from the bounds of Dunegal of Strath Nith to the bounds of Randulph Meschines. And I will and grant that he have and hold that land and its castle well and honourably with all its customs, to wit with all those customs which Randulph Meschin ever held in Carduilh and in his land in Cumberland, on that day in which he had them best and freest. Before these witnesses, Eustace fitz John and Hugh de Morvil, and Alan de Perci and William de Sumervill, and Berengar Engain and Randulph de Sulis, and William de Morvil and Hervi fitz Warin, and Aedmund the chamberlain, at Scone."[1]

Here, again, is a charter of the whole estate of Dundas, near Edinburgh, granted by a subject—I

---

[1] Original charter preserved in the British Museum.

Chap. VII. believe nearly as old as the reign of David. The granter is Waldev, son of Cospatric, Earl of Dunbar or March. The original charter, still preserved, is of course in Latin:—

"Waldev, son of Cospatric, to all his good men and all friends present and to come, greeting: Know that I have given and granted, and by this my charter confirmed to Helias son of Huctred, Dundas, for half the service of a knight (*militis*), to be held by him and his heirs, of me and my heirs in fee and heritage, in moors, in waters, in ponds, in mills, in meadows, in pastures, with all their right bounds and pertinents. I grant also, and will and command, that the foresaid Helias have and hold that land as quietly, as freely and as honourably, as any knight holds of a baron in the whole land of the King of Scots. Done before these witnesses, John son of Orm, Waldev son of Baldwin, Robert of St. Michael, Helias of Hadestanden, William of Copland, William of Hellebot, Aldan the Steward, Gerard the knight, John of Gragin."

A.D. 1153. 1165.

A more important charter of Malcolm IV. gives us the same form and all the essentials of feudalism in a grant of the sovereign:—

"Malcolm, King of Scots, to bishops, abbots, earls and barons, justiciars, sheriffs, bailies, and servants, Frenchmen and English, Scots and Galwegians, clerks and laics, and to all men of his whole land, greeting: Know that, after I received knighthood (*postquam arma suscepi*) I gave and granted, and by this charter have confirmed to Walter fitz Alan, my steward, Birchinside and Leggardswode, by their right bounds, to wit, as fully and wholly as king David my grandfather held the lands in demesne. I have given also to the foresaid Walter, Molle, by its right bounds and with all its just pertinents; To have and to hold to him and his heirs, of me and my heirs in fee and heritage, as freely and quietly, amply and honourably, as any earl or baron in the kingdom of Scotland holds and possesses any land of me: Doing for the said lands to me and my heirs the service of one knight. Given in presence of these witnesses—Ernald bishop of St. Andrews, Herbert bishop of Glasgow, John abbot of Kelso, William abbot of Melross, Osbert abbot of Jeddeworde, Walter, the chancellor, William, the king's brother, Richard de Morevill, Gilbert de Unframvill, Waldev, son of Earl Cospatric, Jordan Ridel, at Rokesburgh."

Some of the old MSS. which used to be cited in court by the Scotch lawyers, before the great work of Stair had banished such *myths*, have a capitular styled "The Laws of Malcolm M'Kenneth," which commences thus—"Here follow the laws of Malcolm M'Kenneth, the whilk was maist victorious king over all the nations of England, Wales, Ireland, and

Norway. And he gaif all the land of the kinrik of Scotland till his men, and nocht held till himself but the kingis dignitie and the Mute hill in the toun of Scone." Sir John Skene, the first editor of our old laws, sets himself to prove that chapter to be the authentic enactment of Malcolm II., who began to reign in 1004, drawing his proofs out of recent acts of Parliament, corroborated by the historical authority of Hector Boece! It is not necessary to controvert his assertion, and to prove that there never can have been a time when all the land belonged to the Sovereign. The story was introduced evidently to support a law fiction—convenient in itself, and the basis of our system of conveyancing—that all property flows from the Crown. Such was the form of conveyancing, undoubtedly, from the earliest of our charter history; and it could not have been more systematically feudal if the country had really been conquered, the natives driven out or enslaved, and the invader, now sovereign, had proceeded to partition the territory among his victorious army. That many of those early charters which we still have of Malcolm IV. and William the Lion, were really new grants of lands fallen to the Crown by reason of forfeiture or otherwise, we have every reason to believe; but many others of them were, beyond all doubt, a mere formalizing of the tenure—grants according to the fashionable feudal manner, of property already held by the grantee. Observe, for instance, the grant by Malcolm IV. to Walter fitz Alan of the office of High Steward and lands which he had held under David I.

"Malcolm, King of Scots, to bishops, abbots, earls, barons, justices, sheriffs, bailies, servants, and all other good men of his whole land, clerks and laics, French and English, Scots and Galwegians, present and future, greeting: Be it known to you all that before I received knighthood (*priusquam arma suscepi*) I granted, and by this charter have confirmed, to Walter fitz Alan, my steward, and to his heirs in fee and heritage, the donation which King David, my grandsire, gave to him, namely Renfrew and Passeleth and Polloc and Talahec and Kerkert and the Drem and the Mutrenc and Eglisham and Lochinavche and Innerwick, with all pertinents of these lands. And likewise, I gave to him in heritage, and have confirmed by this charter, the office of my steward (*meam senescalliam*), to hold to him and his heirs of me and my heirs freely, in fee and heritage, as well and as amply as King David gave and granted to him his stewardship (*senescalliam suam*), and as he himself best and most amply held it. Moreover, I myself gave, and by this same charter have confirmed, to the same Walter in fee and heritage, for the service which he did to King David and to myself, Prethe as much as King

Chap. VII. David held in his own hand, and Inchenan and Steintun and Hadestonden and Legardswode and Birchinsyde, and farther, in every one of my burghs, and in every one of my demesne dwellings (*dominica gista*), through my whole land, an entire toft to make him a residence there, and with each toft twenty acres of land. Wherefore I will and command that the same Walter and his heirs hold in fee and heritage of me and my heirs in chief all the forenamed subjects, both those which he has by gift of King David and those which he has of my gift, with all their pertinents and rights, and by the right bounds of all the foresaid lands, freely and quietly, honourably and in peace, with sac and soc, with tol and them and infangtheefe, in vils and shealings, in plains, in meadows, in pastures, in moors, in waters, in mills, in fishings, in forests, in wood and plain, in roads and paths, as any one of my barons most freely and quietly holds his fief of me; Rendering to me and my heirs for that fief, the service of five knights. Witnesses, Ernald bishop of St. Andrews, Herbert bishop of Glasgow, John abbot of Kelso, William abbot of Melros, Walter the chancellor, William and David the king's brothers, Earl Gospatric, Earl Duncan, Richard de Morevil, Gilbert de Umphramvill, Robert de Brus, Ralph de Sulis, Philip of Colevil, William of Sumervil, Hugh Riddell, David Olifard, Valdev, son of Earl Gospatric,

William de Morevil, Baldwin de la Mar, Liolf son of Maccus. At the castle of Roxburgh, in the feast of St. John the Baptist, the fifth year of our reign."

But I could not give you a better specimen of one of those ancient simple conveyances than a charter of William the Lion—a grant to the ancient family of Seton. It conveys three great baronies—confers all baronial privileges—fixes the *reddendo* at one knight's service—expresses the formal authentication of a goodly array of witnesses—and is comprised in seven short lines. The original is in possession of the Earl of Eglinton and Winton.

Among the essentials of a feudal holding, though not always expressed in our ancient charters, was that the vassal should be bound to give suit and service in the court of his lord (*facere sectam et sequelam curiæ*). In the court, so composed of all the vassals of a baron—the suitors or sectators of a barony—were discussed the affairs of the barony and the suitors, and *there* were tried all causes, civil and criminal, of which the lord had jurisdiction by his tenure.

As by the feudal theory all land was held of the Crown, every estate of land was represented by some one who was the immediate vassal of the Sovereign: and of these Crown vassals was originally formed the King's Court. Such at least was the constitutional theory as early as we can trace any constitutional principle in Scotland. The early Crown charters, however, which specify suits of court as part of the vassal's obligation, for the most part limit it to the attendance and service in the king's courts in the nearest shire, town, or royal residence. It must indeed have been impossible and most undesirable to assemble all the Crown vassals in such a council at once. The attendance, *in fact*, in the king's court, seems to have consisted chiefly of a few churchmen, the great officers of state, and a portion of the nobility and great barons.

A few instances will show both the notion at the time, of the legal constitution of the King's Court, and the actual members who attended it.

In 1184, William the Lion held a court at Perth, of which the members are described in the record as, "the bishops, abbots, priors, earls, barons, and other good men (*probi homines*) of his land."

In the same king's reign, an assize or statute was made, which was sworn to be observed by " the bishops, earls, barons, thanes, and whole community" (*tota communitas*).

So much does this vary, however, that in following statutes, we find the style run : "It is statute by the king, with counsel of his great men" (*magnates*). "The king and the community of the kinrik has statute." There was certainly, then, no means for the commons of the kingdom to express their counsel or assent; and I think all that can be safely inferred from such forms of expression is, that some memory perhaps remained of the old Saxon, and, indeed, general Teutonic principle, which looked to the assembly of the whole nation as the source of law and of all power.

Of the persons noted as actually attending the King's Courts, whether on legislative or judicial business, we may take at random one or two instances.

Between 1190 and 1196, in a Court of King William at Edinburgh, were present, the Bishops of Glasgow and Dunkeld, Earl David the king's brother, the Earls of Fife and Stratherne, the High Constable, two abbots, and ten barons. In 1208, on the octaves of the apostles St. Peter and St. Paul, King William held a *plein cour* (*plena curia domini regis*) at Selkirk, for the determination of an important dispute between the House of Melrose and the Earl of Dunbar, at which were present—the King and Prince; Ralf Bishop of Doune in Ireland, who had formerly been Abbot of Melros, and seems to have had an affection for his old country; Bricius Bishop of Moray (he was a son of the family of Douglas, and the first who raised into importance that afterwards illustrious house); David Earl of Huntingdon, the king's brother; Eustace de Vesci; William and Oliver, two of the king's chaplains;

Chap. VII. Robert de Londin, the king's natural son; William de Boscho, Hugh de Prebenda, Adam de Kingorn, Gilbert de Stirling, the king's clerks (an office of importance and confidence, for several of these rose to be chancellors of the kingdom); and the following barons—Gervase of Avenel, David de Lindesay, Hugh de Normanvil, William de Valoins, Philip de Moubray, Ingelram de Balliol, David the Marshal, Robert de Mortimer, Patrick, son of the Earl (of Dunbar), Patrick de Witham, Nes de Walghton, Roland de Grenelaw, Roger de Merlai, Philip and William de Colevil, Thomas Fraser, with the usual clerkly addition of "many others."

Such information as we have regarding the individuals present in the *national councils* is not to be overlooked. In 1230, we find statutes which bear to be enacted by the advice and consent of the magnates of the realm and of the whole community; but the list of those present, which is preserved in several manuscripts, gives us no more than the names of one bishop, two earls (one of them Justiciar of proper Scotland), one prior, the Justiciar of Lothian, the High Steward, and one other baron. In 1244 the attendance is somewhat larger—two bishops, three abbots, seven earls, of whom one is the High Constable, and eight great barons, one of whom is the Chamberlain. In this assembly, the barons seem to be identified with the "probi homines." In 1255 an important national convention, which, however, from the circumstances in which it met, excluded one great party of the nobles, numbered four bishops, four abbots, four earls, and thirteen great barons. Many of these barons were of equal importance and possessions with several of the earls. At the head of the list are the Steward of Scotland and Robert de Bruce. The assembly of nobles which acknowledged the Maiden of Norway as heir to the throne, at Scone, on the 5th day of February 1283, consisted of thirteen earls and twenty-four great knights and barons. Finally, the great convention of Briggeham in 1289 was composed of the four guardians (two of whom were bishops), of ten other bishops, twelve earls, twenty-three abbots, eleven priors, and forty-eight barons. In none of these is there any mention of representatives of burghs.

Whatever the *communitas regni* meant, it certainly did not imply the presence of a class of burghers or burgh representatives in Parliament. The Burghs, indeed, were already protected by privileges, and several of them were of consequence enough to have been entitled to the honour, or bound to the duty, of sharing in the national councils. But long before the principle of representation was known in the high court of Scotland or in England, the burghs of our country had established their own council apart,

Chap. VII. and sent their deputies to a burgher Parliament, where they framed laws for their own government.

The power to impose taxes is the first criterion of what we consider the constitutional power of Parliament. I have mentioned the ancient and ordinary sources of the revenue of the kings of Scotland. When an emergency occurred requiring more extensive supplies, they were obtained by means of an *auxilium* or " aid," raised from the people. We have evidence of a national aid or tax imposed
A.D. 1161. on Scotland during the reign of Malcolm IV., but no indication of the authority by which it was imposed. Its purpose was to defray the marriage and dowers of the king's daughters—a proper and established feudal burden due by the vassals, and which may have been demanded from a court of vassals, as well as from a parliamentary or legislative
A.D. 1211. assembly. Half a century later, King William held a great council, where he claimed from his magnates (*optimates*) an aid to enable him to pay his heavy debt to King John of England. The magnates—meaning, I think, the clergy and barons—gave him 10,000 marks. The burghs, says our historian, 6000 marks. Lord Hailes remarks, that " from this passage it may be concluded that as early as 1211, burgesses gave suit and presence in the great council of the king's vassals, although the

contrary has been asserted with much confidence by various authors."

With all the reluctance to dissent from Lord Hailes' opinion that every one must feel who has experienced the benefit of his accuracy and learning, I confess I cannot arrive at that conclusion. I think the separation of the sums, and the turn of the sentence in Fordun,[1] lead more to the belief that while the magnates or great men of the king's own court voted their 10,000 marks, the court of the burghs separately and independently granted an aid from their constituents of 6000 marks. The words of Fordun seem to me to indicate that the burgesses did not vote or deliberate in the same assembly with the " optimates."

The *term* Parlement, first used in France, under Louis VII., first occurs in England in the preamble to the statute of Westminster, 3 Edw. I.

The magna charta of John, points to the *theory* of the constitution of Parliament. But the earliest Parliament that can be proved by extant writs to have resembled the present legislative constitution of England by summons of citizens and burgesses is 49 Hen. III.

Middle of twelfth century.

A.D. 1272.

A.D. 1215.

A.D. 1266.

---

[1] Hoc anno rex magnum tenuit consilium, ubi petito ab optimatibus auxilio, promiserunt se daturos 10,000 marcas: præter burgenses regni qui 6000 marcarum promiserunt.—*Ford.* VIII. 73.

Chap. VII.

A.D. 1286.
A.D. 1189.

The first time that Wyntoun gives to the National Assembly of the Estates of Scotland the name of Parliament, is in mentioning that in which the six Wardanes were appointed.[1] By the treaty of Briggeham, it was covenanted that no *parliament* should be held without the boundaries of Scotland, as to matters respecting the kingdom. The term had very recently been introduced in England, and was not, till some time afterwards, the word of style for all solemn National Assemblies of the Estates.

The Parliament assembled by John Balliol at Scone, on the 9th day of February 1292, was probably the first of the National Councils of Scotland, which bore that name in the country at that time, although later historians have bestowed it freely on all assemblies of a legislative character. We have no reason to believe that any change in its constitution occasioned the adoption of the new term, which soon became in Scotland, as in England, the received designation of the great Legislative Council solemnly assembled.

Hitherto we may conclude no burghs had sent representatives to the king's proper court of magnates. But their importance was on the increase, and the circumstances of the country, the long and costly war of independence, required to extend the

[1] Wynt., VIII. 1.

sources of national supply. Still we have no evidence that the representatives of the burghs formed a part of the solemn Parliaments of Robert I. in 1314, 1315, and 1318, although a remarkable change of style in the second of these, seems to indicate the introduction of a new element in the National Assembly. In the parliamentary settlement of the crown on Edward Bruce in 1315, the members present are classed as "bishops, abbots, priors, deans, archdeacons, and other prelates, earls, barons, knights, and others of the community;" and seals are affixed by the prelates and nobles, and by the "*majores communitatum,*" a phrase which it might be rash to assert, meant the burgesses, if it were not for their undoubted appearance so soon afterwards.

Finally, in the famous Parliament at Cambuskenneth, held on the 15th day of July 1326, when Bruce claimed from his people a revenue to meet the expenses of his glorious war, and the necessities of the state, the tenth penny of all rents, according to the old extent of King Alexander III., was granted to the monarch by the earls, barons, *burgesses*, and free tenants, in full Parliament assembled. The change had taken place silently, perhaps gradually; but from thenceforth, undoubtedly, the representatives of the burghs formed the third estate, and an essential part of all parliaments and general councils.

It is remarkable that, in this Parliament, where we can for the first time ascertain the presence of the Third Estate, we have the first development of what are now considered the fundamental principles of a representative constitution. There was a compact between the king and the three Estates; a claim of right, redress of grievances, a grant of supplies, and a strict limitation of the grant. The three estates acknowledge the great merit of the king, and all that he had undergone for restoring the liberties of all. The grievous burdens of the people, through arbitrary taxes, are pointed out; *sustentationem non habuit absque intolerabili onere et gravamine plebis.* The king is to impose no other "*collectas,*" and to mitigate his legal exactions of *prisæ et cariagia.* On the other hand, the Estates grant him the tenth penny of all rents, a gift which they declare shall be null if the king defeats its application to the public service by any remissions granted beforehand; and the grant is to cease with the king's own life.

The next important change in the constitution of our Parliament arose from pure accident.

The frequent meetings of the national council, and their long deliberations, had been felt extremely burdensome, especially by the class of small freeholders, among whom, as yet, no representation was established. Many of these attended with reluctance, and could not continue during the session without much inconvenience. To ease that class, and also to avoid the inconvenience of popular discussion of certain questions, for the consideration of which expressly the national council was summoned, Parliament devised the plan of delegating its power to certain committees of its members.

In a Parliament held at Scone, September 27th, 1367, the record bears, that "convocatis tribus communitatibus regni congregatis ibidem, quedam persone electe fuerunt per easdem ad Parliamentum tenendum, data aliis, causa autumpni, licentia ad propria redeundi." In the Parliament at Perth in the March of the following year, the Three Estates, on account of the inconvenience of the season, and the dearness of provisions, elected certain persons " to hold the Parliament," who were divided into two bodies: one to treat of the general affairs of the king and kingdom, and another smaller committee to sit on appeals from inferior courts—" *super judiciis contradictis.*" And in the following parliament held at Perth, on the 18th February 1369, two committees were appointed; the first, " ad ea que concernunt communem justiciam," namely, appeals, and pleas, and complaints, which of right ought to be decided in Parliament; the other, " to treat and deliberate on certain special and secret affairs of the king and kingdom, previous to their being brought before the whole Parliament; since," says the record, "it is not expedient that the whole body should assist at a deliberation of that kind, nor be kept in attendance." In these arrangements we perceive the origin both of the "Committee of Articles," which afterwards became an essential and remarkable part of the constitution of Parliament, and of that judicial committee which, under various forms and regulations, became in like manner a permanent institution, and terminated in the establishment of a separate and supreme Court of Justice. That these were novelties in the reign of David II., is evident from the words of the records already quoted; and as such they were avowedly used as a precedent in the reign of his immediate successor, Robert II. In a Parliament held at Scone, March 2, 1371, the form of procedure in that of 1368 was literally copied—"Imitando videlicet ordinem illum et modum qui servabantur in Parliamento tento apud Perth tempore venerande memorie domini regis David anno regni ipsius quadragesimo."

There were various attempts to establish a court of supreme Civil Jurisdiction from the time of James I. downwards. In 1425 it was ordained that the Chancellor, and with him certain discreet persons of the Three Estates to be chosen by the king, should sit three times in the year, to examine, conclude, and determine all complaints, causes, and quarrels that may be determined before the King's Council. The Parliament, 1457, enacted that the Lords of the Session should sit thrice in the year, " ilk time forty days, in thir three places: Edinburgh, Perth, and Aberdeen." " The noumer of the persons that sall sit sall be nine, of ilk estate three." In 1503, because there had been great confusion of summons at each Session, so that leisure nor space at one time of the year might not have been had for the ending of them, it was statute that " thair be ane consale chosen be the kingis hienes quhilk sal sit continually in Edinburgh, or quhar the king makes residence, or quhar it plesis him, to decide all manner of sumoundis in civile maters, complaints and causis, daily, as thai sal happen to occur, and sal have the same power as the Lords of Session." All these attempts seem entirely to have failed. Each successive Parliament appointed its judicial committee, or " Dominos ad causas et querelas," who not only exercised an appellate jurisdiction, but decided causes in the first instance. Their jurisdiction is in no respect distinguishable from that of the King's Council. In 1467 it was ordered by Parliament " that all summondis and causis that is left undecidit in this Parliament sal be decidit before the Lords of Counsaile, the summondis standing as they now do." And, accordingly, causes that commenced in the one court frequently were disposed of in the other, while the clerks seem to have had no clear notions of the distinction between them; and frequently, in engrossing the proceedings of the one, use the style and form of the other.

The functions of both these judicial bodies were at length united in the Court of Session or College of Justice, established by James V.

The institution of that court seems to have originated with the king himself, who, intending "to institute ane college of cunning wise men, baith of spirituale and temporale estate, for the doing and administration of justice in all civile actiouns, therfor thinks to be chosen certaine persouns maist convenient and qualifyit therfor to the nowmer of xiii persounes, half spiritual, half temporal, with ane president. . . The Three Estates of this present Parliament thinkis this artikle wele consavit, and therfor the kingis grace, with avise and consent of the said Three Estates, ordanis the samin to have effect."

It was perhaps to be expected that the new "College of Justice" should for some time be unpopular; but the hatred and rage with which its institution and first proceedings were received, are not to be explained either by the dilatory and cumbrous working of a new procedure, nor by ignorance or incapacity of the members of the Court. It may be that the smaller number of judges rendered it more open to solicitation and the coarser modes of influence which at that time, and for very long afterwards, tainted the fountains of justice.

Of the original mode of electing the Lords of Articles there is little evidence. It is probable each estate chose the part to be taken from its own number. James VI. applied his whole ingenuity to secure for the Crown the permanent control of their election; and though he might overstate his power when, in his speech at Whitehall to the Parliament of England, he boasted that in Scotland, " such bills only as I allow of, are put into the Chancellor's hands to be propounded to Parliament; and after this, before I put my sceptre to a law, I order what I please to be erased"—the desired result was fully obtained during the reigns of his successors. In 1621, the Lords of Articles consisted of eight from the clergy, eight from the nobility, seven officers of state, eight small barons, and seven commissioners of burghs. They were appointed to meet every day in the inner house of the Tolbuith, at ten morning. The whole Estates were ordained to await in the town of Edinburgh till the end of Parliament. The Lord High Commissioner and the Lords of Articles sat every day, advising on the articles presented in Parliament, from July 21st to August 4th; on which day the Parliament met and passed one hundred and

AP. VII. fourteen Acts, and was thus concluded. In 1633, the method of election gave rise to much discussion. The King and Estates being convened in the Parliament House, the Parliament fenced and suits called, the king having retired to the inner great room of the Exchequer House, the clergy to the little Exchequer House, the nobility to the Inner House, where the Lords of Session sit; for Lords of the Articles, the nobility elected eight of the clergy, the clergy chose eight of the nobility; and thereafter, the persons chosen of the clergy and nobility, being convened together in the Inner House of Session, chose, jointly, eight of the commissioners of shires, and as many of the free burghs; and the King having entered into the said Inner House in presence of the nobility and clergy, named eight officers of state, besides the Chancellor and President; and the King, clergy, and nobility, re-entering the Parliament House, and his majesty being set upon the throne, and the whole estates having taken their places, publication was made of the election. The King and the Lords of Articles sat daily within the said Inner House of the Tolbuith, and advised on the whole articles, petitions, ratifications, acts, statutes, laws, and others, presented to them in Parliament, from the 20th to the 28th of June; on the which last day the King, with the whole Estates of Parliament convened, concluded the Parliament, the whole Acts being read and voted by the Three Estates to stand as Acts of Parliament; the king assenting and confirming the same by touching them with the sceptre, as presented to him by the Lord Clerk of Register. And in 1663, it was enacted that the same form and order should be kept in all time coming.

A system of representation of the small freeholders was attempted to be introduced by James 1. upon his return from England, which for the time was wholly ineffectual. No representatives were actually returned to Parliament, and acts were passed for more than a century for the relief of the small barons, successively raising the amount of fortune below which they should not be obliged to give personal suit and presence in Parliament. The project was renewed in 1567, and again, with more success, in 1585 and 1587; and from the latter period, the representatives of the small barons or freeholders formed a considerable proportion of every Parliament, where they were classed and treated as a separate estate, though by the theory of the constitution they formed a part of the baronage.

The clergy, as one of the Estates, may be said to have disappeared with the Reformation. The laymen, who continued for some time to sit in virtue of grants of the great Church benefices, were in no respect distinguished in interest or feeling from the other barons. During the periods when Episcopacy was again established, the bishops alone formed the clerical estate.

Each of the royal burghs was at first required to send at least two representatives to Parliament; and though the number actually attending was generally small, it was not till 1619 that they were relieved of a part of the burden. From that time, by an order of the convention of burghs—as it appears, unsanctioned by Parliament—one member was returned for each burgh, except Edinburgh, which continued to send two representatives.

Certain great officers of the Crown had a seat in Parliament in virtue of their offices. The number of these "offices of the State" admitted, was, in 1617, limited to eight.

There was no division of houses in the Scotch Parliament: all the Three Estates sat and voted together; an accident unfavourable to the independence of the Third Estate. The Committee of the Lords of the Articles soon engrossed the whole legislative business and power of the Parliament; a result not so mischievous even from its throwing into the hands of a party the initiative of all measures, as from entirely quelling the freedom of parliamentary discussion, which became impossible when a multitude of bills, hitherto kept secret, were laid at once before Parliament, and forthwith put to the vote in a mass.

The mode of the election of the Committee of the Articles was necessarily a subject of great interest, and, in later and worse times of the Scotch Constitution, the devices of politicians threw it entirely into the hands of the Government. It formed the first subject of the list of grievances presented by the Estates of the kingdom after the Revolution; and in the first Parliament of William and Mary, "the Committee of Parliament called *the Articles*" was abrogated.

Circumstances were most unfavourable to the growth of a sound representative constitution in Scotland. It was James's wish to have a Parliament like that of France, a court to register his decrees; and while the system of representation was still in its infancy, his accession to the English Crown seemed to give him the power to carry his wishes into effect. The succeeding Stuarts, though they never found Scotland so easily governed as James boasted, were successful in extinguishing all parliamentary discussion. The period between the Revolution and the Union was too short to give the habits or the spirit of an independent legislature; and the superior importance attached to the proceedings of the English Parliament, had by that time thrown Scotland somewhat into a provincial position. It was rather from the accidents of its

Chap. VII. government, than by reason of any radical defect in its constitution, that the Scotch legislative assembly never fulfilled the highest end of a Parliament in possessing the confidence of the country. Certainly, at no period of her history can it be said, that the people of Scotland looked to the Parliament for redress of grievances, or as the defender of their rights.

CHAPTER VIII.

From the ancient lives of the saints—our first authority as to the state of the country—we learn something of the dress and manners of the people of Scotland in the seventh and eighth centuries. We find they used chariots, that they manufactured swords and other weapons,—probably those articles of bronze now so commonly dug up, especially in the west of Scotland,—that they used cloaks of variegated colour, apparently of home manufacture, and fine linen, which must have been of foreign production. The bodies of the dead of high rank were wrapped in it.

In the churches there were bells, but only hand-bells probably, and very likely not often cast, but hammered and riveted, a kind of which we have one or two curious specimens remaining.

Adomnan mentions drinking-cups of glass as in use among the Picts. Ale was made at home, and wine, which must have been imported, was also used.

They had boats or coracles of leather on the rivers, and galleys built of oak, and carrying sail.

CHAP. VIII. Even in their leather boats they went to sea, and performed long voyages, at least from Ireland to Orkney. In their galleys, the missionaries of Iona crossed the stormy and dangerous sea to the Shetlands and Iceland.

A.D. 1120. At a later time, we escape from the ideas of mere barbarism, in finding the pearls of Alexander I.[1] (in the beginning of the twelfth century) much celebrated, and the object of envy to a church dignitary of England. The same magnificent monarch bestowed an estate on the church of St. Andrews, and along with it, as the symbol of possession, according to a knightly fashion, an Arab horse, with its furniture of velvet, and a suit of Turkish armour.[2]

> Befor the lordis all, the king
> Gert than to the Awtare bring
> Hys cumly sted of Araby,
> Sadelyd and brydeled costlikly,
> Covered with a faire mantelete
> Of precious and fyne welvet,
> Wyth his armwris of Turky,
> That Princes than oysid generaly,
> And chesid mast for thare delyte,
> With scheld and spere of sylver quhwite,
> With mony a precious fayre jowele.

Some of the privileges granted by King David I. to his burghs bring us acquainted with a manufacture which must have been extensively carried on in

---

[1] Angl. Sacr., II. 236. [2] Wynt., vol. I. p. 286.

several districts of Scotland, and perhaps in all its villages. This was the making of cloth, which we learn from the charters I formerly brought under your notice, was both dyed and shorn (*tinctus et tonsus*). We have, too, the trades of weavers, *listers*, that is, dyers, and fullers, very early enumerated among the burgher classes—all, I think, pointing to a manufacture of our native wool into a cloth of somewhat higher quality than that fabric of *wad* (or wadmail), a coarse home-made cloth which formed a part of the rent of farms in Shetland and Orkney, and I believe all over Scandinavia.

Still, in the reign of David, and even in that time of prosperity of which his reign was the commencement, the native produce of our country, its hides and tallow, its wool and furs, was chiefly exported unmanufactured. It would be something did we find proofs in his reign that there were Scotchmen of enterprise and skill enough to trade to foreign countries; but the foundation of that assertion is scarcely sufficient.[1] It amounts only to an allowance of delay in actions in burgh, in cases where the party is abroad in parts beyond sea, in pilgrimage *vel in negociis suis*, which may, indeed, mean engaged in trade, but may evidently refer to any other occupation or affairs.

From better evidence we learn of an extensive

[1] L. L. B., 48.

CHAP. VIII herring fishery, and of the use of that fish as almost a staple article of food. Off the isle of May was a favourite fishing station, where the vessels of all the neighbouring nations met—English, Scotch, and Flemings. Thither the Abbot of Holyrood, in the reign of William the Lion, was in the habit of sending his own men to fish—a fact we learn from a charter of that king, granting them the common exemptions[1] from distraint for the debts of others while so employed in their fishery.

The Abbey of Dunfermline had a specific grant from David I. of the tithe of the gold produced by Fife and Fothrev (the district surrounding Dunfermline). David had likewise a silver mine in Cumberland; and we have evidence of iron being dug and wrought in the thirteenth century in the forests of Moray.

We gather something of the importance of the trade of the country, and of the revenue derived from the king's customs upon it, from occasional grants made by David I. and his successors, of freedom from custom. Thus he bestowed on Dunfermline—evidently as a considerable boon—the freedom from custom of one ship yearly, wherever it happened to land. It would seem almost certain, from another charter, that this was the abbot's own ship, which he manned for his

[1] S. Crucis, No. 28.

foreign trade, as the Abbot of Holyrood employed his servants in the fishery of May. The extent of trade at an early period is farther shown from the large sum granted out of the custom duties of particular burghs. David gave to the Abbey of Holyrood an annual rent of 100 shillings from his customs of Perth, to be gowns for the canons, and that, says he, from the first ships which come to Perth for the sake of trade. He gave five marks for the same purpose to the monks of Dunfermline, exigible out of the customs of the first ships that came to Stirling or to Perth; and Cambuskenneth had a similar grant.

I have already shown you some indications of shipping carried on by several of the great religious houses. The Abbey of Scone had possessions in Caithness, and apparently found the communication by sea more convenient than that by land, which led through several disturbed districts. But in those northern waters the protection of the Scotch king was insufficient, and William the Lion wrote to the Norse Harold, the jarl of Caithness and Orkney, entreating his favour to the monks of Scone, and protection for their vessel in its northern voyages.

The progress of trade and the wealth derived from it are well marked in the proportion of a national tax borne by the burghs in the end of King William's reign. In 1209 a treaty was made between Scotland and England, partly concerning the marriage of William's two daughters and their dowers, partly for an abandonment by John of England of all right to the trade of Berwick, and his consent to the destruction of an objectionable fort of the Bishop of Durham's at Tweedmouth. We do not know on which of these grounds a payment was to be made by Scotland, but it is certain it amounted to 15,000 marks. Of that great sum the *optimates* (meaning, I presume, the barons and clergy) assessed themselves with 10,000 marks, and the burghs undertook for a contribution of 6000, or somewhat more than one-third of the whole burden of the country.

An English chronicler[1] of the twelfth century describes Berwick as a noble town belonging to the King of Scots. The Norse writers tell us it had at that time many ships and more foreign commerce than any other port in Scotland. An anecdote related by Torfæus gives us a better impression of the merchants of Berwick and their wealth and enterprise, than any general description. A ship belonging to Cnut, who was commonly called the *opulent*, a citizen of Berwick, was taken at sea by Erlend, jarl of the Orkneys. On board the vessel captured was the merchant's wife, perhaps returning from a pilgrimage over sea. Instead of yielding to the panic which those northern pirates

[1] W. Neubr., V. 23.

used to inspire, Cnut bestirred himself. He took from his well-filled coffers 100 marks of silver, and was able with that sum to hire fourteen ships, fully manned, with which he instantly gave chase to the pirate Earl, and (we may hope) rescued his ship and his lady wife.

At a later date, in the middle of the thirteenth century, the Chronicle of Lanercost describes Berwick a " a city so populous and of such trade, that it might justly be called another Alexandria, whose riches were the sea, and the waters its walls. In those days, its citizens being most wealthy and devout, gave noble alms;" and the chronicler goes on to instance some of their beneficences to the Church. A merchant of Gascony, to whom Alexander III. owed £2000 and upwards — a heavy wine account if you consider the relative value of money — was quite satisfied with an assignation to the customs of Berwick ; and of the dowry of the widow of Prince Alexander (the son of Alexander III.) — amounting to 1500 marks a year — there were 1300 yearly made payable out of the customs of Berwick. If it were allowable to go into such details, it would be easy to show the considerable wealth of the burgher and trading class during the thirteenth century in Scotland, from an examination of their numerous gifts of property to the religious houses. I have been particularly struck by the munificence, in this way, of the merchants of Berwick and the burgesses of Roxburgh; the former, by the revolutions of the two kingdoms and of trade, now fallen into comparative insignificance; the latter, once so considerable as to be one of the four burghs of the burghal parliament, now scarcely to be traced by a few heaps of green turf marking the site of its castle and town walls.

We have an interesting fact connected with the other extremity of Scotland. In 1249 the Earl of St. Pol and Blois was preparing to accompany St. Louis (Louis IX.) of France, in his memorable expedition to the Holy Land. The most picturesque account is given of that ill-fated crusade by old Joinville, who, among other particulars, describes very minutely the ships used for carrying the horses of the men-at-arms, with an opening in the side of the vessel for the horses to enter, which was afterwards shut and caulked up for the voyage. Now Mathew Paris,[1] an intelligent and unsuspected testimony, informs us that one of these ships (*navis miranda*) was built for the Earl of St. Pol, a great French lord, in Scotland, at Inverness. A fact like this opens up a wide field for speculation. The place was probably chosen for the convenience of easy access to our Highland pine forests. But consider what various labour and skill were requisite for

[1] Page 771.

building and rigging this ship, the admiration of France! Even if we presume that the master builders were some of the cunning artists of Flanders or the more distant Marseilles or Genoa (for the armament was fitted out from all these ports), it almost sets conjecture at defiance, how the under workmen, the men of the axe and mallet, of the anvil and forge, were to be found in a Celtic village—how even the materials and conveniences necessary for such a work could be brought together without long preparation and too profuse expense, in a place like Inverness.

The earliest mention I have found of coal works in Scotland, is in a charter of 1291, granted by William de Oberwill, lord of Pettincrieff, to the monks of Dunfermline. The monks are to dig for coal wherever they choose, except arable land, but only for their own use, and not for sale.

This has usually been considered the earliest notice of the working of coal in Scotland. The words by no means give the impression of its being a recent discovery, and from the peculiarly exposed situation of the coal in some of our old coal-fields— about Preston and Tranent more especially—it can scarcely be supposed to have escaped notice so long, in a country where fuel was so necessary.[1] But the

---

[1] Sea-coal (*carbones marini*) were bought for the Castle of Berwick in 1265.— *Comp. Camer.* 43.

Chap. VIII introduction of coal is so important as regards the comfort of the people and the advancement of manufacture and the arts, that I wished to call your attention to an early authentic mention of it.

In the old MS. collections of laws already alluded to, is a capitular concerning the rate of custom duty to be taken at the ports of Scotland, which in most of them is described as settled at Newcastle by King David I. The oldest authority we have for this chapter now extant is the Ayr MS., written in the reign of Robert Bruce; but its antiquity is carried a good deal higher when we find that it coincides to a great degree with the customs established at Newcastle, and ascribed to the reign of Henry I. It seems not improbable that the ordinance was passed at Newcastle on Tyne, when that port was within the jurisdiction of David I., and that the tariff was at one time applicable to the ports of Northumberland, as we know it was long afterwards in Scotland. From that ordinance we gather the common exports and imports of the ancient trade of our country.

A.D. 1306-1326.

A.D. 1100-1134.

The first chapter is of Peloure or Peltry, and it is not without interest that in the enumeration of furs upon which duty was to be taken in exporting, along with the common skins of tod, whitret, mertrick, and cat, we have, specially mentioned in all the manuscripts, the skins of beaver and sable.

Corn, meal, salt, and malt, are taxed for export. Iron and madder or woald are common imports. Hides pay a small export duty. Deer skins and skins of hind calves somewhat more. A last of wool or ten sacks paid eightpence. A stone of litted (*dyed*) wool, a halfpenny; and there are rates for the exportation of wool skins, shorlings, hog skins, lamb skins, and goat and hare skins.

There are customs payable on the export of herrings, salmon, and our common sea fish—keling, ling, haddock, whiting, cod, oysters.

The chapter headed "Of Custom of Merchandise," enumerates the commodities of *brasil*, I presume a dye-stuff, wax, bales of pepper, cumming, alum, ginger, seatwell, almonds, rice, figs, raisins, "or other sic thing"—iron, lead and grease or oil.

Another section contains duties for kells which I take to be nets and thread for manufacturing them—linen thread of a different description, boards of timber, knives. Cordwain skins were admitted duty free, and also pans, cauldrons and brass pots.

The constant recurrence of teazel for dressing cloth, and of the dye-stuffs necessary for its manufacture, is worthy of notice.

There seems to have been no duty levied upon wine, and only a small charge for harbour dues.

The first year in which the extant accounts of

the Great Chamberlain of Scotland enable us to form an accurate notion of the extent and proportion of the custom-duties of the ports of Scotland is 1329—the year, you will observe, of the death of Robert Bruce.

The customs collected for the year 1369 present a very extraordinary increase as compared with the last year of Robert, which must be attributed, at least in part, to the excessive depreciation of the currency, and perhaps in some degree to the increased rates of custom.

A.D. 1369.

The Chamberlain received that year, of customs from the burgh of Dunbar, a hundred and fourscore and seventeen pounds. The customs of Haddington yielded £873; Edinburgh, £3849; Linlithgow, £1403; Stirling, £106; Perth, £710; the city of St. Andrews, £172; Aberdeen, £1100; Dundee, £800; Montrose, £244; Elgin, £71; Inverness, £56; Ayr, £25.

These accounts of the Great Chamberlain give us, at least, some materials for estimating the extent of trade, and comparing that of the different ports. We learn even a few points of their internal government and affairs. But our fullest and most satisfactory information regarding burgh matters, and the old burgh life of Scotland, is derived from the fine series of records, still extant, of the burgh of Aberdeen, which commences in 1398, and embraces regulations for trade and the supply of provisions, judicial proceedings illustrating the state of police and manners, transactions between the great burgh and its Bishop and other country neighbours, and a multitude of occurrences exhibiting the whole system of the everyday life of the merchant and tradesman. You find in these records the magistrates in their ancient and proper position as the respected friends and fathers of the community, administering justice and enforcing police with great care and attention, and sufficient authority, asserting the rights of the burgh against overbearing lords, and looking zealously to its best interests; but not thwarting their townsmen in their harmless enjoyments and sports, and even joining their holiday pranks, and thinking it no shame to lead the revels.

A very interesting picture of trade and old burgh life might be composed from these records, but it would be somewhat out of place here; and the meritorious exertions of the Spalding Club have now placed a larger specimen of their contents within public reach than I could pretend to lay before you. I pass on to matter less generally accessible.

Every one who has worked upon a difficult subject of antiquities must have felt the longing desire for access to the actual materials which men used at the period under investigation. What volumes of discussion would be saved if we could step at once into the guard-room where the Roman soldier changed his arms, or laid them aside for the *toga!* What infinite light has been shed upon ancient domestic life by the discoveries at Herculaneum and Pompeii—at Nineveh! In the same way, in speculating and guessing upon the manner of life of our forefathers, and especially upon their trade, I had often desired that in the loads of rubbish crowding our old charter-rooms there might be found some actual merchants' books, to show us how they traded of old, the commodities of export and import, the money, the banking, the exchange, the correspondence of the Scotch merchant four or five centuries ago. I considered myself very fortunate, then, when I lighted upon a fine antique ledger, which, though not going so far back as might be desired, is by far the oldest of actual merchants' books that has been preserved in Scotland. The owner of the book appears, from several entries, to have been Andrew Haliburton, a Scotch merchant, residing mostly at Middleburgh, but carrying on business at the fairs at Berri, Bruges, and Antwerp. He was evidently a person of consideration, since we find letters, accidentally left in his book, addressed to him as " Conservator of the privileges of the Scotch nation at Middleburgh;" and among his correspondents, who were mostly of Scotland, appear persons of all ranks, from the merchants of Dundee, Aberdeen, and Edinburgh, up to the Bishop of Aberdeen, the Prior of St. Andrews, and the Duke of Ross, the king's brother and Archbishop of St. Andrews. The dates in the ledger extend from 1493 to 1503.

Haliburton seems to have been for the most part a buyer and seller on commission, and he states his charges for commission in each account under the name of "*my service.*" His accounts are kept in the most simple and intelligible manner, the one page giving credit for consignments of goods and the value or money produce of them, and the other showing purchases and expenses connected with transmitting goods from the Continent to his correspondent in Scotland. The Scotch exports were but little varied. Thus, in the year 1493, he received on consignment from Lawrence Tayllyefer, three sacks of white wool, which he sold to men of Tournay for thirty-one marks each, equivalent to £61 : 18s. He received a sack of middling wool, which he sold for twenty-six marks, or £18 : 1 : 6. In return, he shipped for Scotland two butts of Malvoisie, which, with all charges, cost £13 : 14s. In 1495, he received out of the Eagle, a ship which either belonged to him, or was a constant trader between Scotland and Flanders, on account of the

Chap.VIII same party, a sack of skins containing 465; and he enters as sold out of this hop, 306, for sixteen nobles the hundred, amounting to £14 : 8s.; and the outshots were sold for £4. He received by the ship Cowasch, and out of the barque Douglas, certain sacks of forest wool, which he sold in Berri, and to a Hollander in Middleburgh. This forest wool seems to be what is elsewhere called white wool. The returns were made in canvas, potyngary, Claret wine and Rhenish vinegar, and a rundel, in which were packed the following commodities—a roll of canvas, three couple of fustian, a stck of velvet, costing 10s. 6d. the ell; a stck of damask, costing 5s. 6d.; a stck of satin, costing 6s. 8d.; three dozen pepper, costing nineteen pence a pound; two dozen ginger, costing seventeen pence the pound; two pound canell, at 4s. 8d. the pound; mace, costing 3s. 10d.; cloves, 3s.; galyga, costing 5s. 4d.; swenvel, 3s. a pound; notmogis, 2s. 2d.; saffron, 1s.

In an account for the year 1498 with Sir John Crawford, evidently a churchman, the discharge of our merchant consists of twenty ducats put into the bank of Cornelius Altonitz to be sent to Rome for the expedition of a bull of dispensation for Sir John Crawford; and of a "letter of change" for a balance of ten ducats required for the same purpose.

Several of his correspondents make voyages from

Scotland to the Netherlands; and one of these, Robert Rind, has the following entry of a charge against him:—" 3d January, 1493, Item, the same night that he passed to Calais I send Rowl after him with a bill to warn of the Lombard that was set to arrest him in Gralyn, the quhilk Rowl cost me five shillings. Paid to the barber's son to convey him by night, twelve gs. Item, given six gs. for drink silver to let them out of the ports of Bruges after ten hours in the night." This same Robert Rhind consigned various kinds of wool, namely forest wool, middling wool, brown wool, and lamb wool, and he took in exchange pipes of tayssillis, soap, spices, much as those I mentioned before, but some with unknown names; rice at 5s. 6d., *I think*, per pound; twelve pounds succer valans, costing six guldens the pound; twenty-four pounds scroschatis at five gs. the pound; succer lacrissye at eighteen gs. the pound; succer candy at twelve gs. In the same ship with these commodities were sent home to the Scotch correspondent in hard cash thirty-four ducats and salutis, price 6s. each; six ongers, price 62 gs.; in auld grots, 39s.

The first account with the Duke of Ross commences with £43 placed to his credit, for the produce of his teind salmon, with £55 of " free money" sent by Cornell Clais of Bruges. The returns sent the Duke to Scotland are, linen cloth at 6 guldens

Chap. VIII the cln; 4 beds stuffed with feathers cost £4; other four of less cost £3; 12 cods, 24 shillings; 12 candlesticks, weighing 29 lb., each pound, cost 5½ gs.; 3 great dozen of powder veschall, with 3 chargeours weighing 354 lb., each pound cost 6 gs.; 28 clls of Dornvyk, 3 ell broad, 27 g. per ell; a dossyn of serviatis cost 9s.; 28 clls of towell, 8 gs. the ell. 3 Aras cowerlats, ilk 20 ell, cost £3. A bankvar cost 18 g. the ell, 16 ells long, sum, 24s. A dozen of cowssings cost 16s.; 6 stekis say, 3 red and 3 gren, cost 23sh. the stek; 2 hingand candyllaris, one cost 12s. and t'other 15s. Another package of the same year contained an odd mixture—10 potts, weighing 343 lb., at 33s. a cwt.; 7 ells of Ryssyll broun at 7s. the ell; 6 ells of blak sattyn, ilk ell cost 8s.; 3 ells cramysse satyn, ilk ell cost 17s.; 3 ells broun satin cramyssit, 14s.; 50 bowglis, ilk stek cost 14 g., sum, £2 : 18 : 4 g.

A certain "Andro Mowbray younger" sends a pak of claith which our merchant sells for him at 5s. the dozen. We may hope this was cloth of Scotch manufacture, sent to compete with the weavers of Berry and Bruges! for undoubtedly another Scotch correspondent sends by the constant trader, the Julyan, a pak of clayth which was sold actually in Bery for 6 guldens the dozen. The same exporter sent large quantities of skins, and got in return awms of Rhine wine and tons of Gascon claret (the latter cost £4 the ton), with 2 buts of Malwissy bought from Jan Bregandin for £12.

Another correspondent, Donald Crown, sent 10 ducats (each 5s. 8d.) to send to Rome for a dispensation betwix the Lord Gram and Archd. Edmeston's dochter ; and Haliburton transacted the affair, remitting the money through the bank de Benny Cassyn, and receiving the dispensation through another banker, with whom he dealt in such remittances, Cornelius Altanite. The expense of the dispensation, and of bringing it from Rome with the exchange, was £17. The same Scotch agent required another dispensation for marriage between the Laird of Mowntgomry's son and Archibald of Edmistoune's daughter, which cost £16.

I notice a small shipment of " ber " for Scotland in 1497 (only £26 worth), chiefly to remark that it is almost the only transaction about corn of any kind to be found in the ledger.

A sack of skins contained several qualities that may be still known in trade. Out of 986 skins, 350 were lentynwar, 300 futfells. The shipper had in return for them,—besides ryssill, probably fine cloths, carefully distinguished as of the ald seil, or of the greit seal or new seal, and velvets,—2 copis of rasynis, cost 5s. the cop., 4 copis of fegis, cost 20 g. the cop.

The second account of the Duke of Ross contains

large remittances from Scotland in money, and a notice of their transmission to Rome. Haliburton paid the expenses of a messenger sent to Venice to my Lady of Burgundy on my Lord's errands. The last two items of the account are for a signet of silver weighing an ounce (4 ang.), the metal costing 6s., and the making 9s.; and a signet of gold, which had a stone in it, weighing one ounce and five ang., which cost, including the making, £3 : 11 : 8. We have afterwards the expenses of making of my lord's round seal, and for mending of my lord's long seal, and what appears to be the expense of the hewing of the Duke's grave-stone, with the sum paid for its "pattern."

Another correspondent was the Archdeacon of St. Andrews, who made his remittances chiefly in money, but sent occasionally a few sacks of wool and dakers of hides, barrels of salmon and trout, which required repacking and pickling at Middleburgh, to the shame of the Scotch curer; and had his value in his own maintenance and expenses during a personal visit, in money sent to Rome for dispensations and for solliciting his affairs in the Roman court, puncheons of wine—claret costing 16s. the puncheon, and the following articles "packit in his kist at Bruges"—two pound of silk to browd with, cost £2 : 4s.; half a pound of gold, cost £1 : 4s.; a challice, half silver and copper owr-gilt, cost 24 shillings; a frontal of red say broderit, cost 18 shillings; twenty-four ell of bord claiths, cost 4 shillings the ell, with towels and serveats of the same.

My Lord of Aberdeen (the bishop) remitted, of course, in the commodities for which his city was renowned—barrels of salmon and trouts (which required no new pickling); lasts of salmon consisting of twelve barrels. The trout must have been, I presume, what we now call grilse; their price was 22 shillings a barrel, while salmon sold for 25s. The returns were made to him in cloths of Flanders, black bonnets, red caps, spices, with small quantities of almonds and rice, and there was sent to Rome, to Master Adam Elphinstone, seventy ducats through the bank de Altanite, and again sixty ducats more; "item, paid for the mending of an oralage, and the case new, the whilk I send to my Lord with James Homyl, 3 shillings;" a counterfeit challice £1:8s.; two silver challices, double overgilt, one weighing seventeen ounces, and costing one shilling and six gs each ounce. Then follow large sums remitted to Rome, including the expenses of expeding a dispensation to John Elphinston.

To the Archdeacon of St. Andrews, Haliburton sent challices of silver, and one of copper, with the cup only of silver; ten dozen of raisit work, the quhilk cost £1:10:6; a gown of ypre black lined with say, a doublet of black chamlet; a bonnet; a pair of hose—altogether costing £3 : 1s.; and sent him with Sanders of Lawder a little kist with iron-work, costing £1 : 17s.; a few other small pieces of plate, and a mat to his chamber, twenty foot long, and as broad, costing seventeen shillings. In the year 1499, he sent him in a ship that passed to Etlyn, tyles for his chamber-floor, costing 16 shillings and 8 gs; a quantity of great pots and pans; a mortar and a holy water pot.

To Dean William Crawfurd, the merchant acknowledges sums of money which he left in his hands when he passed to Rome, and charges him with four pounds paid for a horse, and twelve shillings given him in his purse, at his parting off Middleburgh in December 1500.

The Abbot of Holyrood is charged for a kynkyn of olives and a corf of apple orangis, sent him by the command of Dean William.

John Smollet imported to Scotland woad for dying at £7 a ton, Bryssell, which I take to be the Brasil of the old custom tariff, and tassil at 14 shillings the pipe. But though thus evidently manufacturing and dying at home, and consigning to Middleburgh packs of his Scotch cloth (Scottis gray, Pabyllis quhit), he sends to Zealand his white cloth to be littit or dyed red, paying 4 guldens the ell, and re-importing it into Scotland.

Among the last entries in the book is a memorandum of a little kist sent to Mr. Richard Lawson, "in the whilk ther was 8 volomis contenand the course of baith the lawis, cost 28 guldyns."

Even such trifling entries made three hundred and fifty years ago, are interesting and not uninstructive. The exports of Scotch trade in the reign of James IV. seem to have been scarcely anything but the unmanufactured produce of our country—wool, skins, hides, and the salmon of our rivers. A little cloth of an inferior quality was indeed exported, and we may conclude the common cloths used at home were of home manufacture. But the finer cloths were imported from the Netherlands, as were the more expensive linens for the table. All the other luxuries, comforts and almost necessaries of life, from the velvet and satin, and rich cloths of Bruges to the pots and pans of Yetlin for our kitchens, were of foreign production. Salt appears a strange article of import in a country which has had salt pans from the earliest time of record. During those ten years at least, Scotland seems to have imported no corn, nor, indeed, is there proof of this country at any time depending much on foreign supplies of corn, though it has been so generally supposed that the population was excessive, and agriculture was undoubtedly imperfect. The shipping employed in this trade was, at least, partly Scotch. A good

Chap. VIII many ships are mentioned as belonging to merchants of Dundee and Aberdeen, and the names of some, as the Douglas, the Julian, the Eagle, sufficiently speak their country. The packing together, in a foreign port, of such miscellaneous wares, and in so small quantities, shows want of capital or enterprise in the home merchants, and we may conclude that the retail trade of Scotland in such expensive commodities was very limited. On the whole, the impression this ledger of the Conservator leaves, of the trade of Scotland is not favourable. It stands not quite midway between the time of the Alexanders and our own. It is but 250 years removed from the first bright era of national prosperity. It is 350 from the present. The state of trade, seen through its medium, contrasts painfully with the larger transactions, evident opulence, and trading enterprise of Scotland under the last Alexander, and under the vigorous and prosperous reign of Robert Bruce. But happily we can also compare it with later times, when no wind can blow that does not waft the manufacture of Scotland to the farthest ports of the globe, and our own shipping brings to our rough shores the products of every climate—of lands that were to our forefathers a mystery, or an eastern fable.

CHAPTER IX.

To trace the origin of the language which we call Scotch, we must go back to a period when it was known by another name. Long before the Anglo-Saxon government and language had come to an end, the language and literature of the great and more enlightened kingdom of Northumbria were distinguished from the Saxon of Southern and Western England; and when the language of England passed by that strangely rapid transition from the cultivated, grammatical Anglo-Saxon, into the rude unformed English, the northern people still kept a peculiar and very distinct dialect. Down to the end of the fourteenth century, this Doric dialect of English extended all over the ancient province of Northumbria, which included Lothian, and beyond even those bounds, along the whole east coast and lowlands of Scotland. It would be a mistake to suppose it a mere *patois* or vulgar spoken tongue, uncultivated by men of learning. Not to mention the wealthy abbeys which studded the valleys of Yorkshire and our own Teviotdale—each a little school of good letters—the great Episcopal Sees of York and Durham, and the Royal Court of Scotland, which, down to the fourteenth century, enjoyed more peace and prosperity than fell to the lot of the English monarchs, were the centres of some intellectual cultivation. The northern tongue, so formed and cultivated, possessed a literature which we become acquainted with, in a state of rapid growth, and bidding fair to rival or excel that of the South —spoiled and depressed as it was by the courtly use of French—until the genius of Chaucer turned the balance. Within those wide bounds, from Trent to the Moray Firth, there were, doubtless, numerous small varieties of language and accent, distinguishable among themselves; while to the Kentish man or the Londoner, the epithet "Northern" comprehended the whole; and it is certain that, down to the fourteenth century, a uniform language was used and cultivated, and written by men of education, and for purposes of literature, through that wide district.

Starting from a point of time, a little before Chaucer had given shape and life to the southern dialect—a little before Barbour had composed his national epic, popular from the first among all classes of his northern countrymen, the languages of the northern and the southern were distinct indeed, and marked by recognised peculiarities, but the people of each country understood the speech of the other. This soon ceased to be so. The disputed succession at the end of the thirteenth century interrupted the old friendly communication between the sister nations, and Scotch nationality required her to abandon the English standard of taste as well as policy. The dialects of the two courts, still in their infancy, grew up in independent and separate growth, and differing at first slightly, but both in a state of progress in different directions, came in the course of three centuries to be almost different languages, and that of the one people scarcely intelligible to the other. In this change the southern court naturally drew with it all the district of ancient Northumbria which was not subject to Scotland. London was necessarily the model of speech, from the Land's End to the Tweed; while Lothian and Saxon Scotland looked to the Scotch court as the rule of propriety; and that which had been long known as the northern speech began sometimes to be called "Scotch." Thus it continued, the difference and breach still widening, until the Reformation drew the sympathies of one great class of Scotchmen towards England and English writers as well as statesmen.

At length came the time when the Scotch court moved to England, and adopted English manners and language, and the example of conformity, after a little reluctance, spread over our speech and literature, so that now, in 250 years after the union of the crowns, we have nearly arrived at the position from which we started 300 years before it; and any difference that exists between the spoken tongues of Scotland and England, is held a mere provincialism, and does not equal the difference between the speech of London and that of several of the English counties, while in the written language there is no difference.

In our most ancient charters we meet with a few words of the vernacular language of lowland Scotland, just enough to show that it was a genuine Teutonic speech, as soon as there was any written conveyance, or any writing at all among us. Thus in charters of William the Lion, we have lands bounded by the "standand stane," the "stane cross;" a penalty for destroying wood is *tri-gild*. *Ut-were* is the charter shape of foreign service, as *In-were* of home military duty. In the year 1312, an indenture of lease between the Abbot of Scone and the Hays of Leys was extended, like all deeds of that time, in Latin. But there were provisions of great importance to the tenant, a layman and country gentleman, and not strong in Latin; and for his benefit, a clerkly friend has gone over the deed, and interlined over each phrase its equivalent in the vernacular. There cannot be a more pure Saxon speech, and it is without the redundancy of consonants and many of the peculiarities which in later times gave an air of barbarism to the language of Scotland in Southern ears.[1]

The first actual literary compositions in Scotch must have been in all probability those lays or ballads which are nearly at the beginning of literature in all countries, and have influenced the literature and the people of Scotland more than any other. Old Barbour thinks it needless to give the particulars of a Border exploit, for any one may hear young women at play " sing it among them ilka day." But of the current traditional poetry of that time—of the songs of battle and adventure and infant patriotism, or of the shepherd's lays of love—we cannot pretend to have preserved anything; or if anything, only a shadow or faint outline; now a name, now the burden of an ancient ditty; or in the rare cases where the theme and spirit are preserved, the language passing through the mouths of many generations, has kept no impress of its first shape.

You will observe I do not enter upon the much vexed question of the Ossianic poetry. Not that I doubt that there existed lately in the Highlands some fragments of a very ancient Celtic, bardic poetry, preserved with the necessary imperfection of oral tradition. On the contrary, I think the evidence is complete, both of its antiquity, and that its subjects and heroes were known to the fathers of

[1] See Appendix.

our Scotch literature. But there I think we stop. I cannot find that the Ossianic strain has affected in any degree the tone of our poetry. Archdeacon Barbour reproves John of Lorn for comparing the Bruce to *Gowmacmorn*—the person whom we know in Macpherson as Gaul son of Morni; and says it had been more mannerly to equal him with Gaudifer Delatyse, or some other knight of romantic chivalry. In the curious interlude of the *Droichis*, now attributed to Dunbar, and evidently of his age, the dwarf claims for his ancestry Gogmagog and other heathens, and a native giant—

"hecht Fyn M'Kowle,
That dang the devil and gart him yowle;
The skyis rainit when he wald scowle,
And troblit all the air."

Gawayne Douglas speaks of

"Gret Gow MacMorne and Fin MacCowl, and how
They should be gods in Ireland as they say."

It is easy to recognise under these names our now familiar Gaul son of Morni, and Fingal. Sir David Lindsay makes his hero, Squire Meldrum, name the former personage as a fabulous giant, a sort of rawhead and bloody-bones to frighten children with.

"Thocht thow be greit as Gow Macmorne,
Traist weill I sall you meit the morne."

and his *Pardoner* among the absurd trumpery of the relics—

> "The calum of Saint Brydis cow,
> The gruntil of Saint Antoinis sow,
> Whilk bore his holy bell,"

brings in the Celtic ogre thus—

> "Heir is ane relic lang and braid,
> Of Fyn-mac-Coul the richt chaft blade
> With teith and al togidder."

In all these instances, there is nothing that shows much respect or any tendency to imitate. And, indeed, nothing can be more free than our early Scotch literature, from the inflated, the passionless, the unnatural style and thoughts of the Ossianic poetry, always judging it through the medium of translation.

Closely connected, however, with the popular oral poetry (in some instances, with us, its foundation or prototype) was a class of early metrical romances which it was the custom to commit to writing, and fortunately a few of these, of Northern composition, have been preserved, and furnish us with the oldest written vernacular language of Scotland. Unluckily, the poetry is of that tedious alliterative kind which wearies the ear of the reader, as it must have exhausted the invention, and cramped the thought of the writer. One short specimen I will give from the romance of "Morte Arthur," as found in a MS. of the latter half of the fourteenth century, giving the character of the courteous knight, Syr Gawain,

Chap. IX. as pronounced over his body by his foe, Sir Mordred.

> "Than Syr Modrede with mouthe melis fulle faire :—
> He was makles one molde, mane, be my trowhe;
> This was Syr Gawayne the gude, the gladdeste of othire,
> And the graciouseste gome that undire God lyffede;
> Mane hardyeste of hande, happyeste in armes,
> And the hendeste in hawle under hevene-riche;
> The lordelieste of ledynge, qwhylles he lyffe myghte,
> Fore he was lyone allossede in londes inewe.
> Had thou knawene hym, syr kynge, in kythe thare he lengede,
> His konynge, his knyghthode, his kyndly werkes,
> His doyng, his doughtynesse, his dedis of armes
> Thow wolde hafe dole for his dede the dayes of thy lyfe."

I will adduce one other extract of that period. It is from the romance of "Syr Gawain and the Green Knight," and describes their hunting together.

> "Full erly bifore the day the folk vp rysen,
> Gestes that go wolde, hor gromes thay calden,
> And thay busken vp bilyve, blonkkez to sadel,
> Tyffen her takles, trussen her males,
> Richen hem the rychest, to ryde alle arayde,
> Lepen vp lytly, lachen her brydeles,
> Vche wyze on his way, ther hym wel lyked.
> The leue lorde of the londe watz not the last,
> Arayit for the rydyng, with renkkez full mony;
> Ete a sop' hastyly, when he hade herde masse,
> With bugle to bent felde he buskes by-lyue;
> By that that any day lyt lemed vpon erthe,
> He with his hatheles on hyze horses weren.
> Thenne thise cacheres that couthe, coupled hor houndes,
> Vnclosed the kenel dore, and calde hem ther-oute,

Blwe bygly in bugles thro bare mote;
Braches bayed therfore, and breme noyse maked,
And thay chastysed and charred, on chasyng that went;
A hundreth of hunteres, as I haf herde telle,

To trystors vewters yod,
Couples huntes of-kest
Ther ros for blastes gode,
Gret rurd in that forest
} of the best."

I think, from the language alone, the evidence is complete, that these are more ancient than Barbour; but in such a comparison, of course, we must allow for the period that elapsed between the composition of the work, and the transcribing of the copy preserved.[1]

John Barbour, Archdeacon of Aberdeen, tells us, himself, that he was in progress of writing his great poem of the Bruce, in the year 1375, and he died in 1395. But the only manuscripts extant are a full century later in date. The Scotch Odyssey was popular from its first appearance, and must have gone through many transcribings in that century of fluctuating language, so that it loses one quality of interest; and serves but imperfectly to mark the state of our language when the Archdeacon, with the fire of a patriot and a soldier, was singing the prowess of Bruce. But though the spelling, and even, occasionally, the words, may have undergone

---

[1] The extracts are from Sir F. Madden's admirable collection of ancient romances relating to Syr Gawayne.

much change, we cannot suppose much alteration in the structure and frame of the language, which would imply the serious labour of an entire re-casting of the metre and versification.

I fear "The Bruce" is less read among us now, than when the homely edition on the coarsest paper was among the three or four volumes over the cottage chimney. I assure you he is not deserving of the neglect into which he has fallen. But I must deny myself the pleasure of making you better acquainted with him, and keep more strictly to my object in directing you to a few specimens of Scotch, actually written during his time. Here is a formal public writ, still preserved in the original, among the Melrose charters, and dated in 1389:—

"Robert Erle of ffyf & of Menteth Wardane & Chambirlayn of Scotland to the Custumers of the Grete Custume of the Burows of Edinburgh hadyntone & Dunbarr greting: ffor qwhy that of gude memore Dauid kyng qwhilom of Scotland that god assoillie with his chartir vndre his grete sele has gyvin to the Religiouss men the Abbot & the Conuent of Meuros & to thair successours for euere mare frely all the Custume of all thair wollys as wele of thair awin growing as of thair tendys of thair kyrkes as it apperis be the forsaid Charter confermyt be our mast soucreigne & doubtit Lorde & fadre our lorde the kyng of Scotland Robert that now ys wyth his grete Sele: To yow ioyntly & seucrailly be the tenour of this lettre fermely We bid & commandes that the forsaid wollys at your Portis thir lettres sene the qwilk lettres yhe delyuere to tham again yhe suffre to be shippit & frely to pass withoutyn ony askyng or takyng of Custume or ony obstacle or lettyng in ony point eftir as the tenour of the forsaides chartir & confirmacion plenerly askis & purportis: In wytness here of to this lettre We haue put our sele at Edynburgh the xxvj day of Maij the yhere of god mill ccc iiij^{xx} and nyne."

The language here is unfortunately a very precise translation of a Latin style, and it follows the structure of the original language too much to be a perfect specimen of the common language of the period. You will find another, nearly contemporary writing, in the record of Parliament :—

"In the counsail general of Striuelyn, seyn and consideryt the grete and horrible destructions heyrschippis brynnyngis and slachteris that ar sa commounly done throch al the kynrike, It is statutit and ordanyt with assent of the thre communatez thare beand that ilke schiref of the kynrike sal publy ger crye that na man rydand or gangande in the countre lede ma persons with hym. bot thai that he wil mak ful payment for. Ande that na man use sik destructions slachtir reif na brynning in tyme to-cum under payne of tynsale of life and gudis."

1397.

CHAP. IX.   Three years later, in the last year of that century, the use of our native language had become common in correspondence. The Earl of Dunbar, writing to the king of England, excuses himself for preferring it to either Latin or French—the language of business and the language of the English court:—

8th Feb. /400.

"Excellent, mychty, and noble prince, like yhour realte to wit that I am gretly wrangit be the Duc of Rothesay; the quhilk spousit my douchter, and now agayn his oblisyng to me, made be hys lettre and hys seal, and agaynes the law of halikire, spouses ane other wife, as it ys said. Of the quhilk wrang and defowle to me and my douchter in swilk maner done, I as ane of yhour poer kyn, gif it like yhow, requer yhow of help and suppowall, fore swilk honest service as I may do, after my power, to yhour noble Lordship and to yhour lande.

*　　　*　　　*　　　*　　　*

And excellent prince, syn that I clayme to be of kyn tyll yhow, and it peraventour nocht knawen on your parte, I schew it to your Lordship be this my lettre, that gif Dame Alice the Bewmont was yhour graunde dame, Dame Marjory Comyne, hyrr full sister, was my graunde dame on the tother syde; sa that I am bot of the feirde degre of kyn tyll yhow; the quhilk in alde tyme was callit neir. And syn I am in swilk degre tyll yhow, I requer yhow as be way of tendirness thareof, and fore my service in maner as I hafe before wrytyn, that yhe will vouchesauf tyll help me, and suppowell me tyll get amends of the wrangs and the defowle that ys done me; send and till me, gif yhow like, yhour answer of this with all gudely haste. And, noble prince, mervaile yhe nocht that I write my lettres in English, for that ys mare clere to myne understandyng than Latyne or Fraunch. Excellent, mychty, and noble Prince, the Haly Trinity hafe you evirmar in kepyng. Written at my Castell of Dunbarr, the 18th day of Feverer [1400].

"Le Count de la Marche d'Escoce

"*Au tres excellent, et tres puissant, et tres noble prince, le Roy d'Engleterre.*"[1]

Andrew Wyntoun, the Prior of Lochleven, wrote his rhyming chronicle about 1420, and a MS. of it, almost contemporary, is preserved in the Royal Library, from which M'Pherson's careful edition was given. It is of great value as a chronicle compiled from records at St. Andrews, many of which have long ago perished. But as a poem, the Prior's work has very small pretensions. I will quote one passage, which preserves to us a little fragment of one of those ancient popular songs which I have just mentioned. The ballad had been made on the death of the beloved king Alexander

[1] Pinkerton's History, vol. i., Appendix.

III., who was killed by a fall from his horse, when riding in the dark, over the crag of Kinghorn. The language must have suffered a great change between that time and the period when Wyntoun wrote, and his chronicle was transcribed.

> "Scotland menyd hym than ful sare,
> For wnder hym all hys legis ware
> In honoure quyet and in pes;
> Forthi cald pessybil kyng he wes.
> He honoryd God and haly kyrk;
> And medful dedes he oysyd to wyrk.
> Til all prestis he dyd reverens,
> And sawfyd thare statis wyth diligens.
> He was stedfast in Christyn fay;
> Relygyows men he honoryde ay;
> He luwyd men that war wertuows;
> He lathyd and chastyd al vytyous.
> Be justis he gave and eqwyte
> Til ilke man that his suld be,
> That he mycht noucht til wertu drawe,
> He held ay wndyr dowt and awe.
>
> *   *   *
>
> Be that vertu all hys land
> Of corn he gert he abowndand.
> A bolle of atis pennys foure,
> Of Scottis mone past nocht oure;
> A boll of bere for awcht or ten,
> In comowne prys sawld was then;
> For sextene a boll of qwhete;
> Or fore twenty the derth was grete.
> This falyhyd fra he deyd suddanly:
> This sang wes made of hym for-thi.

> Quhen Alysandyr oure kyng was dede
>   That Scotland led in luwe and le
> Away wes sons of ale and brede,
>   Of wyne and wax, of gamyn and gle:
> Our gold was changyd into lede,
>   Cryst borne into virgynyte,
> Succour Scotland and remede,
>   That stad is in perplexite!

We have thus seen our vernacular language, call it by what name you please, gradually assuming definite shape and system. Barbour's great poem is almost at the beginning of its literary use. From his time down to the union of the Crowns, while Scotland stood aloof from England in policy, feeling, and literature, she produced a national literature, which, judged even by our present canons, was on a footing with that of the Southern people. As at the beginning of the period, Chaucer, so towards its conclusion, Shakspeare, stand separate in genius and out of all competition. But, after these immortal names, it may be allowed to question whether any poets of England of those two centuries and a half can be placed on a level with Barbour, Gawin Douglas, Dunbar, and Lindsay. As has happened in other countries, it was very long after our countrymen had used their native language for poetry, that they first ventured to adopt it in prose writing. John Bellenden's translation of Boece, written in 1533, printed in 1536, may be said to be the first

A.D. 1375.
A.D. 1653.

Chap. IX. classical Scotch prose; and even after it, Buchanan wrote popular history and tragedies, as well as the psalms, in Latin.

It would be painful, and I trust, unreasonable, to suppose that such a literature was addressed to a people unworthy of it. But we are not altogether left to conjecture about the education of the people and the diffusion of learning among our forefathers. I confess the evidence (in early times) is not very complete; but I am one of those who believe that the ignorance of the people, even in the middle ages, has been a good deal exaggerated.

Taking our view from the present position of society, the chief obstacle to any general diffusion of learning would seem to be the want of books. And I do not pretend that any equivalent for the printing press existed. Books were rare and dear—luxuries to be had only by the rich, or through the union of bodies of men in colleges and monasteries. But you must not believe that modes of conveying instruction were ever altogether wanting. Reflect that in Rome, in its Augustan age, when Horace hoped " monstrari digitis prætereuntium, Romanæ fidicen lyræ"—in Athens, when Aristophanes wrote to the mob, and was understood—when Demosthenes, in language and reasoning too severe for popular assemblies now, had the ear of that intellectual people—" wielded at will that fierce democratie"—in those days books were as rare, as costly, as difficult of manufacture, as with us before printing.

As the school of the ancient philosopher served to spread his learning and doctrines over the civilized world of old, so our universities in their first institution were instrumental in spreading the science and knowledge of their age among thousands who could never have obtained means of purchasing the books necessary for private study. It is said that thirty thousand students were attracted to Oxford to hear the lectures of Duns Scotus at the beginning of the fourteenth century, and although much of their time was doubtless bestowed on subjects now lightly esteemed—not unlike those which occupied the devils of Milton, who "found no end in wandering mazes lost"—let us not fall into the vulgar error of undervaluing all but our own manner of teaching. The subtleties of that philosophy no doubt whetted the mind for the work of life, and there was little danger of its becoming too fascinating or popular.

The great means of impressing the popular mind, since the introduction of Christianity, has been through the Church; and we have to regret that we know so little what were the lessons conveyed from the altar and the pulpit in early times. We are not, however, altogether without facts.

CHAP. IX. Here is a little volume of homilies—of sermons actually preached in our ancient mother tongue—in pure vigorous Anglo-Saxon—by one who styled himself monk and mass-priest, and who died in the year 1052. A few sentences may help to show you how our forefathers were instructed 400 years before printing.

"He said again, 'Let there be heaven,' and instantly heaven was made, as he with his wisdom and his will had appointed it.

"He said again, and bade the earth bring forth all living cattle, and he then created of earth all the race of cattle, and the brute race—all those which go on four feet; in like manner of water he created fishes and birds, and gave the power of swimming to the fishes, and flight to the birds; but he gave no soul to any beast nor to any fish, but their blood is their life, and as soon as they are dead they are totally ended. When he had made the man Adam, he did not say, 'Let man be made,' but he said, 'Let us make man in our likeness,' and he then made man with his hands, and blew into him a soul; therefore is man better if he grow up in good than all the beasts are, because they will all come to naught, and man is in one part eternal, that is in the soul—that will never end. The body is mortal through Adam's sin, but nevertheless God will raise again the body to eternity on doomsday.

Now, the heretics say that that the devil created some creatures, but they lie; he can create no creatures, for he is not a creator, but is a loathsome fiend, and with leasing he will deceive and fordo the unwary; but he may not compel any man to any crime unless the man voluntarily incline to his teaching.

"Whatsoever among things created seems pernicious and injurious to men is all for our sins and evil deserts."[1]

I hold it is from such rare specimens that we are to judge of the general instruction of the people, and even of the learning, the judgment, and qualifications of their teachers. The author of those discourses refers to his authorities—St. Augustin, St. Jerome, Beda, St Gregory, and other doctors of the Church, but speaks of the books in the vulgar tongue as confined to those "which King Alfred wisely turned from Latin into English, which are to be had."

Almost contemporary with that Anglo-Saxon preacher, we have notice of a little store of books preserved in the Culdee monastery in the isle of St. Serf, in Lochlevin. They were evidently thought of much importance, for the Bishop of St. Andrews, in granting to his new priory the little island Abbey of Lochlevin and its possessions, enumerates, along

[1] Aelfric's Homilies. See Appendix.

with the lands, mills, rents of cheese and barley, tithes, and valuable properties—the church vestments of the poor Culdees, and their library of sixteen books, each of which he distinguishes separately.[1]

1432.   A long time afterwards, but still anterior to the use of printing, we have a catalogue of the books preserved and used in the Cathedral Church of Glasgow, where the heavy tomes of theology and the philosophy of the schools are relieved by a sprinkling of classics, Sallust and Ovid.

We have abundant proofs of the existence of burgh schools and convent schools, at a period almost as early as our records reach. I mentioned before that there were considerable burgh schools at Perth, at Stirling and at Roxburgh, in the reign of Malcolm IV., and a convent school at Roxburgh was in high fashion at the same period. Reginald of Durham, a monk of the twelfth century, in connection with a miracle of St. Cuthbert, describes a village school at Norham on Tweed, where some of the boys attended for love of learning, and others from fear of the rod in a rough master's hand. He says it was kept in the church, according to a practice, *in his time*, common enough. Nobody can read that story without being satisfied that it was a parish school for the parish boys, one of whom, a tricky fellow, thought to get

[1] See Appendix.

rid of the restraint by stealing the church key and throwing it into a deep pool of Tweed. The schools of Roxburgh, of Perth, of Abernethy, of Glasgow, and doubtless of our other towns, were probably somewhat of a higher kind. In 1418 we find the induction of a schoolmaster of Aberdeen—*Magister scholarum burgi de Abirdene*—on the presentation of the Provost and community, when the chancellor of the diocese, the inducting officer, testifies him to be of good life, of honest conversation, of great literature and science (*magnæ literaturæ et scientiæ*), and a graduate in arts.

It was sometime afterwards, but still long before the reformation, that a master of the grammar school of Aberdeen " inquirit be the Provost whom of, he had the said school—grantit in judgment, that he had the same of the said good toun—offerand him reddy to do thame and thair bairnis service and plesour at his power, and renounceit his compulsator of the curt of Rome in all poyntis, except that it suld be lesum to him to persew the techaris of grammer within the burgh." The " teachers of grammer," were interlopers—poachers in his manor.

Even the Act of Parliament, requiring "all barons and freeholders of substance to put their eldest sons to the schools fra thai be eight or nine years of age, and to remaine at the grammar sculis quhil thai be competentlie foundit and have perfit

CHAP. IX. Latyne"—is sufficient to prove that there was no lack of such schools of grammar, English and Latin, in Scotland, long before the Reformation excited to a more extensive course of learning. What they taught in those schools in more early times, when books were so rare that reading was scarcely an object of desire for any but the man of fortune or the churchman, we cannot perhaps learn with certainty. But let us not forget in our self-complacency that books are but one of the roads to knowledge; and that the higher training of the disposition and the heart, moral and religious instruction, and the discipline even of the understanding and memory, may be successfully prosecuted without them.

Whatever may have been the course of study and training in those remote times, there can be no doubt that the *grammar* schools of Scotland, in the fifteenth century, and even at the beginning of it, taught the elements of letters and of grammar as we now learn them, only perhaps with more earnestness, as having in hand a high and important duty. We find merchants writing and keeping accounts, and corresponding with foreigners in their own language, who must have received their education early in that century. In the year 1520, John Vaus, the rector of the grammar school of Aberdeen, is commended by Hector Boece for his knowledge of Latin, and his success in the education of youth;

and he has left us an elementary work on Latin grammar. A little later, Andrew Simson taught Latin with success, at the grammar school at Perth —the same foundation, doubtless, of which the Dunfermline monks were the patrons three centuries earlier—where he had sometimes 300 boys under his charge; and although it is boasted that these included sons of the principal nobility and gentry, it is more for our present purpose to observe they must have consisted of a large proportion of the burgher and peasant class, and a great number who cannot have been designed for the Church. A sketch of school life of that time, by James Melville, the nephew of Andrew Melville, appears to me one of the most interesting pictures of old domestic manners, but it is too long to be given here.[1]

The introduction of Greek as a part of the Scotch education—its successful teaching at Montrose by Peter de Marsiliers, a French scholar brought over by John Erskine of Dun—the subsequent teaching of Hebrew—are now very generally known.

Down to the beginning of the fifteenth century, the Scotch youth, whether churchman or laic, ambitious of carrying his education beyond the level of those excellent grammar schools, must look abroad. Towards the end of the fourteenth century, Oxford was in the high tide of popularity, and

[1] See Appendix.

crowds of young Scotchmen obtained passports and hurried thither to complete their course of philosophy —among them, Henry Wardlaw, afterwards Bishop of St. Andrews, and founder of that University. But northern men were never popular at Oxford, and it happened that the Papal schism just then made new cause of quarrel. In 1382, Richard II. of England addressed a writ to the Chancellor and Proctors of the University of Oxford, forbidding them to molest the Scotch students, notwithstanding their "damnable adherence" to Robert the Antipope (Clement VII.) Such inconveniences hastened that which must have come without them; and three Universities were founded within the fifteenth century in Scotland—all from the first, teaching successfully the philosophy and higher education which were then cultivated.

But while such was the education for the church, the higher gentry, and the learned professions— including that profession of *scholar*, once well-known among Scotchmen, who for centuries carried their classical learning and native industry wherever a market opened—I think there is no room for doubt that the mass of the people had also a considerable share of education. If other proof were wanting, I should appeal confidently to the manly, homely tone of our Scotch literature. The mere fact of so many leading writers devoting themselves to translate the works of the great authors of antiquity, shows a wholesome tendency to popularity. When Gawain Douglas, the high-born bishop—the associate and equal of princes—declared of his language,

> .... "I set my bissy pane,
> As that I couth to mak it braid and plane,
> Kepand na Suthron, bot our awn langage,"

He certainly looked for readers, not to a little knot of courtiers, or churchmen, or literary gossips, but that his immortal poem should be received as a public good by the public. Lindsay in plainer terms disclaims writing for a learned class. He chooses to write to the people,—

> "Whairfor to coilyearis, carters and to cuikis,
> To Jok and Tam my ryme salbe direckit;
> With cunning men howbeit it wilbe lackit."

CHAPTER X.

Chap. X. LET us examine a little how our forefathers dwelt and were lodged, the mechanical contrivance shown in their habitations, and the rude but interesting beginnings of constructive and masonic skill, which required great development before they deserve the name of ART. At the same time we shall find it convenient to consider that class of antiquities which are at least akin to habitations, the structures of an early age for defence, for religious and legal meetings; and monolithic monuments, whether for commemorating the dead, ascertaining boundaries of estates, or preserving the memory of some historical event.

In thus approaching the proper ground of the antiquary, I trust I may escape falling into the common error of that respectable class. I will not ask my readers to form a rash determination upon any of those points, regarding which, it requires extensive comparison as well as much previous study to justify any expression, even of confident opinion. There are many remains of antiquity, many *classes* of such in this country, which are much less known, and, as to their purposes, much more mysterious than the Cyclopian remains of Greece or the barrows and (now) subterranean palaces of Nimroud and Nineveh. I feel that I shall disappoint my younger readers when I pass by such interesting relics without pronouncing decidedly upon their dates and, still more, upon their original design and use. I cannot help it. The proper study of antiquities is hardly begun among us; and much of the discredit and ridicule that have fallen upon it and its votaries, arises from the crude and presumptuous judgments passed upon individual cases and objects as they arise, instead of investigating each with reference to the family to which it belongs. To do this well requires much previous learning, a knowledge of the history and antiquities of cognate nations, especially a familiar acquaintance with their historical collections. But above all, it requires a careful and patient examination of similar remains, where they exist in our own country. That, at least, the public has a right to demand before adopting a theory or explanation, which may not be untenable as applied to one instance, and yet may become palpably absurd when tried by its application to others.

We do not know from which side the first stream of colonizers took possession of Scotland. If our Celtic forefathers arrived from the South, it must have re-

Chap. X. quired all their skill to make it a comfortable habitation. In some districts, perhaps, the native forest furnished the early squatters with materials for their huts and wigwams. And of these we must not look for any vestiges. But on our eastern coast, where wood is scarce, and yet the soil and neighbouring sea, its fishing and harbours, were attractive, the new-arrived strangers would seek their shelter from the weather, their protection against beasts of prey, as well as concealment from other hostile settlers, in those caves which are sufficiently abundant everywhere. Many such, unassisted by art, are yet found, not unfitted for human dwellings. Where the rock is dry, and the vault spacious enough, these were habitations ready and commodious. Where the arch of the great architect, Nature, was too low for their purpose, their rude tools of stone or brass enabled them to enlarge it. Caves showing abundant traces of this artificial enlargement are to be seen in many districts. I need hardly put you in mind of those of Hawthornden. On the banks of the little river Ale, which falls into Teviot at Ancrum, are a wonderful number of similar caves, all more or less showing the hand-work of their ancient occupants.

From such habitations which they disputed with their legitimate possessors, the bears and wolves, the natives of this country swarmed off into new hives, not very dissimilar in appearance, nor superior in comfort. These were the under-ground chambers which are still found in several places in Scotland. There are some of these of great size, and well defined, near Airlie in Angus. I am acquainted with some in the heights of Aberdeenshire—on the high moorland which separates the valley of the Don from Strathbogie, not far above the ancient castle of Kildrummie. They are almost invisible from without. Within, they are cased with rough stones, and roofed with the same materials, gradually converging and supported by the pressure of the earth upon their outer extremity, with no approach to the principle of the arch. In the Orkney islands such apartments are found, somewhat more artificial in construction. An officer, now engaged in the survey of the northern coast, has bestowed some of the forced leisure of those stormy seas upon opening up some of the remarkable *souterains* of Orkney. I have seen his drawings and very accurate plans of these, which exhibit a more advanced state of society—if we may use the term for that mole or rabbit sort of existence—than any I have met with elsewhere. One consists of a pretty long gallery, with apartments branching off it. The height of the gallery could admit of a man of Orkney stature standing and walking upright. The apartments on either hand, if human dwellings, were for night use. But observe

Chap. X. —in that region of storm, and placed between a coast constantly strewed with drift-wood, and an exhaustless supply of peat fuel on the moor—there is no vestige of a chimney, nor any means of admitting light. At the end of the green hillock, under which he supposes the ancient Orcadians to have lived, Captain Thomas assured me he found the remains of ashes of wood or peat, that must have been accumulated for many years; and interspersed among them, the remains of bones of animals and of the horns of a deer, which he concluded were used for the food of the inhabitants.

Such were no doubt the abodes of the people, chosen for concealment, and little capable of protecting cattle, or bulky property. Their early, and indeed aboriginal strongholds, again, varied with the situation and material. We have the green mound, steeply escarped, and giving barely room on its summit, for the wooden castle of which the material was supplied by the neighbouring forest—the little island of firm land in midst of a mountain lake, or still more impracticable morass—sometimes a structure of piles in the lake where there was no natural island—the circular redoubt, like a larger pen for cattle, placed high on a hill side to guard against surprise, surrounded with a wall of heaped earth, or of stone, and a dry ditch, such as afforded protection for the cattle and their owners, against the hurried onslaught of a foraging enemy. Some of these forts are more elaborate and remarkable. One stands on the striking height of Cathertun, looking across the valley of Strathmore. Another, nearly similar, I had an opportunity of inspecting carefully very lately. It is called the " Barmekyn," and crowns the summit of a conical hill of perhaps 300 feet high, which rises from the hollow of Echt, in Mar. The interior of the fort is not levelled—it is oval, 120 by 100 yards, surrounded by no less than five walls, three of earth, two of stone, and these defences occupying altogether 20 yards across. The outer wall of stone, though much weather worn, appeared to have been built of stones rudely squared, but without mortar. It stands in places still 8 feet high. The entrances to the east, west, and south, were curious. The narrow path of approach is made to wind in a zigzag through the walls, so as not to have the openings of any two of the walls opposite to each other.

Of the same class, were the vitrified forts which crown the tops of many of our hills, and which have exercised the ingenuity of antiquarians too much, and with too little success, for me to speculate upon their mode of formation. I may observe, however, that the vitrified wall in no cases rises to any considerable height, seldom more than a few inches, and that the vitrification is generally very partial;

Chap. X. from which I infer, only, that it was caused by the use of fires for other purposes, and not lighted for saving mortar and producing a concrete and solid wall.

But however these curious vitrifications were produced, all that class of strengths are such as a people in the infancy of the arts would have recourse to. There is little skill or ingenuity shown in their structure. We have a rude outer fence, and no remains nor appearance of any building or habitations for the people who trusted to it in time of need.

Considerably different from these, and still more perplexing as to their origin and purpose, are the bell-shaped circular buildings, vulgarly called, " Picts' Houses," and which are met with, round our northern and western coasts, and in the islands. They are frequently found, several in the same vicinity, and often three or four within sight of each other. The most perfect I have seen, and I believe the most perfect that exists, is on the little island of Mousa in Shetland. The chambers, if they may be called so, of this tower are in the thickness of the walls. There is no appearance that the centre space was ever roofed over; and what adds to the difficulty of appropriating this singular building to any purpose, there is no chimney nor fire-place anywhere, which seems to shut out the possibility of its being used as a permanent residence in the northern climate and exposed situation in which it, and most of the same class are placed. It seems more likely that they were places of occasional resort, perhaps for storing the property or the plunder of a people spending their lives in coasting piratical expeditions; but this leaves the very artificial and uniform shape of these "Picts' Houses" altogether unaccounted for. Mr. Worsaäe, a Dane, and most intelligent and learned in the antiquities of Scandinavia, assures me there is nothing at all resembling them in the old land of the North-men. One of these towers near Dunrobin was carefully examined lately, and, in particular, the rubbish removed from the chambers and galleries; and in one of these was found a skeleton. The ground of the centre area was removed to a good depth, and the search produced only remains of fire in the middle space, and several of the common small querns or hand-mills.

I must be pardoned for this unsatisfactory way of raising difficulties without furnishing or seeking a theory for their solution. I stated in the beginning that it must be so; for in no other country has so little been done for throwing light on national antiquities as in Scotland. No one has even taken the trouble to visit and compare all the specimens of each class in our own country, still less to compare them with the existing monuments of neighbouring or cognate nations. But each pretender blurts out his own crude and undigested theory, formed from a specimen or two nearest to himself, and which is overturned as soon as a few other instances force themselves on the student's observation.

Much more is this rash and ignorant way of observing and theorising of our antiquaries to be regretted in reference to another and still more interesting class of Scotch monuments—I mean those erect sculptured stones of high antiquity which meet us everywhere in the northern shires.

I wish to distinguish between them and the circles of standing stones commonly, though improperly, called Druids' circles, found over all Scotland, and of which the Stones of Stennes, in Orkney, are the type and grandest specimen. Those circles vary in size and number and height of the stones, and in having or wanting avenues of stones leading to them, and, more rarely, concentric circles. But for the most part they will be found, where the soil has not been disturbed, to have cairns of sepulture around them. Many of them have a stone laid flatways in the circumference of the circle, which is generally considered as an altar; and, I believe invariably, the stones are undressed by the mason's tool, and altogether without inscription or sculpture. There is evidence of history or record to show that some of these circles were used, even within a comparatively recent period, as places of public meeting and of justice; and there is reason to believe they were originally the places of those assemblies common to all the Teutonic peoples, where the tribe met to discuss its common affairs, to devise laws, and to administer law. That they were in some way consecrated, and served for temples of religion also, is indeed most probable, though we have no evidence on the subject. But we cannot easily conceive a primitive society which does not blend religion and its rites with law—the lawgiver and the judge with the priest. In this view, the cairns and marks of sepulchre will appear as appropriate to these places of legal and religious meeting, as a cemetery to a Christian church. In one of those circles on the bank above Inverness was dug up a rod of gold, simply crooked at the top like a rude crozier or an ancient *lituus*. A few miles distant, at Clava, in the rocky valley of the water of Nairn, there are the remains of quite a little city of such circles, of small size, some having in their circumference what were long thought to be mere cairns of loose stones, but are now found to cover rudely-formed chambers, the roofs formed by converging stones without arches. A similar chamber has been discovered in the centre of the great circle in the Lews. It would be a considerable boon for our antiquities if any student of our history were to endeavour to fix the limits of the districts of those stone circles; and important results might be derived from it for the history of our original peoples. I have not myself found them in the West Highlands, the ancient territory of the proper Scots; while the greatest and most remarkable are in Orkney and the Lews.

I wish to distinguish from those circles of unhewn stones, a somewhat later, but more interesting and yet more mysterious class of our national antiquities—the sculptured monuments, standing singly or in small irregular groups, which are found chiefly in the North, but of which the most interesting and also the most numerous specimens occur in Strathmore—at Glammis, at Meigle, at Aberlemno. In chronicles and ancient Church records we find mention of setting up great stones and stone crosses to mark the place of death of some great man (Fordun relates that the place of Alexander III.'s fatal fall was marked by a stone cross), and of others to distinguish the boundaries of estates and jurisdictions. Thus the Steward of Scotland marked the marches between the monks of Paisley and his chace of Ferencze; and Lesmahagu, the church of St. Machutus, had the extent of its girth or sanctuary defined by four crosses which stood around it. We could have no difficulty, then, in accounting for the ancient stone cross, was it not often accompanied by a species of hieroglyphics which set the speculations of the antiquary at nought. You must not suppose that it is the mere ornaments of the artist, however grotesque, that appear inexplicable, or, indeed, that excite our curiosity. There is a class of symbols represented on these stones, of such constant recurrence as to preclude the possibility of their being the work of chance, and yet of forms which suggest no feasible explanation or meaning. For the most part, those symbolic sculptures are conjoined with carved crosses (though generally on the other side of the stone), suggesting the idea that they may have existed as monuments before, and that the symbol of Christianity may have been superinduced over those of pagan times. Others have thought that the stones being boundary stones, the cross on one side denoted the possession of the Church, while the figures on the reverse had reference to the occupations or dignities of the conterminous lay lord. I must say, however, that the person who has devoted most study to this subject has arrived at the conclusion that these sculptured pillars are in all cases sepulchral. The sculpture is not in general in a style of good art; but I have been much struck with the freedom, spirit, and grace of some figures of horses and horsemen on the stones in the church-yard of Meigle. There, too, occurs the interesting representation of a chariot—the only real evidence to

Chap. X. support the ancient historians who make the inhabitants of rocky, boggy, woody Scotland, a race of charioteers. The more ancient and ruder of those monuments have no other sculpture but the symbolical figures I have already alluded to. Such are "the Maiden Stone" in the Garioch, Aberdeenshire, and the older of the stones of Aberlemno in Angus.

The later have ornaments of different kinds; processions—as that really majestic monument at Forres—battles, and hunting scenes; but over and through all these representations, the ever-recurring symbols of unknown meaning.[1]

One of these monuments is interesting on several accounts. It is preserved at the church of St. Vigeans in Angus. Owing to having been buried in the ground till lately, it is particularly fresh and sharp in its sculpture, but I think it is of later workmanship than most of the others bearing the symbols. Here, they are as distinct as if cut only yesterday. The animals appear to me curious; we have good figures of the tusked boar and the bear, both, no doubt, objects of the chase. But the most interesting peculiarity of this stone is that it gives a short inscription in legible letters. When I speak of this as a singular instance of an *inscribed* stone of this class, I should mention the

[1] The Stone of Forres is without the mysterious symbols.

well-known stone at the manse of Ruthwell, decyphered by the lamented Mr. Kemble. It is inscribed in what we are now desired to call Saxon Runes, and it resembles monuments found in Man, and also in Scandinavia—quite a distinct family from our northern Scotch sculptured monuments.

But while I profess that nothing is yet ascertained regarding this class of monuments; that no theory or plausible conjecture has been offered respecting their purpose, the meaning of those constantly recurring symbols, the people who made them, you are not to suppose that intelligent inquiry directed to an object is ever without some results. We have learned to limit and define the district in which these symbolical monuments occur. They are confined to the eastern lowland of Scotland, extending from the garden of Dunrobin to the base of Largo Law. In no other country are they found, nor in any other district of Scotland. In the short time to which any attention has been directed to these singular antiquities, it is something to have ascertained that the Irish antiquary is as ignorant of them as the Scandinavian, and that among the monuments of Wales and Bretagne, however nearly they may be approached in general design, there is nothing apparently the same, or equivalent to the two most remarkable of their mysterious symbols. Secondly, by comparison of the ornaments of those sculptured monuments with works of art, and especially with illuminations of Anglo-Saxon manuscripts, we can nearly limit the period of their production to the eighth and ninth centuries.

There remain in some of the remotest of the Western isles, ruins of buildings of the rudest kind, without chiselled stone, without mortar, but plainly ecclesiastical. No history nor real tradition touches these. We love to associate them with the early followers of Saint Columba, the apostles of those isles, and they may be ranked as the most ancient of our Christian edifices.

Great uncertainty, at one time, prevailed regarding the purpose and the era of the round towers of Ireland. That has lately been much removed by the careful researches of Mr. Petrie. The two similar buildings of Scotland, at *Brechin* and at *Abernethy*, may now be without hesitation placed after the introduction of Christianity; and whatever other purpose they were intended to serve, there can be little doubt that, as has been proved of those in Ireland, they were used as belfreys; probably before bells were hung in buildings, and when the mode of assembling a congregation was by a hand bell rung from the top of the bell tower. No record alludes to the erection of these two venerable Scotch towers. They are now surrounded with buildings, which, though of some antiquity, are modern as compared with them. To judge from the comparison of the masonry alone, with the most ancient of our other ecclesiastical buildings, they cannot be ascribed to a lower age than the tenth, or even the ninth century.

I trust it is not expected that I should attempt anything like a detailed or systematic history of Scotch art. Meagre as our materials are for such a history, they would extend far beyond the space which I can devote to the subject. All that I can hope to do is to direct attention to a few of the proper objects of intelligent interest, connected with the arts, at each period of our history, rather to furnish matter of speculation and inquiry, than in the hope or wish of bringing forward fully considered and definite results.

The buildings of a people are perhaps always the oldest specimens of art among them; and the religious buildings called forth so much of the zeal of early Christians, that all the other arts may be considered as ancillary to architecture. Even painting, which now stands so high among the fine arts, was first used only as one of the means of church embellishment. In all discussions upon early art, then, we must look to architecture, not only as the foundation, but as the great end to which other arts were directed, and it is of the greatest consequence to aim at some precision in the history and dates of

Chap. X. the successive styles of architecture, as they developed themselves in this country.

It would, no doubt, be very desirable in such an attempt to rear the architectural edifice upon historical ground, to produce evidence of the foundation of each church, to warrant the assertion we make of its antiquity, and fix even a precise date. But in Scotland, this is not to be hoped for, and we are obliged to take the rudiments of our chronology of architecture from the richer record stores, and longer and more learned investigation of the subject by the scholars of England. We know, indeed, from the best authority, that Saint Ninian, in the fourth century, built his church of stone, contrary to the custom of that time, whose white walls, shining over the waters of the Solway, obtained its name for Whithern, the cathedral of the bishops of Galloway. But that structure and all vestiges of it have long disappeared.

In like manner, the historical and legendary memorials of Iona furnish no clue to the date of the existing architectural remains, or only give negative assistance. Whatever may have been the edifice that cradled the Faith in that stormy region, wave after wave of the Pagan Norsemen had long obliterated that *gloriosum cœnobium*—all that had been hallowed by the presence of Columba and his disciples. We know historically, or rather by the superior evidence of charters, that none, even calling themselves successors of the old "family of Columba," tenanted his little island in the twelfth century. Early in that century the Cluniac monks were introduced into Scotland, planted first at Paisley by the Stuarts, and before the end of it, had obtained possession of Iona. The remains of ecclesiastical buildings on the island are theirs, and the church is a well-marked specimen of the period of transition between the Norman or Romanesque, and the succeeding style of "first pointed," which we need not hesitate to place in its true date, the beginning of the thirteenth century.

I could be well pleased to travel onward in this manner, endeavouring to reconcile the facts of history with the existing appearances of architectural remains; and with later buildings it gets both easier and more satisfactory; but I must not occupy your time with these researches, when I fear I shall hardly be able to communicate some of the foundations of such study, already elaborated to our hands.

I. The first period of our architecture has been usually named the *Norman*, and perhaps more appropriately the Romanesque. It came into England, as is now admitted, a short time before the Norman conquest. In its early stages it is plain and extremely massy.

Short circular pillars, and arches semicircular or

Chap. X. inclining to the horse-shoe, are the distinguishing marks of this style, which preserves its character singularly during an extraordinary progress of mere ornamental embellishment. The style which, at its commencement, was the most simple, like the cavern hewn from the rock—the first efforts of men unused to wield the chisel—became, before it was superseded, ornate, and absolutely overwhelmed in ornaments, mouldings of wonderful variety in the arches, capitals of the most fantastic design, and the walls striped with rows of niches and pannels, often taking the pretty form of arcades of interlacing arches. Even the pillar shafts were broken, sometimes, into zigzag and spiral lines, which did not produce that lightness which seems to have been missed; and the invention of artists could go no farther in mere surface ornament. Through all, the character is preserved—the massy round pillar, the semicircular arch, the unbuttressed wall—and not to be confounded with any subsequent style, any more than a Grecian portico with the architecture of Delhi or of the Alhambra.

The period of this style extends in English examples from a little before the Conquest till late in the twelfth century. Speaking roughly, we may assign to it in Scotland all the twelfth century.

Of this period in Scotland, we can point with some certainty to the nave of Dunfermline, which we know to have been dedicated in 1150; St. Rule's tower at St. Andrews, a very curious and somewhat anomalous specimen, though historically fixed between 1127 and 1144; the cathedral of St. Magnus of Kirkwall, founded about 1138, but taking long years in building, and displaying the changes of style of that period in its architecture; the chancel and the western gable of the abbey church of Jedburgh. Leuchars in Fife, and Dalmeny on this side of the Firth, are two interesting specimens of rural parish churches, both of rich, late Romanesque work, and both exhibiting the peculiarity of the circular apse, which must have been common of old, but of which I am acquainted with very few Scotch specimens still entire. Still later in this style, we have the choir of the cathedral of St. Andrews, begun in 1162; Kelso; a little part of Coldingham; several fragments of the rural churches of the Merse; the western gable of Arbroath; a beautiful remnant preserved within the park at Tyninghame; a single arch, seen on the southern side of the chancel of Holyrood; the little chapel of St. Margaret in our castle; a few arches of Kinloss in Moray, which, if placed in this period, are, I think, the only specimen of Romanesque work in the North.

If you would impress on your minds the character of that most peculiar style, compare these with the specimens fixed and chronologized in

England. Or, whoever is happy enough to have leisure for such studies, and opportunity to follow them in England, will find fine specimens of the earliest and severest Norman in the Tower of London, especially in the chapel in the top of the white tower, the white washing of which formed an item in the expenditure of Henry II., in the crypt of Winchester Cathedral, built before 1100; or, nearer and more cognate, in the gigantic nave of Durham, founded by our own kings, and the kingly lords of Northumbria and Lothian, which is so evidently the pattern and type, on a grander scale, of our Dunfermline. Of the later Norman, the English examples are innumerable. There are none more striking than the beautiful parish church of Iffley, looking up the vale of the Isis to the towers of Oxford; or the Galilee of the cathedral of Durham.

II. The next century gave a new order of architecture; and it is very important for us in Scotland to understand it, since that was the great age of church building in this country. Here again the public history of the country gives and receives light from the study of art. You have seen that the real golden age of Scotland—the time of peace with England—of plenty in the land—of foreign trade flourishing—of internal police—of law and justice—was the period of a full century following the treaty between William the Lion and Richard

Cœur de Lion, comprehending the reign of William and the long reigns of the second and third Alexanders. Now, that century is the time when we can ascertain most of our fine and great churches to have been built, and their style is what Rickman calls the "Early English," and later artists the "First Pointed."

To this period we owe undoubtedly a large part of the magnificent cathedral of Elgin, though so roughly handled by the Wolf of Badenoch in the end of the fourteenth century, that the bishops called their restoration a rebuilding. There are, worthy of note, also, the cathedrals of Brechin, Dunblane (of beautiful work, and still very entire), Whithern, Dornoch; the abbey churches of Arbroath (sadly decayed, and still more spoilt by ignorant restoration), Paisley, Coldingham, Kilwinning, Inchcolm, Restennot, Dundrennan, Ferne, Cambuskenneth, Inchmahome, Sweetheart, Pluscardine; the later parts of Dunfermline and Jedburgh, Holyrood, Dryburgh, and, more important, the great cathedrals of St. Andrews and Glasgow.

This was the era of those enthusiastic fraternities or associations for church building which assisted in erecting most of the beautiful churches of Europe, and which undoubtedly bestowed that singular uniformity which characterizes the ecclesiastical buildings of the same era, during the twelfth and following centuries. We find notice of a society of this kind having for its chief object the restoration of the cathedral of Glasgow, after it had been burnt down in the reign of William the Lion. It was instituted by Bishop Jocelin about the year 1190, and had a special charter of protection from King William the Lion.

Among the accounts of the building of churches of that period, it seems remarkable that we never hear of the architect or the artist who furnished the plan; and yet the symmetry and fine proportions of those old churches bespeak no common design nor vulgar workmen. It is common among us to say those beautiful churches must have been built, or at least designed by foreign artists. But the same defect of information is found in other countries, and this has driven foreign antiquaries to the conclusion that churchmen studied architecture (for which they have indeed some other foundation), and were for the most part the architects of their own buildings, aided and no doubt counselled, in matters of taste, by the members of the church-building fraternities.

The "First Pointed" period is recognized by the pointed arch—the tall and more slender pillar, composed of clustered shafts round a circular pier, often divided by one or more bands, and with capitals plain or wrought in infinite variety—the long, narrow, lancet-headed window, without much feathering, and none at all till towards the end of the period, but often in pairs, or three together—bold buttresses, at first unbroken in height, but towards the end of the period divided into stages—The roof high in the pitch—when of stone, groined, and with the crossings richly ornamented with bosses—wooden roofs frequent, and tall steeples coming into fashion. A frequent and distinguishing ornament of this style is the toothed ornament.

Speaking roughly again, the style of Early English, or First Pointed, lasted during the thirteenth century.

III. The style which succeeded is that which Rickman christened "the Decorated," while later writers have named it, more appropriately, "the Second or Middle Pointed." It was known in England from the beginning of the reign of Edward I., but was chiefly prevalent in the reigns of his successors, Edward II. and III.; and this, the perfection of English Gothic, may be said to have terminated with the fourteenth century. That was not an age of building of churches in Scotland. Occupied with continual wars with a foreign enemy, or domestic feuds and troubles arising from a weak government, people saw with indifference the magnificent churches of the previous age fall rapidly to ruin; while the poor monks of the once venerated

A.D. 1272.

A.D. 1400.

convents were turned out to beg the bread which they had long shared liberally with the poor. A few instances, we have, however, serving to mark the perfect parallelism, during the first part of that time, of the art in England and Scotland.

You recognize the Middle Pointed style by its window-tracery, at first in regular geometrical figures, circles, quatrefoils, etc.; latterly, flowing in elegant waving lines; weather-mouldings, or drip stones, over door and window; often running into triangular canopies richly crocketed; niches everywhere, especially in the buttresses. The mouldings are quite peculiar. Frequent ornaments are a four-leaved flower, and a ball-cup, taking the place of the toothed ornament peculiar to the previous style.

I need hardly mention Melrose as the splendid type of this most perfect style. Its building extended over the latter half of the fourteenth century, and the first half of the fifteenth.

Of this style, too, we have the northern cathedrals of Fortrose and Aberdeen; the latter begun in 1366, and not finished for about a hundred years.

But here I must notice two peculiarities of Scotch architecture:—

1. Some of the features of the Norman style—in particular, the semicircular arch and the round pillar, though not generally in conjunction, continue with us much lower than in England, and break

out occasionally through well-defined specimens of all the later styles.

2. We cannot assign so definite a termination to the "Middle Pointed" style as the English do. With us, it did not so plainly give way before the prevalence of the "Perpendicular," as the next English style is called, but rather underwent a modification in the latter part of the fourteenth century, from our greater communication with France, which introduced a sort of imitation of what has been called the "Flamboyant" style, the architecture of France contemporary with the "Perpendicular" of England. The English architects do not admit this as a separate style, but pronounce it a degenerate "Decorated;" and it has most of the features of "Decorated," running, however, more into extremely waving lines, thin and weak mullions, and groining ribs, and generally inelegant combinations of mouldings. Part of the importation from France was the polygonal apse, not known before in Scotland, and rare in England; while in France and Germany they are of common occurrence.

A fine specimen of the Scotch Middle Pointed period is the Douglases foundation of Lincloudcn, built before 1400. The cathedral church of Dunkeld, we know from Abbot Milne, its historian, was not begun till 1400, though to a hasty examiner this interesting ruin has an earlier appearance.

Chap. X. Another of much interest, and to which we look back with regret, was our own Trinity Church or College Kirk, the foundation of the piety of Queen Mary of Gueldres, which has lately been swept away to give room for a railway coal-store.

Most of our collegiate churches of Scotland came within this period of "Decorated," or Flamboyant—belonging to the fifteenth and beginning of the sixteenth centuries. I need not point out to you Dalkeith and Linlithgow; each within half an hour's distance. Other specimens are Corstorphine, and St. Duthacs of Tain. You will find almost all this class running into the three-sided apse, with double doorways having flattened heads enclosed within a Pointed arch. Battlements are comparatively rare, and the corby-stepped gable begins to prevail towards the end of the period, with gabled or saddle-backed towers.

C. 1430.
C. 1480.

Hitherto I have said nothing of what may be called the surface ornament of our old churches. I hope it will not alarm any one if I venture merely to allude to the science of heraldry—a study which of old engaged the attention of all that were gentle-born—which is now left to the tender mercies of the lapidary and the coach-painter. *Requiescat!* I shall not try to unfold the mysteries of the noble art of blazon. I might indeed suggest the great importance of some knowledge of heraldry to the student of historical antiquities. For the pursuit of family history — of topographical and territorial learning — of ecclesiology — of architecture, it is altogether indispensable; and its total and contemptuous neglect in this country is *one* of the causes why a Scotchman can rarely speak or write on any of these subjects without being exposed to the charge of using a language he does not understand.

But my present object is very limited; nothing more than to bid you observe how heraldic blazoning is mixed up with almost all the fine arts of the middle ages. In architecture it soon took a prominent place among what may be called surface ornament — not affecting the shape and frame, the type and style of building, but furnishing in infinite variety subjects of embellishment, mixed with much of personal interest. If the shield of rich blazoning, or the cognizance of some old name, covered with dust and dirt, still creates an interest on the wall of a ruined church, or as part of the tracery of a monumental tomb, we may imagine what effect was produced by the brilliant colours of the old herald's "tinctures," adorning not only the walls, but repeated in the tiles of the pavement, and glowing in the gorgeous colouring of the windows; when each bearing and difference — the square banner of the knight and the squire's pennon — told a universally understood history of the founders and benefactors of the church, and perhaps called up some memory of battle or siege, and of honour won in the field or tourney-yard.

Of stained glass we have scarcely a fragment remaining in Scotland. All that have come under my own observation are a few handfuls of broken pieces, dug out from the rubbish around our old churches—none of it serving to hint the subject of the painting, but showing often the broad, bold handling, the rich and full colour, the masses of shadow and light—in short, the knowledge of effect, which seemed, until lately, altogether to have deserted the modern worker in this beautiful art.

While the walls and roofs of churches were adorned with heraldic escutcheons and devices, and the windows glowed with the brilliant colours of the herald, and the higher artist thought it no unworthy object to devote himself to the decoration of God's house, all the details of the building became matter of minute and scrupulous attention, which, in later ages, may have sometimes run into superstitious observance. Not only the disposition of the altar and its furniture, the shapes of windows, the position of fonts and screens, the whole form and structure of the sacred edifice, were all studied, as having deep and important symbolical meaning —φωνᾶντα συνετοισι—speaking a language known to the initiated.

The effect of this was evidently to inspire a sentiment, to raise the aim, and improve the taste, not only of the chief artist, the architect himself, but of all those designing or working in the subordinate departments. Under such an influence, even the carpenter and smith become something more than men of rule and hammer. Accordingly old locks, keys, and hinges, old chandeliers and iron railings, though often of workmanship which a Sheffield artisan would contemn, are frequently of admirable and effective designs. Whoever has seen the iron rail that tops the lordly pile of Glammis Castle, will easily understand what I mean.

So it was with the worker in wood. You may sometimes meet with an old church chest, more frequently with doors, with pannels, and with chairs or stools that had been made and used for church purposes; and I cannot think it is the charm of antiquity alone that places these, as works of design, so immeasurably above the conveniences of our modern workshop. Of timber roofs I need not speak. They are often of admirable design, and requiring great scientific skill in their construction. Those of our ancient churches—where, however, timber roofs were not very common—were no doubt planned and directed by the architect, and not left to the invention of the carpenter; while the later

x

Chap. X. roofs of this sort—those of Darnaway great hall and our Edinburgh Parliament-house—are of a period subsequent to our present inquiry, and one of them at least—probably both—the work of foreign artists. In passing, I may allude to the beautiful stucco ceilings of the seventeenth century, though that also is below our period. The castle of Craigievar, in Aberdeenshire—Glammis, in Strathmore—some of the apartments in Holyrood, and many of our old country houses in Angus, Fife, and the Lothians—especially in and around Edinburgh—furnish excellent specimens of that art, requiring more artistic taste than our stucco work of the present day; for you will observe the old work was done by the hand and tool, without the common use of moulds.

But that which chiefly exercised the skill of the worker in wood, and still preserves memorials of exquisite taste and of most dexterous handiwork, is the carving—whether of screens, of stalls, or of pannels—that adorned our ancient churches. Some fine old stall work is still preserved—though most of it not *in situ*—in Dunblane Cathedral; but it is in King's College, Aberdeen, that we have perhaps the most beautiful wood-work that now remains in Scotland. There we find both canopied stalls and a fine open screen of very delicate cutting, and pannels covered with exquisite tracery of varied patterns. The date of this work is the very beginning of the sixteenth century.

Inferior, perhaps, as a work of art, but not of less effect as an architectural aid and ornament, was that manufacture of paving-tiles with which we know that many—I may say, all—of our churches were more or less paved. Of their various kinds it is unnecessary to speak. In many places of Scotland they have been found plain or glazed, but I believe only in one have they been discovered enriched with patterns or designs. These are part of what covered the chapel floor of the Abbey of North Berwick. They are of fine bold designs—not heraldic—and with the pattern raised in such relief that, if really used for the floor, they must have been very inconvenient to walk over.

Another shape or offspring of the architectural taste of the early ages, are the ancient seals, which form an important section of mediæval antiquities. In those of laymen—king, earl, baron, and knight—we can trace the first introduction of heraldic device, and, onwards, all the refinements of heraldry; while the Church seal-cutters have used for their ornaments tracery adopted from the shrine and window work of churches; and in many specimens you find that heraldry and that Gothic tracery combined with the same happy effect which is so often found in the heraldic adornments of our old churches.

Chap. X. As mere works of art, these old seals show great skill in figure and combination, and evince undoubtedly a clear perception of the beautiful. But when you consider that in them we read the first adoption of the cognizance of each noble name—the descent and alliances of most of our old families—while the arms, though commonly surrounded simply with the name and style of the individual, are sometimes in combination with the proud battle-cry of the race, or with a motto of peace and affection, approaching to the sentiment on a modern lady's seal-ring, you will see that a knowledge of them is not only calculated to give precision to history, but to throw light upon the modes of life and thought of our ancestors. In both respects they seem to me more important than the useful study of medals.

Of the artists of our earlier coins we know nothing, except a few of their names; as, for instance, in the reign of William the Lion—Adam and William the moneyers of Berwick, Adam and Hugh of Edinburgh, Folpolt or Folpold of Perth, Raul of Roxburgh, etc.

We have no coins, probably, of earlier date than those of David I., which are rude indeed, but not much inferior to those of the contemporary monarchs of England. In the reign of William the Lion, in like manner, the coinage, now abundant and of many different mints, keeps parallel, and similar to that of England. From such vile representations of humanity, we pass downwards, regularly and steadily improving, both in design and execution—marking, I think, that we could not be much indebted to foreign artists. At some periods, however, we do find foreigners employed, and we can still point to some of our early gold of good workmanship, minted by Bonaccio of Florence, in the reign of Robert III. But such foreign superintendence must have ceased long before the best period of our coinage; and I cannot see any reason to doubt that it is to native skill and taste, we owe those beautiful coins of James V., which may bear a comparison with those of any country at any time.

Without inquiring too curiously whether this is its right place, I must be allowed now to notice among the objects of art of the twelfth century in Scotland, one of singular interest. I have given some specimens of our ancient charters, which were usually very brief and very small. In some instances, however, as charters of foundation, or general confirmations to religious houses, the king or chancellor of the day, indulged in greater verbosity and breadth of parchment. When Malcolm IV. saw fit to ratify all former endowments to his grandfather's great abbey of Kelso, it seems to have been his wish to do it with all solemnity. The

Chap. X. writing of charters of that period is always careful and elegant; but this great charter was to be distinguished by a novel ornament. The Gothic initial M of the king's name, formed of intertwined serpents, as is common in Anglo-Saxon MSS., is made to serve as a frame of two compartments, in each of which is painted a portrait of a crowned king in his royal state, in the most brilliant colours, and relieved with gold. On the right hand sits an aged monarch with a beard of venerable length, bearing in his hands the sword and globe of sovereignty. On the other, a youthful king with fair beardless face, holding in his right hand the sceptre of actual rule, and having the sword of office laid across his knees. This superb charter is dated in 1159. David I., the venerable founder of the Abbey, had died, full of days and of honour, six years before. Malcolm the IV., the reigning king, was then seventeen; and when we consider the object of the charter, and the circumstances in which it was granted, it really leaves no room for the most sceptical to doubt that these are portraits executed in 1159 of the reigning prince and of his grandfather, who must have been still fresh in the memory of his people.

It is seldom that we can have a work of art of so high antiquity, stamped thus precisely with its date and subject. One other instance I may mention of art, of yet more early date, well ascertained. I wish I could fix the place or country of manufacture as definitely.

In the summer of 1857, some boys playing on the sands of the Bay of Skaill, in Orkney, turned up several small pieces of metal which they showed, and soon discovered to be silver. There was speedily no want of diggers, and the little *cache* on the Orkney sea-shore, produced in all about sixteen pounds weight of silver. It was chiefly in the shape of torques and massive mantle-brooches, worked with careful, and sometimes pretty ornaments; but with a singular uniformity of design, as if the artist had but little invention, or considered himself bound to a conventional type or style. There were a few little ingots or bars of silver—suggesting the idea that the deposit contained the treasure of a silversmith's work-shop—and there were (fortunately) a number of silver coins. Some of the coins are Oriental, of that kind which were in common currency over Northern Europe in the middle ages. One is a coin of Khalif Al Motadhed, bearing to be struck at Al Thash (a town of Transoxiana) in the 283d year of the Hegira, corresponding with A.D. 896. But two of the coins are English, of which one, a "St. Peter's penny," coined at the city of York, numismatists place, with confidence, in the early part of the tenth century; the other, bearing the impress " *Æthelstan rex totius*

Chap. X. *Britanniæ,"* is limited by that king's reign to the years 925-941.

It was not a case of old wreck. There were a few grey stones ingeniously disposed, so as to point and lead to the spot, when one knew where about to look, and that is all. I conjecture it to have been the hoard of a northern pirate of the tenth century, fresh from the plunder of a good town where the silversmith's booth had naturally attracted his chief attention, who had buried his spoil to wait his return from another cruise, and had returned no more. The silver brooches and ornaments—the best and most authentic guide we have to Northern art of the tenth century—and the coins found along with them, are now in the museum of the Scotch Antiquaries.

To return from this long digression from the subject of architectural art — our field is much narrowed when we come to civil and domestic architecture. Of the rude dwellings of our *aborigines* I have already spoken. In them is little art, and nothing that can be called architecture. But in the reign of David I., and even earlier, history and contemporary charters notice numerous royal castles, and we cannot doubt that the masons who were erecting Dunfermline and St. Rule's for the saintly king, must have applied their new-born art to constructing those places of dwelling and defence for their patron, and for many of his Southern followers—each a prince in possessions and magnificence. We can point where those dwellings were. We know that on the rocks of Edinburgh and Stirling—at Roxburgh, Perth, Forfar, and other usual residences of royalty, as well as at the chief places of the greater earldoms, March, Fife, Athol, Angus, Strathern, Mar—castles were built for security and enjoyment, at the time when such sumptuous fabrics were erecting for the Church here in Scotland; and while castles and houses were building in England for the very brothers and cousins of our Northern settlers. But of such civil structures of the Norman or Romanesque period, we have only the vestiges remaining—a mass of shapeless masonry, disclosing marvellous strong mortar, or more frequently a mere foundation, faintly distinguishable through the green sward. I believe that, of the secular buildings of the eleventh and twelfth centuries, we have not a fragment affording any architectural feature.

Of the thirteenth and the following century, we have somewhat more. That was the age of those stately garrison piles, still the pride of England and Wales, and it was a time when men's minds were more turned to castles than to church building. Many of the events of the wars of Wallace and Bruce turn upon the attack and defence of our Scotch

Chap. X. castles. Barbour has thrown a romantic interest around Turnberry, Douglas, Brodick, Bothwell, Kildrummy; and the history of that glorious war perpetuates Dunstaffnage, Forfar, Brechin, Linlithgow, not to mention the great strengths of the kingdom, Edinburgh, Roxburgh, Stirling, Dunbar, and indeed a royal castle, as the proper and almost necessary accompaniment of each royal burgh. Most of those castles of residence and defence were sacked and burnt and demolished many times during that fierce struggle. But the masonry of that time was much enduring; and enough remains of Kildrummy, of Lochindorb, of Bothwell, of Caerlaverock, to show the style and plan of those fortresses, and to satisfy us that they followed the English model in everything but size. Some remaining parts, such as the round tower and chapel, of the ill-used castle of Kildrummy (which has served as a quarry for the country round), and some parts of Bothwell and Dirleton, all reaching back to the period we are studying, and all, be it observed, in striking situations, show the characteristic architecture of that castle-building age with much beauty of composition and detail. But like Edward's Welsh castles, those Scotch thirteenth and fourteenth century castles, are too much of the nature of fortresses for receiving garrisons, to furnish what we are chiefly seeking, some indications of domestic life.

These are found much more in the fifteenth century baronial tower, so peculiar to our country, although evidently built after the model of the primitive Norman *donjon*, long antiquated and disused in England. Take the middle of the fifteenth century—the chief time of these square towers—and observe the condition of Scotland. Since the death of Robert Bruce, a century of cruel wars and the most wretched misgovernment had impoverished the country almost to starvation. Many of our great families were extinguished; all the old grand way of life forgotten. The chivalrous manners—the noble simplicity of knights and ladies, so charmingly, and I think so truly, painted by Barbour—had been swept away. When again, with some breathing time of peace, and by the efforts of James I., agriculture had a little revived, and the Government encouraged building and "policy" in the desolate country—the buildings were like the people, poor and mean in taste. The chief thing aimed at was security against marauding bands and unfriendly neighbours. I need not describe to you the Scotch castle of that time—the single, square, gaunt tower, rising story above story, each floor consisting of but one apartment, the door placed high for safety, the walls thick, the window-openings narrow and jealous. Such a dwelling, and we have plenty of them, though few in their unmitigated bareness, recalls

Chap. X.

A.D. 1329.

A.D. 1424.

Chap. X. the time when the rural baron and his family, visitors, vassals, retainers, servants rural and domestic, lived and scrambled for their food, all crowded together in the one hall—a gloomy cold apartment—when the offal of the board was fought for by the dogs below it, and the garbage was hid among the foul straw which might be renewed when harvest produced a supply—when the furniture was limited to the moveable boards on which the meat was served, and a few stools and settles of deal—when carpets, curtains, window-glass, comfort, cleanliness, were unknown—when the women had no separate apartment but their sleeping-room, and no tastes that made such life irksome.

This style, which contrasts so unfavourably with the ruins of that which had preceded it by a century, fortunately did not continue long in its utter rude nakedness. As security increased, and the education and tastes of the people improved, dwelling-houses of more comfort were built up beside the sixteenth century tower—tall, lean, high-roofed, *single* dwellings, full of small rooms and small windows; and such additions and re-additions were constantly taking place in the century which succeeded the period of square towers, and preceded the next marked change of domestic architecture.

James III. was addicted to masonry and other art, and his son and grandson were men of princely taste, and showed it in their dwellings—Witness the remains of old Holyrood, Falkland, Stirling, and Linlithgow. But, except by one or two great courtiers, such palatial architecture could not be imitated; and it required skilful modification to adapt that over ornate style to the modest means of the Scotch gentry. It was not till the storm of the Reformation had subsided under the peaceful sway of James VI.—scarcely, indeed, before his accession to the English throne had given stability to government, and opened a way of riches to many a Scotch lord and laird—that a style of country house was introduced in Scotland, which, preserving the rude ancestral tower, surrounded it with graceful ornament, and added convenient accommodation in good keeping with the now decorated castle. The two leaders of the new style were their own architects, and both men of excellent taste. The Lord Chancellor (Alexander Seton, Lord Dunfermline) taking as his *nucleus* two ancient ecclesiastical mansions, produced the beautiful house of Pinkie, and the lordly pile of Fyvie, besides minor edifices at Elgin and elsewhere. His rival in architecture, the first Earl of Strathmore, applied his taste—may we not call it genius?—to supplementing, raising, grouping, lighting, ornamenting without, decorating within, the rude mass of an old Scotch keep. His first essay was upon his tower in the Carse of Gowrie, then known as Castle Lyon, now called Castle Huntly. But his great triumph was in producing from such materials the castle of Glammis, an edifice out of the common rules of art, and perhaps contrary to them, but which no artist can approach without admiration.

Those two master builders were but the type of their age. Castle-building, or castle-adorning, was in high fashion in the beginning of the seventeenth century; and, strangely, it fixed on Aberdeenshire as its favourite field, where castle mansions of Frasers, Gordons, Forbeses, Burnetts, and Urquharts still exist to teach our presumptuous age a lesson of humility. All those *chateaux*, and the less adorned country houses of that period, mark a great improvement in the comfort and in the tastes of our gentry. We cannot figure houses like Castle Fraser to have been built and inhabited by any who were not gentlemen and ladies, in the best sense of the word.

I wish it were possible to trace changes in the dwellings of the people—the middle and lower ranks—corresponding to those well marked steps of progress in the higher. But the cottage and the old farm house were of too perishable materials to furnish the outline of their history. One thing is sure. Looking back through all the time that record or chronicle can show us, the manner of life of the labourer may have been depressed by wars and famine, and pestilence—may have been kept stationary by hopelessness; but, as compared with the unlabouring class, it has never retrograded. This is not the place to notice the efforts of the modern Scotch agriculturist which have not only increased beyond all former belief the produce of the soil, but are mitigating our climate, and improving the health of the people. The improvement in their own dwellings was slow to follow; but it has come. Old men still remember when the dwelling of the Scotch peasant farmer was not secure against wind or rain with no window, or none made to open —with the damp earth for floor, with dunghill and green pestilent pool at the door. The "black hut" that is still to be seen in a few glens of the Highlands, is a less unhealthy abode than the houses of the yeomanry and peasantry of three-fourths of Scotland were half a century ago. The change is still going on universally over Scotland, not in fancy cottages, dressed up to please the lord or the lady, but in the acquisition of habits of cleanliness and comfort, which require better accommodation for our cattle now than was bestowed on human beings in the last generation.

Of burgh domestic architecture, I suppose we have none older than the sixteenth century. But of that we have good specimens around us, in those solid stately houses that seem likely to survive many changes of fashion, and which show that the burgess of the Reformation period lived in greater decency and comfort than the laird, though without the numerous following, which no doubt gave dignity if it diminished food. I am not sure that this class has gone on progressively, either in outward signs of comfort, or in education and accomplishment, equal to their neighbours. The reason, I suppose, is obvious. The Scotch burgher, when successful, does not set himself to better his condition and his family within the sphere of his success, but leaves it and seeks what he deems a higher.

POSTSCRIPT.

Since these chapters were written, there has been discovered in the public library at Cambridge a MS. of the Gospels, which bears to have belonged to the Abbey of Deir, in Buchan. I have not myself seen the book, but I am told it contains, besides the Gospels, some portions and forms of church service—among which the service of the visitation of the sick—and, on the margins and blank vellum, are entered a few charters and memoranda of grants to the Church of Deir. These entries are of high antiquity—more ancient than any extant Scotch chartularies—and recording facts still more archaic, reaching, indeed, a period of history which neither charter nor chronicle among us touches, and of which we have hitherto had only a few glimpses from the older lives of the saints, or from the meagre notes of foreign annalists.

The first of the remarkable entries is one of that class of memoranda of transactions which must have been used in all countries before the introduction of charters of gift. They are of common occurrence in church registers of France and Italy, and are not unknown among ourselves. The memorandum is in a Celtic dialect, and runs as follows:—

"Columkille and Drostan, son of Cosgrech, his disciple, came from Hy, as God had directed them, as far as Aberdover, and Bede, a Pict, was then Mormaer of Buchan on their arrival, and it was he that granted to them that city in freedom for ever, from the Mormaer and his sub-chief. They came afterwards to another city, but the king of it gave refusal to Columkille, for he was not endued with the grace of God, and the Mormaer ordered that it should be given to him; but it was not. And, after refusing the clerics, a son of his [the king's] took a disease, and it wanted little but he died. Afterwards the Mormaer went to entreat the clerics, and [undertook] that he and Domnail and Cathal would make all offerings to God and Drostan from beginning to end, in freedom from the Mormaer and his sub-chief till the day of judgment."

An imperfect note of two other benefactions gives us the names of Colban, Mormaer of Buchan, and Eva, daughter of Gartnait, his married wife, "and the Clan Magan."

Among the grants are two charters of Gartnat, son of Cannoc, and Eta, daughter of Gillemichel, his wife, and a grant by Doncad, son of MacBead.

The MS., whether judged from the handwriting or its contents, appears to be of the tenth century;

and the interest and importance of the discovery will be felt when it is considered that we had not previously any charter or grant of lands in Celtic language in Scotland, nor any written Gaelic of Scotch production earlier than the sixteenth century, unless we except eight leaves of an almost illegible pedigree, said to be as old as 1450; that all we knew of the Picts was a naked list of some seventy kings, without dates or events; that the title of Mormaer, learnt from the Irish annals, does not once occur in any Scotch charter, and the name of the Picts only once (in a description of boundaries).

Its dedication to St. Drostan, and, in part, the tradition of the church (preserved in the Aberdeen breviary) had informed us that Aberdouer in Buchan was one of St. Drostan's churches: but the early history of Deir was quite unknown.[1]

Ferrerius, the historian of the sister Abbey of Kinloss, asserted it to be the foundation of William, Earl of Buchan, in the beginning of the thirteenth century, and no doubt truly, as regards

[1] A fair used to be held at Deir on St. Drostan's day (14th December) and called "Drustan fair" in our old almanacs. It is curious how often a chapter of old history is preserved in such memorials. The dedications of many of our churches to the first preachers of the faith, despised and forgotten in Scotland, are often preserved by the name of a well beside the church, at first hallowed as the baptismal source, or by the name and the day of the village fair, which was of old held on the festival of the patron saint.

the establishment of the Cistercian convent. But, as had happened in many of our monasteries,[1] and, indeed, in some of our bishoprics also, the so-called foundation was perhaps an importation of new religions, probably a new and more liberal endowment, of a church which certainly had been founded and endowed ages before.

We know three charters of Deir about the period fixed by Ferrerius as the foundation of the Cistercian house, none of them a foundation charter, but all showing the interest taken in the abbey by Marjory, Countess of Buchan, the heiress of the old race, who carried that earldom into the family of Cumin. Two of the Countess's charters are witnessed by "Magnus, son of Earl Colben," and "Adam, son of Earl Fergus."

Without rushing too hastily at conclusions, we must think that these charters, together with the book of Deir, leave little doubt that the Colbens and Ferguses, old mormaers of Buchan (and with them the mormaers of Angus, Moray, Ross, etc.) latterly changed their style to Earl; and that Marjory, whom we know in record as Countess in her own right, was the descendant and representative of those old mormaers of Buchan. Who, then, were the Magnus and Adam, sons of "Earl Colben" and "Earl Fergus?" Were they simply illegitimate sons

[1] As Melrose, Dunfermline, Glasgow, Aberdeen.

of the family, while their niece or cousin Marjory was alone legitimate? Or do we see here a remnant of that system of succession through females alone, which has been asserted of the Picts, and treated as fabulous? It is enough merely to indicate subjects of such curiosity and interest.

If I have been rightly informed, and have correctly represented its contents, it is evident that the discovery of this book sets the whole discussion which excited the Scotch antiquaries of the last century on an entirely new footing. But it is premature to reason upon its contents. It is to be hoped that Mr. Bradshaw, who has undertaken the task, will not long delay giving them fully to the public.

APPENDIX.

I.—P. 29. CAPITULAR OF CHARLEMAGNE, *De villis imperialibus.*

This ordinance was made in the year 812. It runs in the name and person of the Emperor, and bears marks that much of it is his own in meaning, if not in words.

[The *Judex* was the steward upon each *Villa*. The *Maior* under him was not to have more in charge than he could oversee in one day. The *Villæ*, or estates of the Emperor, many of them of great extent, are here (for convenience) rendered *Manors*.]

C. 8. The Emperor commands each Judex to have care of the vineyards in his manor, and to put the wine in good casks, and diligently care that there be no miscarriage (naufragium).

C. 9. Measures of liquid and dry to be kept of the same standard as those of the palace.

C. 11. No Judex to take quartering for himself or his dogs upon our men (*super homines nostros*) in forests.

C. 13. Stallions to be provided.

C. 14. Care to be taken of the stud mares, and the colts to be separated at the proper season.

C. 17. Bees to be kept at every manor.

C. 18-19. Poultry to be kept at mills and at the royal stables; in the chief manors, not less than a hundred poultry and thirty geese.

C. 21. Every Judex to keep up fish ponds, and increase them by all means.

C. 23. In every manor the Judex to have byres, piggeries, houses for sheep, goats, and kids. Lame oxen, and cows or horses, free of scab or disease, to be given for the dogs' food, but so that neither our byre nor our plough be deprived of cattle.

C. 27. Our houses to have continually fires and watches for safety.

C. 32. The best seed each season to be prepared by purchase or otherwise.

C. 34. It is especially to be cared, that all things made with the hand, as lard, preserved meat, wine, vinegar, mustard, butter, malt, mead, honey, wax, flour, shall all be made and prepared with extreme cleanliness (*summo nitore*).

C. 35. Tallow to be made of fat sheep as well as pigs; and not less than two oxen to be fattened in each manor, either for tallow or for sending to us.

C. 36. Our woods and forests to be well kept. The Judex to superintend needful grubbing of wood, and not to allow our wood to be turned into arable. To preserve well our beasts of chase in the forests, and to protect hawks' nests. To collect diligently the dues of the forest, and if he send his own swine into our wood to fatten, let himself be first to pay the tithe for good example.

C. 37. To manage skilfully our fields and farms, and set up our meadows for hay in due time.

C. 38. To have plenty of fed geese and fatted poultry for our use.

C. 39. The poultry and eggs paid by the labourers and cottars (*servientes et mansuarii*) to be received, and where more than required for use, to be sold.

C. 40. On all our manors, the Judex to have swans, pea fowls, pheasants, geese, pigeons, partridges, turtles, for ornament (*pro dignitatis causa.*)

C. 41. The stables, kitchens, bake-houses, wine-presses, to be carefully prepared, in order that our servants may properly, well, and cleanly perform their offices.

C. 42. Every manor to have in the mansion (*camera*) beds, feather-beds and bed-clothes, table linens, dish towels, seat covers, vessels of brass, lead, iron, wood, fire dogs (*andedos*), chimney chains and hooks, hatchets, wedges, shovels, and all other utensils, so that it may not be necessary to borrow. And weapons used against the enemy, so far as useful at home, should be placed in the mansion on their return from war.

C. 43. In the women's work-room should be lint, wool, woad, vermilion and other dye stuffs, wool combs, teazles, soap, grease, vessels, and other necessaries.

C. 45. Every Judex to have in his employment good artificers, that is, blacksmiths, workers in gold or silver, shoemakers, turners, carpenters, shield makers, fishers, falconers, soap-makers, brewers who can make cider, beer, perry, and other drinks; bakers able to make fine bread for our use; makers of nets for hunting, fishing, and fowling, and other artisans whom it would be too long to enumerate.

C. 46. The Judex to take great care of the fences of our parks, mending from time to time, not waiting till a complete new fence is required; and so in all our buildings.

C. 48. Wine-presses to be prepared. No one to presume to press our grapes with the feet, but all to be done cleanly and decently.

C. 53. Every Judex to take care that our men in their employment be not thieves or criminals.

C. 54. That our family labour industriously, and do not go idling to fairs.

C. 55. Accounts to be kept and sent us of income and expense.

C. 56. The Judex to hold courts and administer justice.

C. 57. Not to prevent complaints made to us from reaching us.

C. 62. At Christmas, yearly, every Judex shall report to us, separately, distinctly, and in order, what he has out of his administration, what of land tilled for himself; what from rents and duties; what from fines; what from beasts of chase, taken in our forests without our permission; what from diverse compositions; what from mills; what from forests; what from breweries; what from bridges or ships; what from free men, and *centeni* who are attached to our estate; what from markets; what from vineyards; what from those who pay wine; what from hay; what from timber, faggots, and shingles, and other produce of the woods; what from peat mosses; what from pulse; what from millet and panic; what from wool, lint, and hemp; what from the fruits of trees; what from nuts larger and smaller; what from grafted trees; what from gardens; what from rape-lands; what from fish-stanks; what from hides, skins, and horns; what from honey and wax; what from tallow, lard, or soap; what from mulberry drink, made wine (*vino cocto*), mead, and vinegar; what from beer; from wine, new and old; from corn, new and old; what from chickens and eggs, and geese; what from the fishers; what from the blacksmiths; from the shield-makers or shoemakers; what out of the great chest, and the smaller boxes; what from the turners or saddlers; from smelters of iron or lead; what from tributaries; what from colts and fillies—that we may know what or how much we have of each thing.

C. 63. In all the foregoing, let it not seem harsh to our *Judices* that we require these accounts, for we wish that they, in like manner, count with their subordinates, without offence. And all things whatsoever any man should have in his house or in his "villa," our *Judices* ought to have in our "villas."

C. 64. Our cars for war to be litters well made, covered with hides so closely sewed, that if necessity occur for swimming rivers, they may pass through (after being lightened of their contents), without water entering. We will also, that flour be sent for our household in each car, 12 bushels of flour; and in those which bring wine, 12 *modia* of wine, according to our *modius*. And with each car let there be a shield and a lance, a quiver of arrows and a bow.

C. 65. The fish of our ponds to be sold for our profit when we are not resident, and others put in their place.

C. 68. Good barrels, hooped with iron, to be used both in expeditions with the army, and for sending to the palace; and no butts to be made of skins.

C. 69. The *Judices* to report to us, always, how many wolves each has caught, and send us their skins. And in the month of May, to search and take the cubs with poison and hooks, as well as with pits and dogs.

C. 70. *Volumus quod in horto omnes herbas habeant, id est lilium, rosas* (then follow about seventy names of plants, mostly herbs, and even those now valued as flowers, perhaps then used in the kitchen or still-room). *Hortulanus habeat super domum suam Jovis barbam.* Of trees, we will that the *Judices* have apple-trees, pears, plums, service trees, medlars, chestnuts, peaches of diverse kinds, quinces, filberts, almonds, mulberries, laurels, pines, figs, cherries of diverse kind; the names of the apples, *gozmaringa, geroldinga, crevedella, spirauca*; some sweet, some more acid; one sort for keeping all winter, another for immediate use; early and late.

Pertz, monumenta Germaniæ historica. Legum. tom. i. p. 181.

II.—P. 269. AELFRIC'S HOMILIES IN ANGLO-SAXON.

Aelfric, monk and mass priest, as he calls himself, in his preface to his homilies, was afterwards Archbishop of York, and died in

1052. His reason for writing in Anglo-Saxon, rather than Latin, was, that he "found much error in many English books, because his countrymen had not the Gospel lore among their writings, except only the men who knew Latin, and except the books which King Alfred wisely turned from Latin into English, which are to be had." For the same reason, he says, he used no obscure words, but simple English (*sed simplicem Anglicam*), that it may more easily reach the hearts of readers and hearers, to the weal of their souls; for they cannot receive instruction in any other language than their native tongue.

Aelfric's "Sermones Catholici," are forty discourses on the solemn days of the Christian year, with a few in commemoration of the Virgin, St. John Baptist, Michael the Archangel, and the greater Apostles and Saints. They are for the most part plain intelligible explanations of Christian doctrine, and narratives of Bible history, suited to people who drew their instruction chiefly from the priest's sermon. But the language is always pure and vigorous, and sometimes rises with the subject to considerable rhetorical power. The translation is by Mr. Thorpe, who has edited the book with his usual care, but leaves his readers disappointed that he does not bestow on them more of the rich stores of his ripe learning. Here is a sentence from the homily of Easter Sunday, as translated by Mr. Thorpe.

"Unhappy was the Jewish people that they were so unbelieving. All creatures acknowledged their Creator, save only the Jews. Heaven acknowledged the birth of Christ; for when he was born, a new star was seen. The sea acknowledged Christ when he went with dry feet on its waves. Earth acknowledged him, when it all trembled at Christ's resurrection. The sun acknowledged him, when it was darkened at Christ's passion, from mid-day to the ninth hour. The stones acknowledged him, when they burst asunder at their Creator's departure. Hell acknowledged Christ, when it led forth its captives through the *harrowing* of Jesus; and yet the hard-hearted Jews, through all these signs, would not incline with faith to the merciful Jesus, who will help all men who believe on him." l. p. 229.

> *Sermones Catholici*, or *homilies of Aelfric*, in *Anglo-Saxon, with an English version by Benjamin Thorpe*. London, 1844.

III.—P. 270. Library of the Culdees of St. Serf's. A.D. 1152

The charter granting the isle of Lochleven to the Priory of St. Andrews, is without date, but the granter, Bishop Robert, and the witnesses, mark it to have been made about the year 1152. It conveys to the Canons regular, the abbey of the island, hitherto held by the Culdees, with all its pertinents, namely, Findahin; Portemuoch; the mills at the Bridge; a mill in Findahin; Chireness; Half Urechan; Sconin; twenty *melis* of cheese, one pig from Markinche; twenty *melis* of cheese, and four *melis* of malt, and one pig from Admor; twenty *melis* of barley from Balcrystin; twenty *melis* of cheese, and one pig from Bolgin son of Torfin; the tithes of our house of the island; the tithes of the whole rent which we are to receive at that house; the church vestments which the Culdees had; these books, namely,—

A pastoral.
A gradual.
A missal.
An Origen.
The "Sentences" of the Abbot of Clairvaux (St. Bernard), a commentary upon the famous collection of theological subtleties.
Three quires concerning the Sacraments.
A part of a collection called the "Bibliotheca," probably the Vulgate of St. Jerome.
A "Lectionarium," which seems to have been a collection of the portions of St. Paul's Epistles used at mass.
The Acts of the Apostles.

The text of the Gospels after St. Prosper (a follower of St. Augustin).
Three books of Solomon.
Glosses on the Song of Solomon.
Interpretations of phrases.
A collection of the "Sentences."
A commentary on Genesis.
Exceptions of Ecclesiastical rules.

Registrum prioratus Sancti Andreæ, p. 43.

IV.—P. 255. LEASE BETWEEN THE ABBOT OF SCONE AND HAY OF LEYS. *Anno* 1312, with a translation interlined.

The interlineation is, of course, more recent than the body of the indenture; but the hand and the reason of the translation preclude the idea of its being more than a few years later.

The words translated are :—

Concesserunt	*Has grantit.*
Dimiscrunt	*Has lettin.*
Pertinenciis	*Purtenauncis.*
Rectis divisis	*Richtuis diuisis.*
Solebant	*Was wont.*
Linealiter	*Euin in line.*
Ex latere	*On side.*
Procreandis	*To be to gitt.*
Descendentibus	*Descendit.*
Triginta	*Thritti.*
Annuatim	*Iere bi iere.*
Hyeme	*Wyntir.*
Immediate sequentes	*For utin oni mene foluand.*
Quod molent	*That thai sal grind.*
Pro sustentatione sua	*For thair fode.*
Molendinum	*Miln.*
Vecesimum quartum vas	*Four and twentiand fat.*
Jure seruientis molendini	i. e. *cnaveschipe.*

APPENDIX. 335

Prestabit .... *Sal gif.*
Genere .... *Kynd.*
Natiui .... *In born men.*
Preparacionem .... *Grayting.*
Sustentationem .... *Vphalding.*
In circuitu .... *Abute thaim.*
Forinsecum .... *Forayn.*
Percipient focale .... *Sal tak fuayl.*
Alienabunt .... *Do away.*
Eorum successoribus .... *Tha that comis in thair stede.*
Vsufructu .... *Gres water and other profitis.*
Indiguerint .... *Thay haf mister.*
Exorte fuerint .... *Haf grouyn.*
Decidentur .... *Haf fallin* (a misreading).
Reseruari .... *Be yemit.*
Dominio .... *The lauerdscape.*
Requisiti .... *Requerit.*
Simulatione .... *Feyning.*
Accedere .... *i.e.* venire.
Contingat .... Impersonaliter.
Revocare .... *Cal agayn.*
Sui recessus .... *Of thair parting.*
Recedent .... *Sal depart.*
Edificia .... *Biging.*
Construi facient .... *Sal ger be made.*
Competentia .... *Gaynand.*
Dimittent edificata .... *Sale lene bigit.*
Cyrographi .... *Hand chartir.*
Confecti .... *Made.*
Penes .... *Anentis* (a mistake).
Residenti .... *Duelland.*
Appensum .... *Hingand.*

    Liber de Scona, p. 104, where the original indenture is represented in *fac-simile*.

V.—P. 270.   CATALOGUE OF BOOKS IN GLASGOW CATHEDRAL.
A. 1432.

This list of books is preserved in the ancient Register of the Bishopric.

The first section, of books for the use of the choir, consists chiefly of church service books. We find ten missals; seven breviaries, some of them small *portiforia* or *portuas books*, used for carrying abroad; five psalters, having nothing joined with them; seven *antiphonaria*, or anthem books, some with psalters added; six *gradalia*, grails, or books of offices; five *processionaria*, or books giving the formulæ and the services used in church processions—each distinguished by being covered with white leather or red, being *magni* or *parvi voluminis*, *solennes* or *non multo solennes*, *notati* (with music), or *non notati*, *cathenati*, chained to the desks, or preserved in chests and presses. Then we have a *collectarium*, or book of the collects; an *ordinarium*, *ordinale*, or ritual book—*continens ordinem divinii offici*; two *libri pontificales*, or pontificals, books of the part of the ritual appropriate to the Bishop; a *catholicon* which, if it be the glossary of Joannes de Janua, and I can give no other conjecture, is oddly placed among the service books of the choir, and noted as chained beside the high altar; the Old Testament, in two large volumes; an *Epistolare*, or book of the epistles (perhaps those of St. Paul only), with the gospels at the end; another volume of the epistles of St. Paul; two copies of *Legenda Sanctorum*, books more commonly called passionaria; a small volume containing lives of St. Kentigern and St. Servan. One of the breviaries is placed outside the choir for chance comers who may be able to read it.

A *processionarium* was in the hands of the binder, and for the honour of Glasgow we have his name, Richard Air. But his prefix of *dominus*, marks him to be a churchman. The greater number of these volumes remained constantly in the choir, and

APPENDIX. 337

were chained to the desks or stalls of the canons and vicars. Books are frequently met with, still bearing the mark of this species of durance, in two holes bored through the lower corners of the oak boards next the binding.

The next class, kept in presses, not within the library, is very miscellaneous. It contains two parts of the Pandects, described by their well-known, but hitherto unexplained symbol of *ff*; the Institutes of Justinian; the Acts of the Apostles; a book of hymns, collects, and *capitula;* Saint Augustin's treatise on the psalms; a book of the decretals and decrees; a book on the *quodlibets*, by a Mr. John Poysley; the venerable Bede's book of forty homilies on the gospels (are these the originals of our friend Aelfric's homilies?) a book of theology, with the arms of the Cardinal of Scotland painted in the first letter (this was undoubtedly Cardinal Walter Wardlaw, Bishop of Glasgow); a book of the sermons of St. Bernard; two volumes of the sermons of Pope Leo; a book of St. Augustin's; St. Jerome on the creed; Valerius Maximus; Peter Damian's book, *Græcismus;* the statutes of the Council of Tours; an exposition of the psalter; a large book beginning, *Reverentia Preclare Virtutum;* Ovid's metamorphoses; Aristotle's rhetoric, in Latin; *Armanorum Questiones*, a book by Richard Fitz Rauf, Archbishop of Armagh, against the Armenians; Friar Richard on the ethics of Aristotle; Friar Peter on the fourth book of the Sentences; the third and fourth books of Bonaventure (upon the Sentences); Saint Augustin against Faustinus the heretic; Francesco Petrarca (probably either *De Remediis Utriusque Fortunæ* or *De Vita Solitaria*); a book beginning, *Est Margarite:* the works of Sallust, whose name, Caius Crispus Sallustius, the scribe has understood to be the names of three persons; a number of little books of paper, whose names were unknown; a work of Henri Boye, a commentator on the Decretals, who flourished at the end of the fourteenth century; *Braco*, which should perhaps be *Brito*, who wrote *Super Leges Anglie;* *Speculum Judiciale*, perhaps the *Speculum Juris* of Durandus; the *Summa Casuum Conscientiæ* of

z

Bartholomeus Pisanus; Boetius *de Consolatione*, with the gloss of Nicholas Trivet, a Dominican friar—the last five in the hands of canons of the Cathedral, either for their life, or during the pleasure of the Chapter.

The books in the library, chained, beginning at the north corner of the west shelf, are as follows:—A book of theology "of faith and its object," illuminated with gold, the binding defective; a book of theology of Saint Thomas, probably Thomas Aquinas's *Compendium Theologiæ; Historia Ecclesiastica*, probably the work of Bede; the morals of Aristotle, in Latin; Treatises of Thomas Aquinas, Duns Scotus (Doctor Subtilis), and Bonaventure, chiefly on various parts of the sentences of Peter Lombard; *Summa Confessorum;* a book of Canon Law; a concordance of the Bible, illuminated with gold; a commentary on the Five Books of Moses; the commentaries of Nicholas de Lira on the gospels; a Bible complete, illuminated with gold—a beautiful volume; a book of questions in theology; the treatise of an Anglican doctor on the four books of the Sentences; De Lira's commentary on the Psalter; St. Paul's Epistles, with a gloss; an explanation of the Prologues of the Bible; a commentary on the Psalter according to St. Augustin.

The second shelf in the library contains first a collection of civil law, consisting of the code of Justinian; the Pandects, which it was the fashion to divide into three parts, the *Digestum Vetus, Digestum Novum,* and *Inforciatum,* a name of unknown meaning and etymology; the Ten Collations, with the Authenticæ. Secondly, works on the Canon Law, viz., the *Speculum Judiciale* of Durandus; *Summa Copiosa,* a treatise on the Decretals, known also by the names of *Summa Charitatis, Summa Aurea,* and *Summa Hostiensis,* from its author, Henri de Suze, Cardinal Bishop of Ostia; *Liber Innocentii,* probably the constitutions of Pope Innocent IV., in the Council of Lyons, 1245; a book of *Decreta*; another; *Liber Clementis,* the constitutions of Pope Clement IV.; a book of the Decretals. Then follow a volume containing the epistles of Bernard, Abbot of Clarevalle, and the treatise of Isidore, Bishop of Seville, on Etymologies; a commentary on Genesis; Friar Gregory's lecture on the book of Sentences ; the *Historia Ecclesiastica* of Bede ; a volume of Master Hugh of Paris, probably Hugo de Sancto Victore, who wrote *De vanitate rerum mundanarum*, etc. ; a Bible complete ; Saint Augustin on the gospel ; *Liber questionum Ermenorum compositus per Ricardum Radulphi*, a copy of which was noticed in the second class ; a fair volume of Mechanics (perhaps it should be metaphysics), with treatises of heaven and earth, generation and corruption, and many others, treatises of Aristotle ; a volume commencing *Finis et Fabula Rerum ;* the *Liber Collationum* of Odo, Abbot of Cluny (printed in the Bibl. Patr. Latin, t. 10, p. 236); a volume in red binding, having in the first line, *Quoniam secundum Apostolum.* And so the second shelf is full.

On the third shelf were placed, a book of Sermons ; the book of Sentences, perhaps the original work of Lombard ; *Epitaphium Senecæ*, containing the Epistles of St. Paul to Seneca, which were received as genuine by St. Jerome and other ancient fathers (the commencement is probably a mistake of the scribe for *Lucius Annæus Seneca*) ; a book of the sermons of St. Austin ; the book of Archbishop Bradwardin (which Leland calls *Divinum Opus*), *De causa Dei contra Pelagium ;* the Rhetoric of Aristotle ; Epistles of St. Austin ; a small volume, *De Peccato Ade*; the Epistles of Clement (perhaps Pope Clement IV.) to several princes ; the second book of Duns Scotus, called Doctor Subtilis ; a book of Landulphus, on the second book of the Sentences ; a book on St. Austin's work *De Civitate Dei ;* a book of the Quodlibets, or commonplaces of scholastic disputations ; the treatise of a John Forrest on the first book of the Sentences ; the first part of the *Summa Sancti Thomæ*, a treatise of Thomas Aquinas on the Sentences ; Saint Austin's *De regulis veræ fidei ;* Friar Gregory's lecture on the first book of Sentences ; the *Liber Pastoralium* of Saint Gregory the Pope ; a book of the Collations, probably that commonly quoted as *Authenticæ* or *Novellæ Constitutiones ;* a book on Faith, written against divers errors ; Bonaventure on the third book of the Sentences ; Saint Austin on the Trinity; Peter of Torento on the fourth book of the Sentences; a volume containing the works of two authors, Jocelin—perhaps the monk of Furnes—and William de Monte Haudon, of whom I know nothing but the title of his book, *Super apparatu Clementis;* a Lucidarius, which is described in the catalogue of the ancient library of the Louvre—Le Lucidaire est un ouvrage de Théologie en vers du 13ième siècle sans nom d'auteur, traduit de Saint Ambrose. —*Registrum Episc. Glasg.*, vol. II., p. 334.

VI.—P. 273. JAMES MELVILL'S DIARY.

Sa I was put to the scholl of Montrose, finding of God's guid providence my auld mother Mariorie Gray, wha, parting from hir brother at his mariage, haid taken vpe hous and scholl for lasses in Montrose; to hir I was welcome againe as hir awin sone. The maister of the scholl, a lerned, honest, kynd man, whom also for thankfulnes I name Mr. Andro Miln;[1] he was veric skilfull and diligent. The first yeir he causit us go throw the Rudiments, againe therefter enter and pas throw the first part of Grammer of Sebastian, therwith we hard Phormionem Terentii, and war exercisit in composition; eftir that entered to the second part, and hard therwith the Georgics of Wirgill, and dyvers vther things.

I never got a strak of hys hand, whowbeit I committed twa lourd faults as it were with fyre and sword. Haiffing the candle in my hand on a wintar night, befor sax hours, in the scholl, sitting in the class, bernlie and negligentlie pleying with the bent, it kyndlit sa on fyre that we had all ado to put it out with our feet. The othir was, being molested by a condisciple wha cuttit the strings of my pen and ink horn with hys pen knife; I minting with my pen kniff at his legges to fley him, he feared and lifting now a leg now the othir, rasht on his leg on my pen kniff and strak himself a deip wound in the schin of the leg qubilk was a quarter of a yeir in curing. In the tyme of the trying of this matter, he saw me sa

[1] Minister at Fedresso.

humble, sa feard, sa grieved, yield sa manic teares, and ly fasting and murning in the scholl all day, that he said he could not find in his hart to punish me fordar. Bot my righteous God let me not slipe that fault, bot gaiff me a warning and remembrance what it was to be defyled with blude, whowbeit negligentlie; for within a schort space eftir, I had causit a cutler new come to the town, to polishe and scharpe the sam pen knyff, and haid bought a pennie worth of aples, and cutting and eating the same in the linkes, as I put the cheine in my mouthe, I began to lope vpe vpon a little sandie brae, haifling the pen kniff in my richt hand, I fell and therwithe strak myselff, missing my wombe, an inch deep into the inwart syde of the left knie, even to the bean, wherby the acquitie of God's judgement and my conscience strak me sa, that I was the mair war of knyffes all my dayes.

In Montrose was Mr. Thomas Andersone, minister, a man of mean gifts, bot of singular good lyff. God moved hym to mark me and call me often to his chalmer, to treat me quhan he saw anie guid in me, and to instruct and admonise me otherwise. He desirit me ever to rehearse a part of Calvin's Catechism on the Sabothes at efter noon, because he hard the peiple lyked weill of the clernes of my voice, and pronuncing with some feeling; and thereby God moved a godlie honest matron in the towne to mak meikle of me thairfor, and callit me hir lytle sweit angle. The minister was able to teach na ofter but ance in the ouk; but haid a godlie honest man reidar, wha read the scripture distinctly and with a religius and devot feiling, whereby I fand myself movit to gif good eare and learn the stories of scripture, also to tak pleasure in the Psalms which he had almost by heart in prose. The Lard of Done, mentioned befor, dwelt oft in the towne, and of his chairitie entertenit a blind man, wha had a singular good voice, hym he causit the doctor of our schole teatche the whole Psalms in miter, with the tones thereof, and sing tham in the kyrk; be heiring of whome I was sa delyted, that I lernit manie of the psalmes, and toones thereof in miter, quhilk I have thought evir sen syne a great blessing and comfort. The exerceise of the ministerie was keipit oukly then in Montrose, and thair assemblies ordinarly, whilk when I saw I was movit to lyke fellon weil of that calling, bot thought it a thing vnpossible that evir I could haf the abilitie to stand vp and speik, when all held thair tongue and luiked, and to continue speaking alean the space of an houre. There was also there a post that frequented Edinburgh, and brought hame Psalm-books and ballats, namely of Robert Semple's making, wherein I tuk pleasure, and learnit something baith of the state of the country, and of the missours and cullors of Scots ryme. He schew me first Wedderburn's songs, whairof I lerned diverse par ceur, with great diversite of toones. He frequented our scholl, and from him also I lerned to understand the callender efter the common use thereof. And finallie, I receavit the communion of the body and blud of the Lord Jesus Christ, first at Montrose, with a greater reverence and sense in my saule than oft therefter I could find, in the 13 yeir of my age; whar, coming from the table, ane guid honest man, ane elder of the kirk, gaiff me an admonition concerning lightnes, wantonnes, and nocht takin tent to the preatching and word read and prayers, quhilk remeaned with me evir sen syne. Sa God maid every person, place, and action to be my teacheris, bot alas! I vsed tham never sa fruitfullie as the guid occasiones servit, bot was carryit away in vanitie of mind with young and fullishe conceats quhilk is the heavie challange of my conscience.

The tyme of my being in Montrose was about twa yeirs, during the quhilk the common newes that I hard was of the grait praises of the government, and in end, the heavie mean and pitifull regrat amangs men in all esteatts, for the traiterus murdour of James Erle of Murro, called the Guid Regent.—*The diary of Mr. James Melvill.* Edinburgh, 1829. P. 17-19.

The whole is of the greatest interest for all who desire to see the old Scotch scholar life. But the book is now well known.

GLOSSARY.

Agayn, 262, against, contrary to
Algatis, 172, *omnimodo*
Allossede, 258, praised
Alswa, 156, also
Amerciament, 172, fine, penalty
Analy, 172, alienate
Anent, 184, towards
Appelis, 183, accuses
Appelyt, 183, accused
Armuris, 228, arms
Askit, 172, asked
Assoillie, 260, pardon
Assythment, 191, compensation for slaughter
At, 155, that
Avise, 220, advice
Aw, 155, owe, ought
Awn, 172, own
Ayre, 172, heir

Baith, 220, both
Bak, 190, back
Bak-berand, 182, bearing on his back (the stolen goods)
Bankvar, 244, a bench with cabinet
Bord claiths, 247, table-cloths
Bare, 259, plain
Be, 262, by
Bedde, 172, bed
Behovit, 172, behoved
Beis, 183, is
Ber, 190, bear
Ber, 245, bear, barley
Bilyve, 258, quickly
Blonkkes, 258, steeds
Blude, 181, blood
Borch, 184, bail or surety
Bot, 156, but
Bot, 187, unless
Bots, 182, compensation, atonement
Bowglis, 244, bugle beads
Braches, 259, hounds
Braid, 251, broad
Breme, 259, fierce
Browd, 246, broider
Brugh, 190, burgh
Busken, 258, dress

But, 172, unless
Brynnyngis, 261, burnings

Cacheres, 258, hunters
Cald, 264, called
Calden, 258, called
Canell, 242, cinnamon
Candyllaris, 244, chandeliers
Cariagia, 216, carriages exacted as service
Chaft, 257, jaw
Chalangit, 188, challenged, accused
Chargeours, 244, large dishes
Charred, 259, led
Chastyd, 264, chastised
Chesid, 228, chose
Clene, 188, clean, innocent
Clenge, 184, cleanse, acquit
Clengying, 183, acquitting
Collectas, 216, levies
Communatez, 261, estates
Compulsator, 271, process of compelling
Consavit, 220, conceived
Constreignit, 172, constrained
Convickyt, 193, convicted
Costlikly, 228, costly
Cosynnage, 156, cousinship, relation
Cowerlats, 244, coverlets
Cowssings, 244, cushions
Cuk stuil, 190, cucking-stool or pillory
Cumly, 228, comely
Cummys, 172, comes
Curt, 271, court
Customys, 155, customs

Dang, 256, beat
Dedde, 172, death
Dedes, 264, deeds
Defowle, 262, indignity
Delyte, 228, delight
Deyd, 264, died
Dome, 156, judgment
Doubtet, 260, redoubted
Dowt, 264, fear
Drede, 155, dread
Dungen, 190, beaten
Dykpot, 188, ordeal pool

GLOSSARY.

Efter, 188, after
Eftir, 172, after
Eld, 188, age
Er, 190, ear
Erl, 181, earl

Faderis, 172, fathers
Falyhyd, 264, failed
Fang, 182, stolen goods
Fay, 264, faith
Feirde, 262, fourth
Ferding, 190, farthing
Fewte, 155, fealty
Fore, 262, for
Forfalt, 193, forfeit
For-qwhy, 260, because
Forsuer, 190, renounce
Forthi, 264, wherefore
Foul, 188, guilty
Fra, 264, after
Fra, 191, from
Furthwartis, 191, forward
Futfells, 245, a kind of skins

Gaif, 204, gave
Galyga, 242, some kind of spice
Gamyn, 265, play
Gangande, 261, going
Gatharion, 193, horse (?)
Ger, 261, make
Gert, 228, made
Gevyn, 188, given
Geyf, 172, give
Gif, 172, if
Gle, 265, merriment
Gome, 258, man
Grantit, 271, admitted
Gretly, 172, greatly
Greyff, 188, magistrate
Grots, 243, groats
Gruntel, 257, snout
Gud, 156, 188, good

Habit and repute, 184, held and reputed
Haf, 190, have
Halde, 155, hold
Halden, 172, held
Haldyn, 190, held
Halikire, 262, holy church
Halpenny, 190, halfpenny
Hand-habend, 182, having in his hand (the stolen goods)
Hangit, 188, hanged
Haterit, 155, hatred
Hatheles, 258, nobles
Hawle, 258, hall
Hecht, 256, hight, named
Hed, 190, head
Hele, 172, health
Hem, 258, them
Hendeste, 258, fairest
Her, 258, their
Het, 187, hot

Hevene-riche, 258, heaven
Heyrschippis, 261, robberies
Hing, 190, hang
Hingit, 190, hanged
Hor, 258, their
Hortus olerum, 125, "kail yard," cabbage garden
Huntes, 259, huntsmen
Hym, 190, him
Hyrdman, 183, *hered-man*, a noble
Hyrr, 262, her
Hys, 262, his

Ilk, 219, each
Ilk, 172, same
Ilk ane, 190, each one
Inquirit, 271, examined
Into, 265, in
Inewe, 258, enough
Iuges, 193, judges
Iugit, 193, judged

Jarl, 231, earl
Jowele, 228, jewel
Justis, 264, justice
Justified, 182, brought to justice

Kail, 125, colewort
Keip, 193, keep
Kinrik, 204, kingdom
Kist, 246, chest
Knawen, 262, known
Konynge, 258, skill
Kow, 181, cow
Ky, 181, cows
Kyn, 262, kindred
Kynrike, 261, kingdom
Kythe, 258, country

Lachen, 258, take
Laff, 190, loaf
Lathyd, 264, loathed
Lauch, 155, law
Lede, 265, lead
Ledynge, 258, men
Leil, 183, *legalis*, lawful, trustworthy
Leflull, 188, lawful
Lemed, 258, gleamed
Lengede, 258, dwelt
Lentyrn, 188, lent
Lentynwar, 248, a kind of skins
Lesum, 271, lawful
Leue, 258, loved
Leyff, 187, leave
Londes, 258, lands
Lordis, 228, lords
Luve, 155, love
Luwe, 265, love
Luwyd, 264, loved
Lyande, 172, lying
Lyf, 186, life
Lyffe, 258, live
Lyffede, 258, lived
Lyking, 183, choice

GLOSSARY. 345

Lym, 186, limb

Mair, 191, more
Makless, 258, matchless
Makys, 193, makes
Males, 258, trunks
Medful, 264, praiseworthy
Mekil, 190, much
Melis, 258, speaks
Memore, 260, memory
Menyd, 264, bemoaned
Merciament, 186, penalty
Mertrick, 236, martin cat
Meuros, 260, Melrose
Molde, 258, earth
Mony, 228, many
Mote, 259, blasts
Mute, 155, meeting of court
Mute-hill, 204, mount of council and judgment

Na, 155, nor
Nede, 172, need
Nevo, 181, nephew
Nocht, 172, not
Nocht, 204, nought
Nother, 156, neither
Noumer, 219, number

Oblisyng, 262, obligation
Obolus, 190, a halfpenny
Of, 190, off
Offerand, 271, offering
Of-kest, 259, off-threw
Ogettheyrn, 181, a young lord
Ongers, 243, a coin
Ony, 155, any
Ouder, 193, either
Outan, 193, except
Oysed, 228, used

Pece, 193, peace
Peraventour, 262, peradventure
Perfit, 271, perfect
Perseu, 271, prosecute
Pes, 264, peace
Pessyhil, 264, peaceful
Plenerly, 261, fully
Poer, 262, poor
Potyngary, 242, apothecary stuff
Pouer, 172, power
Poverte, 172, poverty
Prisæ, 216, exactions
Prys, 264, price
Purchest, 172, acquired
Puttis, 172, puts
Pewder veschall, 244, pewter plates

Quha, 188, who
Quharfor, 172, wherefore
Quhether, 172, whether
Quhilkis, 190, which
Quhil, 271, till
Quhilk, 155, which

Quhit, 188, quit
Quhwite, 228, white
Qwhete, 264, wheat
Qwhilom, 260, formerly
Qwhylles, 258, while

Radness, 156, fear
Rainit, 256, rained
Realte, 262, royalty
Rechen, reach
Redyly, 172, readily
Remede, 265, help
Requer, 262, require
Renkkes, 258, knights
Reyflake, 188, robbery
Richt, 156, right
Rurd, 259, noise
Rychtwysely, 172, righteously
Rydand, 261, riding
Ryssyll brown, 244, fine cloth (?)

Sairly, 190, surely
Sal, 155, shall
Sall, 188, shall
Salute, 243, a coin
Samyn, 193, same
Sare, 264, sore
Sawfyd, 264, protected
Sawld, 264, sold
Say, 244, silk
Sayand, 172, saying
Schew, 262, show
Scheep, 190, sheep
Scheriff, 187, sheriff
Schorn, 190, cut
Scroschats, 243, sweetmeats
Seke, 172, sick
Serviatis, 244, table napkins
Sculis, 271, schools
Seyn, 261, seen
Shone, 190, shoes
Slachteris, 261, slaughters
Sons, 265, plenty
Spek, 193, speak
Stad, 265, placed
Stanche, 172, stop
Statut, 188, enacted
Sted, 228, stead
Stek, 242, piece
Sua, 172, so
Succar valans, 243, } sugar of different crystalisations.
Succar lacrissye, 243,
Succar candy, 243,
Suer, 155, swear
Suppowall, 262, support
Swenvel, 242, a kind of spice
Swilk, 190, such

Thai, 156, they
Takles, 258, garments
Takyn, 193, token
Tane, 188, taken
Tayntet, 188, proved
Tayssillis, 243, teazle

Techaris, 271, teachers
Tendys, 268, tithes
Than, 172, then
Thar, 187, there
Ther, thare, 258, where
Theyff, 190, thief
Thir, 219, these
Throu, 172, through
Thruch, 156, through
Thyft, 183, theft
Till, 204, to
Tod, 236, fox
Traist, 256, trust
Trowhe, 258, troth
Trussen, 258, pack
Trystors, 259, hunting stations
Twa, 190, two
Twapert, 181, two-thirds
Tyffen, 258, arrange
Tyn, 172, lose
Tynsall, 156, loss

UPLANDMAN, 184, a man dwelling out of burgh

VCHE, 258, each
Verray, 172, true
Veray, 172, true
Visnet, 193, *vicinage*, trial by jury
Vewters, 259, trackers

WALDE, 172, would
War, 172, were
Watz, 258, was
Weill, 256, well
Weren, 258, were
Wers, 182, *capitis æstimatio*, the prices at which every man was valued by the Saxon law
Whilk, 203, which
Wit, 262, know
Wites, 182, the king's fine for violation of the law
Withouten, 172, without
Withoutyn, 261, without
Wollys, 260, wools
Wranget, 262, wronged
Wrangwisly, 172, wrongfully
Wyrk, 264, work
Wyt (it is for to wyt), 172, be it known
Wyze, 258, goeth

YHE, 261, ye
Yhete, 172, yet
Yhour, 262, your
Yod, 259, went
Yowle, 256, howl
Yrn, 187, iron
Ys, 260, is

INDEX.

ABERDEEN...Its origin; situation; harbour and fisheries; Scotch Hanse towns mentioned in early charter, 164 ...A second charter granting burgesses new privileges, 165...William holds his court at, 120...Its burgh school; induction of a master in 1418, 271... John Vaus, rector of grammar school, 272...Customs, A.D. 1369, 238...Fine series of burgh records, 238...Magistrates in fourteenth century, 157.

Aberdeen Cathedral an example of "The Middle Pointed Style," 300 ... King's College contains beautiful "wood work," 306.

Aberdeen, Bishop of; a correspondent of Haliburton, 247.

Aberdeenshire...Ancient dwellings, 279... Famous for its castellated mansions, 318.

Aberdouer, in Buchan, 322.

Aberlemno, sculptured stones at, 286, 288.

Abernethy, a Culdee house founded at, in the fifth century, 108...Round tower, 290...David holds his court at, 120... Its grammar school, 271.

Aceard (a witness), 88.

Adam, a moneyer of Berwick; an artist of the reign of William the Lion, 308.

Adam, a moneyer of Edinburgh, 308.

Adam of the Hog, a serf, 141.

Adam, son of Earl Fergus (a witness), 324, 325.

Adelphius, bishop of Lincoln, at council of Arles, 46.

Admor, 333.

Adomnan on the use of glass cups among the Picts, 227.

Adomnan and Cumin, 98...Biographers of St. Columba, 107.

Adrian in Britain, 43.

Ædan consecrated bishop to the Northumbrians; founds Lindisfarne; conducts the education of twelve youths, 103... His daily life, 104...His good works and death, 105.

Aedmund the chamberlain at Scone, 201.

Ælfred, 56.

Aelfric, archbishop of York, 69...Homilies, 268, 331-333, 337.

Aelfric the steward (a witness), 88.

Aelfwyn (a witness), 88.

Ælred; characteristics of David I., 112, 115, 116; account of the battle of the Standard, 90-96.

Aeta, bishop of Lindisfarne, 105.

Æthelbert of Kent and his people converted; compiles the earliest code of English laws, 57.

Ætheling, or king's son, at times excluded from the succession, 51.

Æthelm, nephew of Aethelred, 66.

Æthelnoth, archbishop of Canterbury, Cnut's letter to, 69.

Æthelwold, nephew of Aethelred, 66.

Æthelstan, his investiture, 56.

Æthelred, 66.

Æthered, ealdorman, 66.

Aetius, consul, 47.

Agricola quoted, 82.

Agriculture, 145-7...Custom sanctioned by Alexander III., of depasturing in travelling, 146 ... Agriculture of monks; monks of Melrose improving their lands of Bele, 147...Revives in reign of James I., 315...Charlemagne's ordinance regarding, 328.

Ailred, see Ælred.

Air, Richard, an early Glasgow bookbinder, 336.

Airlie in Angus, ancient dwellings, 279.

Alan de Percy at the battle of the Standard, 93.

Alaric, king of the Visigoths; his compendium of Roman laws, 23.

Alcuin, 26.

Aldan the steward (a witness), 202.

Ale in use among the Picts, 227.

Ale, caves on the banks of river; ancient habitations, 278.

Alexander I. of Scotland marries a daughter of Henry I., 87...His magnificence, 228.

Alexander II.'s statute regarding ordeals, 188...Reign of, unexampled period of prosperity, 296 ... Architecture encouraged, 297.

Alexander III; household, 121...Income and household expenses, 122, 123...His wine account, 122, 233...Law regarding the tenth penny, 215...Deer park at Stirling, 125...Establishments for rearing horses; his death near King-

horn, 131...Commemorated in a ballad preserved in Wyntoun's chronicle, 263 ...Also by a sculptured stone cross, 286.
Alexander, prince, son of the preceding; dowry to his widow, 233.
Alfader, the creator and ruler, in the Norse mythology, 10.
Alfred, 62...Hero of the Anglo-Saxons; champion of Christianity; "the lawgiver," 62 ... Rebuilds towns; makes roads; reforms ship-building, 63 ... Restores religious houses; "friend of the poor," 64 ... His scholarship and promotion of learning; his translations into Saxon, 65...His death, 65, 66...His will, 66-67...An illustration of a deceased king's brother being elected in preference to his son, 51.
Algar the priest (a witness), 88.
Allan, 73.
Almonds imported, 237, 247, 331.
Al Motadhed, khalif, 311.
Alps, 7.
Altar, swearing upon, 183...Offerings, 131, 133.
Al-Thash, coin of, found in Orkney, 311.
Altonitz (Altonite), Cornelius, banker, 242, 245...Bank of, 247.
Alum, 237.
Alimanni, 22.
Alnwic, 93.
Alwin Fitz Arkil, the progenitor of the race of Lennox, 89.
Ancient dwellings, 276-279.
Ancona, march of, 5.
Anderson, Thomas, minister of Montrose, 341.
Anglia Sacra, quoted, 87, 228.
Angles, from the district of Angeln, 48... Occupy Northumberland, East Anglia, and Mercia, 49.
Anglo-Saxon institutions, 51-6...Missionaries, 61.
Anjou, 91.
Apollo's temple on the Thames, the site of the Abbey church of St. Peter of Westminster, 45.
Apparel, wearing, imports and price, 248.
Apples in Charlemagne's reign, 28...Names of varieties, 331.
Apse, circular, examples in the Norman parish churches of Leuchars and Dalmeny, 295.
Apulia, 91.
Aquinas, Thomas, on the Sentences in Glasgow Cathedral library, 338, 339.
Aquitaine, 91.
Aras cowerlats imported; their price in 1493, 244.
Arbroath abbey church, an example of "First Pointed" style, 297...Its western gable of Norman architecture, 295.
Arbroath burgh, 169.

Architects of the thirteenth century, names unknown, 298.
Architecture, 291-320 ... Moorish, 16 ... Dwellings of the Scotch aborigines, 312...Early fortifications, 281...Picts' houses, 282-3...Sculptured stones, 284 ..."Druidical circles," 284-6...Round towers, 290 ... No examples of secular architecture of the eleventh and twelfth centuries, 313...Examples of the thirteenth and fourteenth, 313-14 ... Norman or Romanesque, and its characteristics, 295-6..." Early English" or "First Pointed," 296 ... Its characteristics, 298 ... "Decorated," "Second," or "Middle Pointed," 299, 301...Its characteristics, 300...Peculiarities in Scotch architecture, 300-302...The "Perpendicular," etc., 301.
Architecture of our old burgh towns; the prevalence of the tall gables of the Flemings, 173.
Architectural societies during the twelfth and thirteenth centuries, 298...Bishop Jocelin institutes one to restore Glasgow Cathedral, 298.
Arian heresy, 18.
Aristophanes, 266.
Aristotle's books in Glasgow Cathedral library, 337, 339.
Arms; the price for cleaning king Alexander's during Norwegian invasion, 123.
Arnulph's death, 36.
Arrows, shield and lance, part of the furniture of a war car, 331.
Artisans employed by Charlemagne, 329.
Artishberka, the sacred hill of Woden, 15.
Arthur, king, 50...Share in the last struggle of his countrymen; his knights of the round table, 50...Brings an image of the Virgin to Wedale, 196.
Articles, Lords of the, mode of their election, 221-2.
Art, Scottish, 291.
Asaland, 8.
Asgard, 8.
Asser quoted, 55, 64.
Athelstane, 51 ... Coin of, discovered in Orkney, 311.
Athole, Duke of, chief of the Perthshire De Moravias, 127.
Atlas, ridge of, 16.
Atonement or compensation, laws of, from the king to the carl, 180.
Augustine, a missionary from Rome to England, A.D. 596, 17, 57...Endeavours to win over the bishops of the ancient British church, 60...His conferences; conditions; his denouncement and its consequences, 61...Oak, 60.
Augustin, Alexander III.'s tailor's purchases, 124.
Augustus, or *Basileus*, titles copied by the later Saxon kings, 51.

Aurlig, first Christian missionary to Iceland, 101.
Auxilium to Malcolm IV. to defray the marriage dowers of his daughters; do. to William to pay his debt to the king of England, 212.
Avenel, family of, 89, 128...They grant Eskdale to the monks of Melrose, reserving the right of game, 129... Roger's stud of horses in Eskdale, 131.
Avon Water, 159.
Awms of wine, 244.
Ayrshire, 128.
Ayr, customs, A.D. 1369, 238; MS. of old Scotch burghal laws, 80, 188, 236... William builds a castle there in 1197, and grants to the burgesses a charter, 166-7...Its nature, 158.

BAGDAD, plains of, 15.
Bak-berand, or hand-habend, thief caught in the act, 182.
Bakers, 329.
Balcrystin, 327.
Baldwin de la Mar (a witness), 207.
Ballads, 255.
Ballad literature, its prevalence among the people, 255...Ballad on king Alexander quoted by Wyntoun, 265...Semple's mentioned by Melville, 342.
Balliol, 89...Ingelram de, 210...And Bruce, competition between, 178...Parliament at Scone, 214.
Bamburgh castle, 103.
Banff, David's court at, 120.
Banffshire, sheriff of, tries a fugitive slave, 145.
Bangor, formerly a place of Druidical worship, 45.
Bankers, foreign, 245, 247.
Bankvar, 16 ells long, imported, 244.
Baptism a badge of slavery to the Saxons, 38...After the manner of Rome required of the British church, 60...Icelanders baptized in the hot springs, 102.
"Baptismal churches," 132.
Barbour, John, archdeacon of Aberdeen, 81 ..."The Bruce," 252, 259, 260, 261... "The Bruce," an early instance of the use of the vernacular, 265...His remarks on Border exploits; testimony to the universal use of ballad poetry among the people, 255...His reproof to John of Lorn, 256...His rank as a poet, 265.
Barcelona, municipal charter, 150.
Baron's court, 207.
"Barmekyn" of Echt in Mar, an ancient fort, 281.
Barrels hooped with iron, 331.
Barrows, 277.
Bartholomeus Pisanus, works of, in Glasgow Cathedral library, 338.

Battle, trial by, 185.. Wager of, 182... Burgesses of Inverness exempted from, by charter, 166
Bavarians, 8.
Beaver fur, 236.
Bede, referred to in Aelfric, 269...On the Germanic kings, 51...On the conversion of the West Saxons, 58...On the Caledonians, 82...On St. Ninian and Columba, 97, 106...On Ædan, 103... Mentions Roman towns, lighthouses, roads, and bridges, 45...Roman walls, 84...His book translated by Alfred, 66 ...Studies at Wearmouth and Durham, 64...Homilies on the gospels, in Glasgow Cathedral library, 337...History in do., 338, 339.
Bede, Pictish mormaer of Buchan, grants Aberdour to Columba, 322.
Beds, feather, imported in 1493; their price, 244...In use in Charlemagne's manors, 329.
Beer, 329, 330.
Bees, 327.
Bole lands improved by Melrose monks, 147.
Bellenden, John; his translation of Boece, 265...First classical Scotch prose, 266.
Bells in use, 227.
Benny Cassyn, the bank of, 245.
Benyn, Simon de, 157.
Ber or Bere, its price; an import in 1493, 245.
Bergen, 152.
Bernard, abbot of Clairvaux; epistles. See St. Bernard.
Berne MS. of Scotch laws, 80.
Bernicia, 102.
Berri, 242.
Berthynsak, ancient law of, 190.
Berwick, 140, 232...Its wealth, 233... Value of its customs, 233...Munificence of its merchants, 234...David's court at, 120...Burghal privileges, 159 ...Its ferme to the Crown, 161...Statutes of the gild in thirteenth century, 156.
Beverley church, frith-stol at, 195.
Bewmont, Dame Alice, 262.
Bible, illuminated, and a concordance, in Glasgow Cathedral library, 338.
Birchinside, 203, 206.
Bishops of ancient British church presided at the Gemot, 55...Augustine endeavours to win them to Rome; conference under an oak; Augustine's demands; the bishops refuse compliance, 60...Their fate, 61.
Blackhall a hunting residence of the Stuarts, 130.
"Black hut," 319.
Blacksmiths, 329, 330.
Blood, atonement or compensation for, 181.
Boars, wild, 123, 129.
Boats or coracles of leather, 227, 228.

Bocland or charter land, 54
Boece, Hector, 204, 265...Commends the rector of the grammar school of Aberdeen, 272.
Boetius on the consolation of philosophy, translated by Alfred, 65...A copy with a gloss of Nicholas Trivet in Glasgow Cathedral library, 338.
Bolgin, son of Torfin, 333.
Bonaventure's works in Glasgow Cathedral library, 337.
Bonaccio of Florence, a moneyer in the reign of Robert III., 309.
Bond, see serf.
Boniface of Devonshire, missionary to the Frisians, 18, 61 ... His catechism, 13 His letter to Ethelbald, 12. See Winfred.
Bonnet-laird, 140.
Bonnets imported, 247, 248.
Books, catalogue of, in the cathedral of Glasgow A.D. 1432, referred to, 270 ...Detailed list, 336...Chained books, 338...Preserved in the Culdee monastery of St. Serf, 269...Detailed list, 333 ...Imported in the fifteenth century; their nature and price, 249...In the vulgar tongue; Alfred's translations, 269...Rare and dear, in Scotland, 266.
Bookbinder, early, in Glasgow, Sir Richard Air, 336.
Boscho, William de, 210.
Bothwell castle, architecture of, 314.
Bowden barony, rents paid by tenants in thirteenth century, 139.
Bowglis, an import in 1493, cost per stek, 244.
Bow-staves, 128.
Boyc, Henry, book by, in Glasgow Cathedral library, 337.
Boyle family, 128.
Brabant, 7.
Braco, 337.
Bradwardin, archbishop; his book in Glasgow Cathedral library, 339.
Brasil imported, 237, 248.
Brass work duties, 237...Vessels, 329.
Breach of sanctuary, notice of, 195.
Brechin, round tower at, 290...A Culdee establishment in the thirteenth century, 110, 111...Castle, 314...Cathedral an example of First Pointed style, 297.
Bretagne, monuments of, 289. See Brittany.
Breviaries in Glasgow Cathedral, 336.
Brewers, 329...And breweries, 330.
Briau, 73.
Bridges, 330.
Bricius, bishop of Moray, 209.
Briggeham convention, 211.
Britain in Charlemagne's reign, 3...Elements of old British society under Roman rule; in Lowlands or east coast, primitive language preserved in the names of rivers and mountains, 41...On the west coast the case different; in Cornwall, called Bretland by the Norse, the British tongue spoken; in Isle of Man and Galloway until a later date, and at present in Wales and the Highlands, 42 ...Roman occupation; their forty-six military stations and twenty-eight cities; natives amalgamate, 43...Helplessness of the natives after the departure of the Romans, 47.
Brito (?) in Glasgow Cathedral library, 337.
Brittany, bards of, 50...Celtic inhabitants of, 22...Monuments, 289.
Brodick Castle, 314.
Brompton's chronicle, 90.
Bronze swords, 227.
Brooches, silver, found in Orkney, 311.
Bruce family, 89...Acquire Annandale from David, 127 ... Robert de, his speech at the battle of the Standard, 94...Assists David in obtaining his appanage, 87 ... Robert de, 211 ... Charter of David in favour of, 201... A witness, 206...Robert, 128, 315...His Parliament, 215...and Balliol, competition between, 178...Edward, crown settlement, 215.
Bruges, 152.
Brunswick, 152.
Buchan, mormaers of, 321, 325...Buchan, Wm., Earl of, 324...Buchan, Marjory, Countess of, 324...Earl Colban; Earl Fergus, 324.
Burgesses, Scotch, 173-4...In Parliament, 215...Their education and status, 174.
Burghal laws, 172.
Burghs, 152, 174....Regulations, 154... Their antiquity, 154...Usages of Newcastle in the time of Henry I., 154... Election of magistrates, 155 ... Berwick statutes of the Gild, 156...The electors, 156...Ayr, 158, 166-8...Berwick, 159...St. Andrews, 159....Edinburgh, 159...Rutherglen, 160...Perth, 161...Aberdeen, 164...Inverness, 165 ...Burgh union, 170...Union of, Edinburgh, Berwick, Roxburgh, and Stirling, make the Four Burgh Parliament ...After 1368, Lanark and Linlithgow were substituted for Berwick and Roxburgh, 170...Court of the Four Burghs, 171...Convention of Burghs, 171...Burgh Towns, their beauty, 172 ...Their sites, 173...Their architecture, 173...Their riches, 232...Churchmen's burghs; St. Andrews, Dunkeld, Dumblane, Rosmarkie, Dornoch, Arbroath, and Paisley, 168-169.
Burgher life, 239, 319...Parliaments, 170, 212...Share in national councils, 211.
Burgh haugh granted to the people of Inverness, 165.
Burgundians, 22, 23...Princes, 7.
Burgundy, the Lady of, 246.

Burleigh, see Cecil.
Burnett family, 318.

CADYHOW, David's court at, 120.
Caefi, the Pagan high-priest, destroys the altars of the gods, 58.
Caerlaverock, 314.
Calabria, 91.
Caledonians or Picts described by Bede; their possessions, 82.
Cambria, 54.
Cambuskenneth Abbey; its founder, 119 ...An example of "First Pointed" style in architecture, 297...Bruce's Parliament at, 215.
Camden, 80.
Camera, W. de, an alderman of Aberdeen, 157.
Candida Casa built by Ninian, 97.
Candlesticks imported; price in 1493, 244.
Caudyllaris "2 hingand" imported; their price, 244.
Canell (cinnamon), its price in 1493, 242.
Canmore, Malcolm. See Malcolm.
Canute, see Cnut.
Canvas, an import, 242.
Capet, Hugh, 38.
Capitulars of Charlemagne, 29, 327-331.
Caps imported, 247.
Cars, Charlemagne's, for war, 330.
Caracalla in Britain, 43.
Carberry, 144.
Carduilh and Cumberland, 201.
Carl, see Serf.
Carloman, 5, 6.
Carlovingians, 35, 38.
Carpenters, 329.
Carriages in thirteenth century; plaustrum, quadriga, charete, biga, 146... "King's wain," 124.
Carving of woodwork in churches, 306.
Castles of the king and the nobles, 312, 313.
Castle, Scotch, described; its domestic life, 315-16...Its improved architecture, 316.
Castle Fraser, 318.
Castle Lyon, or Castle Huntly, built by Lord Strathmore, 318.
Catalogue of books in monastery of St. Serf, 333...and in Glasgow Cathedral, 336.
Cat skins exported, 236.
Catechism for the new converts of the Thuringians and Saxons, from a MS. in the Vatican, 13.
Cathal, a Pict, 322.
Cathcart, 128.
Cecil, Lord Burleigh, 80.
Cedde, a pupil of Edan, bishop of Mercia, known in later days as St. Chad, 104.
Celtic races, 7...Speech, 85...Emigration, 277.
Chairs and stools of carved work, 305.
Chalices imported, 246, 247.

Chamberlain, office of, 121.
Chamlet doublet imported; its price, 248.
Chariots used in seventh and eighth centuries, 227...In thirteenth century, 146.
Charlemagne, 2, 4, 6, 10, 24-34, 115...Einhard's description; dress, manners, 25 ...Eloquence and scholarship, 26...Conquests, 33...Saxon war, 32...Love for strangers' society; builds palaces and fleets; his charity and veneration for the Christian faith, 27..His ordinances, 28...Law regarding the Pagans, 11... Domestic and court life in the eighth century; directions regarding the vintage, harvest, hay-making, and rural life generally, 28...Regarding Sunday observance, 29...Pastors, 30...Attachment to the Church of Rome; its champion; unity of the empire and the Church, 31...His creed, 32...Capitular de villis imperialibus, 327-331.
Charles the Fat, 36, 37.
Charles the Simple, 37, 39.
Charles Martel's victory at Tours, 5.
Charters; ancient, 200...Memoranda of grants to the abbey of Deir, etc., 321 ...Contain a few words of the vernacular, 254...The oldest by Duncan, 78, 79 ...Edgar's, 79...Alexander I.'s to Scone Abbey, 186...David's to St. Andrews, 111...To Kelso respecting the sanctuary at Lesmahago, 197...To Robert de Brus, 201..To Dunfermline, of a tithe of gold, 230...Malcolm IV.'s to Walter Fitzallan, his steward, 202...A second, 205...To Kelso; its beauty and portraits, 309-10...William the Lion's to Rutherglen, 160...To Perth, 162...To Aberdeen, 164 ... To Ayr, 166 ... To Seton family, 207...To Holyrood Abbey, 230...To Inverness, 165, 166... Charles I.'s to Glasgow, 170 ... Of Robert, bishop of St. Andrews. to the Priory of Lochleven, 269, 327... Waldev, earl of Dunbar's, of the estate of Dundas, 202...William de Obervill of Pittencrieff's to the monks of Dunfermline, 235...Spanish, named Fuero, 150...Of Winchester, 154.
Chase, 129.
Chaucer, 252, 265.
Chesnuts, 331.
Chester an Episcopal see, 54.
Chests, carved, 305 ... Charlemagne's "great chest" and "smaller boxes," 330.
"Child of Elle," 58.
Childeric, 5.
Chirtness, 333.
Choristers' education, 136.
Christianity in Britain, 57...Extinguished, in England, by Saxon conquest, 56 .. Preserved in Wales, Ireland, and Scotland, 57...Early history in Scotland, 97-113.

Chronicles, 79, 80... Fragment, dated circa 1165, in Cottonian Library, 79... Melrose, 79, 80...In Paris Library, 80.
Church, Christian; its power, 18-20... State alliance, 5...The great promoter of education, 267....Specimen of its lessons in the 11th century, 268...Its clergy, 131...Its courts, 189...Ancient Scottish, 97-112...Girth or sanctuary, 195... Vassals, their social position, 140...Terms of tenure, 141.
Churches, internal decoration, 303-4.
Churl, his rank and value, 53.
Cinnamon, see Canell.
Citizens of Edinburgh, their education, 174.
Clackmannan, William's court at, 120.
Clais Cornell, merchant in Bruges, 243.
Claret; its price in 1493, 242, 244, 245, 246.
Clarilaw cottages, 139.
Clava; "Druids' circles," 285.
Clement IV., constitutions of, 338; epistles, in Glasgow Cathedral library, 339.
Clergy, as one of the Estates, disappear at the Reformation, 223...Secular and regular, 132.
"Clenging by six hand," 184.
Clitherow, field of, 92.
Cloaks of variegated colours used, 227.
Cloth, 229...An export in 1493, 244...An import, 247... Scottis gray (*Pabyllis quhit*) sent to Zealand to be dyed; its cost, 248..."Ald seil," greit seal or new seal, 245.
Cloves, price in 1493, 242.
Clovis, his victory at Soissons, 22.
Cluniac monks introduced by the Stuarts; their monastery at Paisley, 293...A colony in Iona, A.D. 1214, 111, 293.
Cluny, Odo, abbot; his book in Glasgow Cathedral library, 339.
Cluny, lake of, famous for eels, 124.
Clyde, shores of, plundered by the Norsemen, 83.
Cnut, or Canute, 62...A type of a different race from the Saxon; acquires the crown by fraud and murder; his government and character, 67-69... Murder of his brother-in-law, Ulf Jarl, 68...His laws for the regulation and protection of the Church and the clergy; letter to his English subjects, 69-71...Prefers England to his Danish dominions, 69.
Cnut of Berwick chases the Jarl of Caithness, 232.
Cnut, Carl (a witness), 88.
Coal; sea coal in use; coal fields of Preston, and Tranent, and Pittencrief; their antiquity; coal works, earliest mention of; their importance, 235-6.
Cochrane family, 128.
"Cods," pillows imported; their value, 244.
Coins, earliest, 308-9...Athelstane's, found in Orkney, 311...Mancus, 66...Ores, 181...Obolus, 190...Ducats and salutis, ongers and grots; their value, 242, 243, 247...Marks, their value, 241, 213, 233...Oriental coin discovered in Orkney, 311...Guldens, 248.
Colban or Colben, mormaer of Buchan, 322, 323.
Colbrand-peth, 159.
Coldingham, almoner of, emancipates Stephen Fitz Waldev, a serf, with his following, 142...Redeems Patrick de Prendergest, who purchases the freedom of Renaldus, 142...Also Joseph, son of Elwald, and others, 143... Abbey church, an example of "First Pointed" architecture, 297...A portion of Norman architecture, 295.
College of Justice, 220.
College Kirk, Edinburgh, 302.
Colman, bishop of Lindisfarne, 105.
Cologne, 152.
Columba...His followers, 61...He settles in the island of Hii, or Iona, 97... His life and preaching; biographies by Adomnan and Cumin, 98... Obtains Iona from Conal, 99...And Aberdouer from the mormaer Bede, 332...Life in Iona, 99...His successors devote themselves to education, 100... They send missionaries to the mainland; to the Orkneys; Shetland; the Faroes and Iceland, 101...Oswald of Northumbria applies for a missionary, 102 ...The monk Corman is sent; he returns to the island; and Ædan takes his place as bishop on Lindisfarne, 103 ...After four centuries, a colony of Cluniac monks their successors in Iona, 292-3...Remains of early ecclesiastical buildings of his time, 290.
Colevil, Philip of (a witness), 206, 210.
Colevil, William de (a witness), 210.
Columkille, see Columba.
Committee of Articles, origin of, 218.
Communitas regni, 211.
Compota Camerariosum Scotiæ (the Chamberlain's accounts), 235.
Compensation for bloodshed, system of, 180-181.
Compurgators, number of, 183.
Comyne, Dame Marjory, 262.
Conal, king of Scots, grants Iona to Columba, 98.
Conrad, emperor, 36, 70.
Constantine, born at York, 43.
Constantinople, emperors of, 20.
Constantius Chlorus, 43.
Convention of burghs, 171.
Conventions, national, 211.
Convent life; an estimate of its good and evil, 133...Culture of the fine arts; architecture; painting and sculpture; inmates; Conventual establishments suited to the times, 136, 138...Rural population under the monks, 138-139 ...Learning in convents, 135...Con-

vents and rural vicars, disputes between, 133.
Conversions by conquest, 58.
Copper and silver challices, 247.
Coracles, 227.
Corby-stepped gables, 302.
Cordwain skins, 237.
Coricsceat (the first fruits of things sown), 71.
Corman, the Iona monk, disgusted with the Northumbrians, returns to the island, 103.
Corn, growing, 145, 330...Export duties on, 237...Not an import from 1493-1503, 249.
Cornwall, called Bretland, 42.
Cornwall, Devon, and Staffordshire, slavery in, 53.
"Corporations by prescription," 158.
Corstorphine parish church, an example of the "Decorated" period, 302.
Cospatric, see Dunbar.
Cottonian Library, 79.
Coucy, De, 125.
Councils, national, 210.
"Count of the Saxon shore," title of a Roman officer, 48.
County Courts, 55.
Court of the Four Burghs, 170-172.
Court of the kings of Scotland, a centre of intellectual cultivation, 252.
Court of Session or College of Justice, established by James V., 220.
Cows, 1000 compensation or value of the king; 16 of a villein, 181.
"Cowssings," a dozen imported, 244.
Crafts incorporated by Henry V., 131.
Craigievar Castle; its fine ceiling, 306.
Cramysse satin imported in 1493; its price, 244.
Crawford, Sir John; his transactions with Haliburton; his bull of dispensation from Rome; its cost, 242.
Crawfurd, Dean William, a correspondent of Haliburton; his travelling expenses, 243.
Crebarryn (Carberry), 144.
Crown Donald, a correspondent of Haliburton, 245.
Crown officers; Chancellor, Constable and Justiciar, Marischal, Great Chamberlain, 120.
Crown vassals, 207.
Culdees; claimed as protestants, 108... Culdee houses; Abernethy (translation of the Pictish see to St Andrews), 108 ... Dunkeld; Dumblane, 109...Brechin; Muthil; St. Servanus on Loch Leven; Monymusk, 110... Catalogue of the books in the library of St. Serf, 110, 333... Discipline of the Culdees in the reign of David I.; he tries to reform them; and finally supersedes them by monastic orders from France and England, 111...

David's charter concerning them, 111 ...Many of David's monasteries decayed houses of Culdees, 113.
Culross, 119.
Cumbria, 83.
Cumin family, 89...Marjory, Countess of Buchan, carries the earldom into, 334.
Cumin's, John, account as bailiff to Alexander, 125.
Cumin's life of St. Columba, 107.
Cummin duties, 237.
Custom duties, 122, 230, 236, 237, 238.
Cuthbert, a shepherd boy; brought up at Melrose; his ministry; Bishop of Lindisfarne; his body carried away by the monks; his canonization, 105. See St. Cuthbert's.
Cwichelm, king of the West Saxons, 58.
Cyning or king, 51.

DAMASK; its value in 1493, 242
Dalkeith Church; an example of the "Decorated" or "Flamboyant" period, 302.
Dalmeny parish church, example of late "Romanesque architecture;" its circular apse, 295.
Damian's, Peter, book in Glasgow Cathedral library, 337.
Dantzick, 152.
Danes and English, 70-71.
Darnaway Hall, timber roof, 306.
David I.; characteristics of, by Elred, 115-117...Portrait in the Kelso charter, 310...Brought up at the court of England, 87...Charter respecting the Culdees, 111...Founds six new bishoprics, 112... Many monasteries founded by David were restorations of decayed houses of the Culdees, 113...Laws regarding compurgation, 182-187... Code of burghal laws, 80, 154... Burghal charters, 158...His assize of twelve good men, 189... Statutes regarding trials by assize or jury, 189... Introduces a new aristocracy, 153... The founder of law in Scotland; habits of activity; continual change of residence, 119...His courts at Dunfermline, Stirling, Scone, Perth, Edinburgh, Berwick, Roxburgh, Traquair, Elbottle, Glasgow, Cadyhow, Strathirewin, Abernethy, and Banff, 119-120 ...Newcastle-upon-Tyne, a favourite residence, 90... Makes Rutherglen a burgh, 159...Gives the Bruces the Valley of Annandale, 127...Attention to the settlement of boundaries, 147... Charter to Kelso granting Lesmahago church as well with privilege of sanctuary, 197...Grants of freedoms from customs, 230-31... Plans for civilizing his people, 96...As earl of Huntingdon, 205, 209.
David, the marshal, 210

De Benyn, Simon, 157.
De Coucy, 125.
"Decorated style" of architecture, 301... Characteristics, 302.
Deer Park at Stirling, 125.
De Boscho, William, 210.
De Camera, William, an Aberdeen alderman, 157.
De Feschamp, Remi, 73.
De Gizors, Luke, king Alexander III.'s saddler, 122.
De Grenelaw, Roland, 210.
De Hamyl, Alexander's falconer, 123.
De Lindesay, David, 210.
De la Mar, Baldwin, 207.
De Lira, *see* Lira.
De Montealto, Edward, sheriff of Forfar, 123.
De Moravias, 127.
De Mortimer, 210.
De Morvill, 88...Hereditary high constable, 120...Hugh (a witness), 201...Richard (a witness), 203...Disposes of his serfs, 141...William (a witness), 201, 207.
De Mowbray, 210.
De Normanvil, 210.
De Perci, Alan (a witness), 201.
De Prendergest, 142.
De Sulis, 89...Ralph (a witness), 206... Randulph (a witness), 201.
De Sumervill, William (a witness), 201, 206.
De Suze, *see* Suze.
De Umphravills. 88...Gilbert, 203, 206.
De Vescis, 89...Eustace, 209.
Deir, Abbey of, charters and memoranda in ancient MS. of Gospels, 321-325.
Devonshire, slavery in, 53.
Diana's temple at London the site of St. Paul's, 45.
Dicson, William, an Aberdeen bailie, 157.
Dirleton Castle architecture, 314.
Dish towels, 329.
Dispensations from Rome, 242, 245, 246, 247.
Ditch and hedge, the earliest notice of, 126.
Dodin and Dodingston, 89.
Dogs, greyhounds, etc., of the monks, 131.
Domestic life in the Scotch castle. 316... Do. in Charlemagne's villas, 327-331.
Domnail, a Pict, 322.
Donald, usurper, 95.
Donead, son of MacBead, 322.
Donjon, Norman, 315.
Doomsday census of slaves, 53.
Doors with carved panels, 305.
Dornoch cathedral, an example of "First Pointed" style, 297...Burgh, 169.
Dornvyk, 28 ells, imported in 1493, 244.
Douglas, family of, *see* Bricius, bishop of Moray, 209...Their foundation of Lincluden, 301...Castle, 314.
Douglas, Archibald, lord of Galloway, 193.

Douglas, Gawain, 256, 265... His use of the vernacular, 275.
Drem, 265.
Doune, Bishop of, in Ireland, 209.
Dress and manners during the seventh and eighth centuries, 227-250.
Drinking cups, 227.
Drostan, son of Cosgrech, a disciple of Columba, 322.
Drostan, or "Drustan Fair," 323.
"Druids' circles," 284-5...Near Inverness, a rod of gold found in, 285.
Drummond, the family of, 127.
Dryburgh Abbey, some later portions examples of "First Pointed" style, 297.
Ducats, 243, 247.
Dumfries, a meeting place for the Galloway judges, 193.
Dunbars, descended from the Earls of Northumberland, 88.
Dunbar, Patrick (or Gospatrick), Earl of, 202, 203, 206, 210...Sells his stud of brood mares to the monks of Melrose, 131...Earl of, letter to the king of England, 8th February 1400, 262... Waldev grants a tribe of serfs to Kelso, 141. *See* Gospatrick.
Dunbar Castle, 314.
Dunbar, William, the "Droichis," 265.
Dunblane Cathedral, an example of "First Pointed" style, 297...Dependent upon the great Earls of Stratherne, 169... Burgh, 169...Fine stall carved work, 306.
Duncan, king, 95...Charter granted to the monks of St. Cuthbert's at Durham, 79.
Duncan, Earl (a witness), 206.
Dundas; charter by Waldev, granting it to Helias, son of Huctred, 202.
Dundee; customs, A.D. 1369, 238; fair of, 124.
Dundrennan Abbey, an example of "First Pointed" style, 297.
Dunegal, of Strath Nith, 201.
Dunfermline Abbey, 312...A ship yearly, custom free, granted by David, 230... Monks patrons of a school in Perth, 273...A favourite residence of David, 119...Had schools in Perth in reign of William the Lion, 185...Receives a grant of the tithe of gold from David I., 230...Register containing genealogies of the slaves, 142...Inquest concerning the liberties claimed by the Abbot's men, 143...Abbot Alexander declares by charter the freedom of several persons, 144...William's court at, 120... Nave of Norman architecture, 294... Its date, 295... Copied from Durham Cathedral, 296...Some later portions examples of "First Pointed," 297.
Dunfermline, Lord, Alexander Seton, 317.

Dunkeld founded by St. Columba, and refounded by the Culdees in the ninth century, 109, 111... Diocese, 132... Cathedral, an example of the "Middle Pointed" style, 301... Bishop of, at king's court, 209...Burgh, 169.
Dunrobin, examination of a Pict's house at, 283, 289.
Duns Scotus, his teaching at Oxford, 267 ... Treatise in Glasgow Cathedral library, 338, 339.
Dunstaffnage Castle, 314.
Durandus, works of, in Glasgow Cathedral library, 337, 338.
Durham, bishop of; his sentence upon Nicholas le Porter for violating church girth, 195; his fort at Tweedmouth, 232...Cathedral, a centre of intellectual cultivation, 252... Its nave of early Norman; the type of Dunfermline, 296...The Galilee, an example of later Norman, 296... Shire, 54 ... Reginald of; account of a village school, 270.
Duties of export and import, 237.
Dwellings of the Scotch peasantry, 319.
Dyers and fullers, 229.
Dye-stuff duties, 237.

EALDORMAN, the style of a chief of a great district, 51...His office and duties, 52, 55, 66.
Ealhswith, the wife of Æthelred, 66.
Earl, compensation for the slaughter of, 181.
Earnulf, 88.
Easter, 60 ... The Scotch clergy heretical regarding the time of celebration, 86.
Eborius, bishop of York, at Arles, 46.
Edda, 10.
Edgar, Duncan's brother, 88....Charters before 1106, 79.
Edgebucklin brae, 159.
Edinburgh; its site, 120...Castle, 58, 314... Parliament House timber roof, 306... "Edinburgh Principal," sheriffdom of, 160...Favourite royal residence of St. Margaret, 159...David, his dwelling on the rock; his garden; his grant to the citizens of a right to exclusive trade over a district extending from Colbrandspath to the water of Avon, 159...The customs paid in the middle of the fourteenth century; its ferme or rent, 161, 238...William's court at, 120...Education of citizens, 174.
Edmonston, Archibald; daughters; dispensations required from Rome, between them and the Lord Graham and the Laird of Montgomery's son, 245.
Edmund and Edmunston, 89.
Edmund Ironside, 86.
Education in the middle ages, 266.
Edulf and Edilston, 89.
Edward, son of Edmund Ironside, aids Malcolm, 86.

Edward the Confessor, 75, 86.
Edward's Welsh castles, 314.
Edwin of Northumbria; gives his daughter to be baptized; renounces his idols when he conquers Quichelm, 58... Bede's account of the conference with his people; Caeti, the heathen high priest, gives his opinion and destroys the altars and shrines of the gods, 58 ...His children and nobles baptised, 59.
Eels, 124.
Eggs and poultry, 328.
Eglintoun, house of, 128.
Eglinton and Winton, 207.
Eglisham, 205.
Einhard quoted, 10...Description of Charlemagne, 24-28.
Elbe, islands at the mouth of, inhabited by Saxons, 47.
Elbottle, David's court at, 120.
Elephant sent by Harun Al-raschid to Charlemagne, 33.
Elfin and Elphinston, 89.
Elgin customs, 238... Cathedral "Early English" or "First Pointed" style, 297 ...William's court at, 120.
Elphinston, John, dispensation required, 247.
Elphinstone, "Master Adam," 247.
English settlers in Scotland, 88, 89.
Engravers of church seals, 308.
Erlend, Jarl of the Orkneys, 232.
Ernald, Bishop of St. Andrews (a witness), 203, 206.
Erskine of Dun, John, introduces a teacher of Greek at Montrose, 278...Mentioned in Melville's Diary, 341.
Espec, Walter, speech at battle of the Standard, 91...At Carlisle, 95.
Espedare river, 131.
Essex, 54.
Estrahanent (Strathannan) granted to De Brus, 201.
Eta, daughter of Gillemichel, 322.
Etlyn, or Yetlin, 248.
Eudes' sons, Brian and Allan, 73.
Eustace de Vesci, 209.
Eustace Fitzjohn, Lord of Alnwic, 93.
Eustace of Newbigging, sells four serfs for fifteen shillings, 143.
Eva, wife of Colban, mormaer of Buchan, 322.
Exports from Scotland from 1493-1503, 241, 249.
Eyries of falcons and tercels, 129.

FAGGOTS, 324.
Falconer or De Halkerston, and others; knights performing feudal service for the Stewarts, 128.
Falconers, 329.
Falcons, 129...Of Alexander III., charges for, 123.
Falkland, 317.

Fallow deer, 125.
"Fang," "bak-berand," or "hand-habend;" law regarding the thief, 182.
Faroe islands, 101.
Faustinus the heretic, Augustine's treatise on, in Glasgow Cathedral library, 337.
Fereneze chace; the steward of Scotland's boundary, 286...Forest, 130.
Fergus, Earl (of Buchan), 324.
Ferine or rent paid by different burghs to the king, 121, 161.
Ferne Abbey Church an example of "First Pointed" style, 297.
Fernyhurst bank at Jedburgh, 126.
Ferrerius, the historian of Kinloss abbey, on the foundation of Deir, 323.
Ferthyngmann, 157.
Fertre, the shrine of relics, 195.
Feschamp, Remi de, bishop of Lincoln, 73.
Feudal institutions, growth of, 36.
Fife, Robert, earl of, 209...Melrose charter, 260.
Fife, gold found in, 230.
Figs, cost, duties on, 237, 245...Mentioned, 331.
Filberts, 331.
Finan, bishop of Lindisfarne, 105.
Findahin Mill, 333.
Fines and escheats of the king's court, 122.
Fingal (Fin Mac Coul), 256, 257.
Finlay, brother of Maolbride, 177.
Fire dogs, 329.
Firths of Forth, Moray, and Tay, 85.
Fish curing, 246.
Fish ponds, Charlemagne's, 327, 330, 331.
Fish used in Scotland in the thirteenth century; salmon, lamprey, sturgeon, herring, eels, 124...Duties on, 237.
Fitz-Alan family hereditary stewards, 89... Charter of Malcolm IV. granting Bircheuside and Leggardswode, 203... Second charter of Malcolm, 205... Their gifts to the monks of Paisley, 130. See Stewart.
Fitz-Arkle Alwin, 89.
Fitz-John, Eustace (a witness), 93, 201.
Fitz-Rauf, archbishop of Armagh; his book on the Armenians, in Glasgow Cathedral library, 337.
Fitz-Warin, Hervi (a witness), 201.
Flamboyant architecture, characteristics of, 301, 302.
Flanders, 7...Counts of, 37...Cloth imported, 247.
Flour required by Charlemagne, 331.
Folcland or public land, 54.
Folkright, 66.
Folpolt or Folpold, a moneyer of Perth, 308.
Forbes, name of, 318.
Fordun, John, his Scoti-Chronicon, 81, 108, 213.
Forest, Caledonian, 124.

Forest customs, 129-130...Charlemagne's laws, 327, 328, 330.
Forfar, 123.
Forfar castle, 314 ... Sheriff of, 123 ... Ancient demesne of the crown, 123... William's court at, 120.
Forres, sculptured monument at, 288... William's court at, 120.
Forrest, John, on the Sentences, in Glasgow Cathedral library, 339.
Forts, ancient, 280-84.
Fortrose cathedral an example of the "Middle Pointed" style, 300.
Fothrev gold mines, 230.
Fragmenta Collecta (in Acta Parl. Scot. vol. i.), 190.
Franks, their empire, 7, 21, 37.
Frankish royal ordinances, 9.
Franklin, 74.
Fraser castle and family, 318.
Fraser, Thomas, a witness, 210.
French language used at court, 252.
Frisland, 9.
Frisians make a settlement in Britain, 50 ...Sailors taken by Alfred to man his ships, 63.
Frith-stol or seat of peace; its violation, bot-leas, 195.
Fruit-trees grafted, 330, 331.
Fuero, or original charter of a Spanish community, 150.
Fullers, 229...And weavers excluded from the merchant guild of Perth by William's charter, 163.
Furs and wool, 229, 236.
Fustian, an import, 242.
Futfells (skins), 245.
Fyvie built by Lord Chancellor Seton, 317.

GAELIC, once the language of Scotland, from the Mull of Galloway to the Moray firth, 85.
Galleys built of oak, 227.
Gallo-Franks, kingdom of, 37.
Galloway, British or Logrian spoken in modern times, 42, 85...Celtic "customs" prevailing, 176...In possession of the Picts or Caledonians in the eighth century, 82...Church dues paid in David's reign, 132...Later, the only province in Scotland asserting peculiar customary laws; scarcely under the king's government in the reign of Malcolm Canmore, 192...William the Lion's code of laws for its government; the judges; their places of meeting; their decisions; continued to be governed under its own laws; rules for the "Mairs;" trial by jury not acquired in the reign of Robert Bruce; but process by purgation and acquittance (the laws of the Brets and Scots): as late as 1385 Archibald Douglas protests for the liberty of the

INDEX.   357

law of Galloway, 193...Judges enactments regarding trial by battle, 186.
Galwegians, atrocities of, 92...Claim the right to form the first line at the battle of the Standard, 92...Their flight, 96.
Galyga, its price, 242.
Gaudifer Delatyse, a hero of romance, 256.
Garden herbs, roots, and fruits, in Charlemagne's reign, 331.
Gardener of Alexander III. at the castle of Forfar, 124.
Gargano Mount, 70.
Garioch, "the Maiden Stone" in the, 288.
Gartnait, son of Cunnoc, father-in-law to Col an, 322.
Gascon claret imported in 1493, 244.
Gascony, a wine-merchant of, paid by Alexander III. by an assignation of the customs of Berwick, 233.
"Gaul son of Morni," 256.
Gaulish territory, 22.
Gauls, fate of, when brought into collision with Teutonic nations, 6.
Gavel-kind, 42.
Gemot, or county court, constitution of, 55.
German free cities, 150.
Gesiths or Thanes, 52.
Geta in Britain, 43.
Gilcongain, 177.
Gillemichel, 322.
Ginger, duties and price, 237, 242.
Girth or sanctuary, 183, 190, 195...Wedale, 196....Lesmahago, 197....Tyningham, 198...Inverlethan, 198.
Gizors, Luke de, 122.
Glammis, a royal demesne, 123...Castle, built by Lord Strathmore, 318....Iron rail, elegance of the design, 305...Its stucco roof, 306...sculptured stone at, 286.
Glasgow, a bishop's burgh, 169...Included in the privileges of Rutherglen, 160 ...David's court at, 120...William's charter granting the privilege of a market on Thursday; oppressed by Rutherglen; struggles against Renfrew and Dumbarton; represented in Parliament in 1576; emancipated at the Reformation; became a royal burgh in the reign of Charles I., 1636, 169...Its progress since the beginning of last century, 170...Bishops of, at king's court, 209...Bishop Herbert, a witness, 203, 209.. Its grammar school, 271...Cathedral burnt down in the reign of William the Lion; Bishop Jocelyn's society for its restoration, 298...An example of "First Pointed," 297...Its library in fifteenth century, 270.
Glass drinking-cups mentioned by Adomnan, 227...Stained, 304.
Glendale, 59.
Gloucester, slavery in, 53.
Gogmagog, 256.

Gold, signet, imported, 246...Mines near Dunfermline, 230.
Gold and silver artificers, 329.
Gordons, 318.
Gospatric, Earl, 206, 210, see Dunbar.
Gowmacmorn, 256.
Graham, and Archibald Edmonston's daughter; a dispensation sent for from Rome; its price, 245.
Grammar schools of Scotland, 272.
Grange, the chief house of each of the abbey baronies, 138, 139, 141.
Grave stone imported for the Duke of Ross, 246.
Grease duties, 237.
Greek as a part of Scotch education; its introduction, 273.
Grenclaw, Roland de (a witness), 210.
Gregory, Friar, on the Sentences, 359.
Gregory's injunction to Boniface regarding converts eating horse flesh, 11...Sends Augustine to the Anglo-Saxons, 57... His leniency to the Kentish Neophytes, 59...His pastoral letter translated by Alfred, 65...A copy in Glasgow Cathedral library, 359.
Grenton the scribe (a witness), 88.
Grilse, see Salmon.
Grots, auld, 243.
Groves, worship of, 4.
Gueldres, 7.
Guizot on the clergy, 19-20.
Gunner, the master, expenses at Ayr in 1264, 123.
Gyllecriste, a serf, 144.
Gyllemycael, a serf, 144.
Gylmahagu, a serf, 144.
Gyrth, see Girth.

Hadfeln, 47.
Haddington customs, 238; Burgher Parliament met at, 170; William's court at, 120.
Hadestanden, 202, 206.
Hailes, Lord, quoted, regarding Bruce and Balliol's competition, 178; his opinion regarding burgesses' presence in the great council, 212-213.
Halden and his brother serfs, 141.
Half Urechan, a pertinent to St. Serf, 333.
Haliburton, Andrew, conservator of privileges of the Scotch nation at Middleburgh; his ledger, 240....His correspondents and transactions, 241-250.
Hallam, Henry, on municipal administration, 152.
Hamburg and Lubeck League, 151.
Hamlet of the church, 139.
Hamyl, De, Wm., 123.
Hand-fasting, system of, 178.
Hand-habend, thief caught in the act, 182.
Hanse league, 152...In Scotland, 151, 170 ...Mentioned in the Aberdeen charter, 164...Hanse towns, 154.
Harald, 74.

Harold, the Norse Jarl, written to by William, 231.
Hart and hind, 129.
Hârûn-al Raschid, 33.
Hassenden estate, 128.
Hasting baptised, 39.
Hawks' nests to be protected, 328.
Hawthornden caves, early habitations, 278.
Hay meadows, 145.
Hays of Leys, an indenture of lease with the Abbot of Scone, 254.
Hebrew a branch of Scotch education, 273.
Hebrides, 82...Laid waste by the Danes, 110.
Hellias of Hadestanden (a witness), 202.
Hemming, a witness, 88.
Hemp, 330.
Hengist and Horsa, 48.
Henry I. of England marries Maud, Malcolm and Margaret's daughter, 87.
Henry V. of Germany first emancipates the German cities, 150.
Henry, David's son, at the battle of the Standard, 93...At court, 120.
Henry the Fowler, 36.
Heraldic devices on seals, 307.
Heraldry neglected, its uses, 302-3.
Herbert, bishop of Glasgow (a witness), 203.
Hereditary nobility, 53.
Hereford, 54.
Heretoga or army leader, 51.
Hermer (a witness), 88.
Herrings in western lochs, 124...Fishery off the Isle of May, 230.
Hexham frith-stol, 195.
Hides and tallow, 229...Dakers of hides exported, 246...Charlemagne's directions, 330.
Hii, Hy, see Iona.
Hildebrand, 72. See Gregory.
History, first authentic materials of, 2.
Holland, 7.
Holstein, 47.
Holyrood, 317...Its twenty-seven parish churches, 132...The abbot sends his men to the herring fishing off the Isle of May, 230-31...He imports a kynkyn of olives, and a corf of "apple-orangis," 248 ... The chapel has a single arch of Norman architecture, 295...Some later portions examples of "First Pointed," 297...The palace contains examples of stucco roofs, 306.
Holy water-pot imported, 248.
Honey and wax, 330.
Honorius, pope, gives the pall to Paulinus, first bishop of York, 59.
Homyl, James, 247.
Horologe sent abroad to be mended, 247.
Horses, price of, in 1500, 248...Attention bestowed on their breeding, 131 ... Charlemagne's directions, 329, 330.
Hortus olerum, 125.

Hosbernus, styled "Homo noster" by the Abbot of Kelso, 140.
Hose imported, 248.
Household of the king, 120...Expenditure, 122.
Household economy of Charlemagne, 329.
Hrolf the Ganger, see Rollo.
Hugh, a moneyer of Edinburgh, 308.
Hugh Capet, 38.
Hugo de Sancto Victore's book in Glasgow Cathedral library, 339.
Hundreds, division of, used by the Saxons, 50, 54, 63.
Hungary, 86.
Hunting expenses of the king, 123.
Huntingdon, no slaves in, 53...Maud of, 87. See David.
Huntly Castle, 318.
Husband and, value of, 139-140.
Husbandmen under the church, 139-141.
Hutchinson, Mrs. Lucy, 78.
Hy, see Iona.

Iceland, missionary sent from Iona to; the first Christian church in Eisinberg, dedicated to St. Columba; Aurlig, first missionary to, 101...Christianity established, A.D. 870; policy of the founders, 101...Many converts object to cold water baptism, 102.
Icolmkill, see Iona.
Iffley, parish church of, in Oxfordshire, an example of later Norman, 296.
Illuminated charters, 309.
Imports in 1493, 241-250.
Inchaffray abbey endowed by the Earl of Stratherne, 127.
Inchenan, 206.
Income of the Scotch king, 122.
Inchcolme abbey church, an example of "First Pointed," 297.
Indulfus, 83.
Innerwick, 128, 205.
Innocent IV., constitutions of, in Glasgow Cathedral library, 338.
Inverlethan church a sanctuary, 198.
Inverness, 165 ... Burghal history; charters of William the Lion; Exemptions granted and privileges conferred, 165-6 ... Customs, 238 ... Early shipbuilding, 234 ... William's court at, 120.
Iona or Icolumkill, 97-102, 107, 322...Laid waste by the Northmen, 110...Lost sight of for 400 years, when it appears as a seat of Cluniac monks, 111 ... Architectural remains, 292.
Ireland, Christianity preserved in, 57.
Iron : duties, 237 ... Imported, 237 ... Wrought in Moray in the thirteenth century, 230...Trial by hot iron, 186.
Ironmongery goods imported in 1493; their cost, 244.
Isidore, Bishop of Seville, on Etymologies, in Glasgow Cathedral library, 338.

INDEX.

Islesmen at battle of Standard, 93.
Ivar Huida slays the Jarl Ulf, 68.

JAMES III., IV., and V.; their love for architecture, 317
James VI.; improved dwellings in his reign, 317...Wish to have a parliament like that of France, 225.
Jedburgh, a residence of Alexander III. and his queen, 125...Church, Norman architecture, 295...Some later portions, examples of "First Pointed," 297.
"Jeddeworde," Osbert, abbot of (a witness), 203.
Jedworth meadows, 126.
Jewellers' work imported, 246...Silver and gold; its price, 247.
Joannis Arii scheda de Islandia cited, 101.
Joannes de Janna's glossary (?) in Glasgow Cathedral library, 336.
Jocelin of Furnes; his book in Glasgow Cathedral library, 340.
Jocelin, Bishop, rebuilds Glasgow Cathedral, circa A.D. 1190, 298.
John, king of England, 232... King William's debt to, 212.
John, abbot of Kelso (a witness), 203, 206.
John of Gragin (a witness), 202.
John, Pope, 70.
"Jove's beard," 28.
Judæa, sanctuaries of, 194.
Judicial combat, 182-5...Parties exempt from it, 184-5.
"Judicium Dei," 185.
Judices; Charlemagne's directions for their guidance, 327-31.
Jura Mountains, 7.
Jury trial; date of introduction unknown, 189.
Justinian's Institutes, in Glasgow Cathedral library, 337, 338.
Jutland, 8, 9...Jutes colonise Kent, 48.

KAIL, 125.
"Kain and conveth; prisæ et cariagia," 121.
Kedwel, king of Cumbria, 102.
Kells, duties on, 237.
Kelso Abbey; Earl Waldev's gift of a tribe of serfs, 1170, 141...Another benefactor, A.D. 1289, makes over lands in Gordun, with Adam of the Hog and all his following, 141...Has a road for its waggons to Berwick and Clydesdale, 146...Hosbernus, "our man," 140... Their granges, mills, hamlets, cottars, 138...Their tenants at Clarilaw farm steadings, 139...Rental of, in 1290, 138 ...Had twenty-seven parish churches, 132...Register quoted, 141...Malcolm IV.'s charter, 309.
Kelso, John, abbot of (a witness), 203, 206.
Kemble, John M., 209.
Kenneth MacAlpine, 82.

Kent, 54.
Kerkert lands, 205.
Kildrummy Castle, 314...Ancient dwellings near, 279.
Kilwinning Abbey church an example of "First Pointed," 297.
Kinghorn, Adam de, 210.
Kinghorn, William's court at, 120.
King, election, of, 6...Origin of, 51...Elective within the range of certain families among the Anglo-Saxons, 51...Of Scots valued at 1000 cows, 181...His court, 208 ... Its composition, 209... Household, 121...Country life, 125... Peace, 183, 192...Penalties for breaking, 197.
King's College, Aberdeen; beautiful carved work; its date, 306.
Kinloss, in Moray, contains a few arches of Romanesque work, 295...Mentioned, 323.
Knightly occupations; war and chase, 129.
Knights and vassals in the time of Alfred, 55.
Kirkwall, 295.

LAMPREY, 124.
Lanark, William's court at, 120.
Lanercost, chronicle of; description of Berwick, 233.
Landulphus on the "Sentences," 339.
Langdene, Witenagemot at, 66.
Language of the ancient Britons; traces of in the names of places, 41...Of old Scotland, 85, 251...Specimen of the oldest written vernacular of Scotland, 257-263... Morte Arthur, 258 ... Sir Gawain, 259...The Bruce, 259...Melrose charter, 260...Parliamentary Record, 261...Earl of Dunbar's letter, 1400, 262.
Lard, 330.
Lappenberg quoted, 67, 71.
Largo law, 289.
Largs, battle of; expenses for the national defences during the Norwegian invasion, 123.
Lathes, or districts of Kent, 49.
Laurel trees, 331.
Lavernans at battle of Standard, 93.
Law in Scotland; earliest common law, 175, 6...Celtic law; law of succession (Tanistry); introduction of laws of Saxon England, 179...Oldest written laws of Scotland, 180...System of compensation for crimes, 180...Ancient Scottish law terms, 181...Laws regarding theft and murder, 182...Law of evidence; compurgators for different ranks, laity and clergy, 183-4 ...Laws regarding wager of battle, 185 and 182...Of ordeal, 186, 187...Of sanctuary, 198 and 183.
Laws of Scotland, oldest collection of, 80, 81...Burgh laws, 80, 176...Laws of

marches, 80...Of the Br t and Scots, 184.
Lawson, Richard, imports "a little kist" of books, 249.
Lead duties, 237.
Learning in convents, 195.
Leases granted by the monasteries of Teviotdale, 117.
Leather boats used between Ireland and Orkney, 228
Ledger, antique, of Andrew Haliburton, 240-249.
Leek, the house, 28.
Lege Iswode, 205, 206.
Leges Burgorum, L.L.B., quoted, 172, 229.
Lennox family from Fitz-Arkle, 89.
Lent, conference regarding, 86.
Len ynwar (skins), 245.
Leising, 89...Lesing (a witness), 88.
Leo's, pope, sermons, in Glasgow Cathedral library, 337.
Leon, municipal charter, 150.
Lesmahago church a sanctuary, 197... Bounded by four crosses, 286.
Letters and state-papers in Charlemagne's reign, 2.
Leuchars parish church, Norman architecture of late Romanesque with apse, 296.
Leving and Livingston, 89.
Lewis "Druid circle," island of, 285.
Ligulf of Bamburgh (a witness), 88.
Lincluden, a fine specimen of Scotch "middle pointed," 301.
Lincoln, 54, 73...No slaves in, 53.
Lindisfarne founded by Ædan, 103-107.
Lindsays, the family of, 89.
Lindesay, David de, a baron of king William, 210.
Lindsay, Sir David, extract from, 256-7, 265...Address to his readers, 275.
Linen of foreign manufacture, 227...Duties, 237...Imported, 243.
Linlithgow, 314, 317...Church an example of the "Decorated" or "Flamboyant" period, 302...Customs, 238...Ferme paid to the king in 1331, 161...William's court at, 120.
Liolf, son of Macens, 207.
Lira, de, commentary on the Psalter, in Glasgow Cathedral library, 338.
Litters, 330.
Litsters, i.e., dyers and fullers, 229.
Living, abbot of Tavistock, afterwards Bishop of Crediton, 69.
Lint, 329, 330.
Lochinavehe, lands of, 205.
Lochindorb castle, 314.
Logrian or British tongue, 42.
Leggy chapel, 143.
Lombard, see Peter Lombard.
Lombardy, iron crown of, 33
London, 152...Rebuilt by Alfred, 63.
Longobardi, the rivals of the Franks, 17.

Lords of the Articles, 221...Their powers, 224.
Lords of Session; their number and places of meeting, 249.
Lorn, John of, 256.
Lothian, as part of Northumbria, 90... Men of, at Battle of Standard, 93.
Louis le Debonnaire, 35.
Lubeck and Hamburg league, 151.

Macalpine, Kenneth, 82.
MacBead, 322.
Macbeth, 177... Abundance during his reign, 118...Death, 86.
Macens, the original of the Maxwells, 89.
Macpherson, James; his translation of Ossian, 256.
M'Kenneth, Malcolm, the laws of, 203.
M'Pherson's edition of Wynton, 263.
Mactiern, the sons of the chief, embark with William of Normandy, 73.
Mace, its price in 1493, 242.
Macormi, a serf, 144.
Madden, Sir F., his edition of ancient romances, 259.
Madder or woad imported, 237.
Magon, the Clan, 322.
Magistrates, election of, Aberdeen, 157.
Magna Charta of John, 213.
Magnus, son of Earl Colben, a witness, 324, 325.
Mail of foreign manufacture from Flanders or Italy, 128.
Mails of the Burghs, 121.
Mainard, a Fleming, the first Provost of St. Andrews, 159.
Mairs of the province of Galloway, 193.
Malcolm, son of Maolbride, 177.
Malcolm, king Duncan's brother, 88.
Malcolm Canmore, 78, 85, 86, 95, 159, 179.
Malcolm IV., charter to Inverlethan, 198 ... His portrait illuminated in the Kelso charter, 310.
Malcolm M'Kenneth, the laws of, 203.
Malis, Earl, see Strathern.
Malkariston, John, shepherd of, 80.
Malmuren, a serf, 144.
Malt duties, 237.
Malvoisie wine, 241...Its price in 1493, 245.
Man, Isle of, British or Logrian spoken, 42 ...Scandinavian monuments in, 289.
Mancus, value 30 pence, 66.
Manufactures, early, 227-9.
Maolbride, the maormor, 177.
Maormors, 177...Of Buchan, 322, 5.
Marches, laws of the, 80.
Mar, Baldwin de la (a witness), 207.
Maiden stone in the Garioch, Aberdeenshire, 288.
Margaret, queen of Canmore, conference with the Scotch clergy regarding Easter, 86.
Markinche, 333.
Marks, 212, 213, 232, 233.

Marischal, office of, 121.
Marriage, feudal casualties, 122; law of, 178; hand fasting, 178-9.
Marsiliers, Peter de, teaches Greek in Montrose, 273.
Mart, killed at Martinmas, 124.
Mary of Gueldres; fate of her church, 302.
Maud, Queen, 87.
May, Isle of, a famous herring station, 230.
Mead, 330.
Meal, duties on, 237.
Measures, liquid and dry, 321.
Meat used in the thirteenth century in Scotland, 124.....At Martinmas the goodman killed his mart, 124.
Mediterranean, 7, 16.
Medlars, 225.
Meigle sculptured stone, 286, 287.
Melrose, a decayed Culdee establishment, restored by David, 113...Abbot purchases from Alexander II. the right of straighting a stream that bounded their lands of Bele, 147...Dispute with Earl of Dunbar, 209...Rules for the house of Home Cultram, 135 ... Abbey has twenty-seven parish churches, 132....Monks acquire the lands of Eskdale, also territories in Ayrshire, 129-130...Are not allowed to hunt except for wolves, 129...Purchase the Earl of Dunbar's brood mares, 131 ... Charter, specimen of early written Scotch, 260...Chronicle of, 79 ..An example of the "Middle Pointed." 300...William, Abbot of (a witness), 203; William's court at, 120.
Melville, James, nephew of Andrew Melville; his sketch of school life in the sixteenth century, 273, 340, 42.
Merlai, Roger de, 210
Merovingian kings, 5.
Merse, the, 128... Husbandland, 139 ... Several rural churches; the fragments of which are Norman architecture, 295.
Mertric fur, 236.
Mervyn, a serf, 144.
Meschines, Randulph (a witness), 201.
Metal work imported, 246.
Metrical romances, 257.
Middleburgh, 242.
Millet, 330
Mills belonging to the monasteries, 138.... Twelfth century, 333...In thirteenth century; water and windmills; handmills, 146...Charlemagne's mills, 330.
Milne, Andro, minister at Fedresso, 340.
Milne, Abbot, the historian of Dunkeld, 301.
Mines, 230, 235, 236.
Missals in Glasgow Cathedral, 336.
" Mold, the good queen," 87.
Molle lands granted to Fitzalan, 203.

Molle, Lady of, resigns to Kelso, lands to secure her son education, 135.
Monastic institutions, 133-147.
Monasteries; of Teviotdale, great extent of pasture land belonging to; monks' attention to farming, 147.....The patrons of a great number of the parish churches, 132.
Moneyers of Scotland, 308, 309.
Monopolies of the early burghs, 163.
Montealto, Edward de, 123.
Montgomery, family of, 128.....The laird's son and Archibald Edmonston's daughter send to Rome for a dispensation; its cost, 245.
Montrose customs, 288....Greek taught at, by Peter de Marsiliers, 273.
Monymusk in Mar, a Culdee house, 110.
Moors in Europe; civilization, 15.
Moravias, de, founders of the Athole family, 127.
Moray, Bricius, bishop of, 207...Province of, pays church dues in David's reign, 132.
Moraymen at battle of Standard, 94.
Moreville, Richard de, 203. See De Morvill.
Mormaers. See Maormors.
Mortancestry and novel diseisn, 189.
Mortar, a, imported, 248.
Morte Arthur, 257...Extract from, 258.
Mortimer, Robert de, 210.
Mote Hill of Scone, 204.
Moubray, Andro, a correspondent of Haliburton, 244.
Moubray de Philip, 210.
Mousa in Shetland, " Pict's House" in, 282.
Mulberries, 325...Mulberry wine, 330.
Municipal institutions, 148-174.
Munth, the, 164.
Murray, Regent's death, noted in Melville, 342.
Mute or Mote Hill of Scone, 204.
Muthil, a Culdee establishment, 110.
Mutrene, 205.

NAIRN, William's court at, 120.
National councils, 210.
Nativus or Neyf, the legal name for the villein or serf, 141.
Newbigging, Eustace of, sells William of Newburgh, his wife, and children, to Prior of Coldingham, 143.
Newburgh, William of, 90, 232.
Newcastle burgh; usages of the reign of Henry I ; connection between Scotland and Northumberland, 154.
Newcastle-on-Tyne, David's favourite residence, 90.
Nimroud and Nineveh, 277.
Ninian, a missionary to the southern Picts in the fifth or sixth century; founds the see of Whithern, 97.
Nobility, hereditary, 53.
Non-entry; among feudal casualties, 122.

Norfolk, 54.
Normans in England, 72-76...System of vassalage and feudal tenures, 40... Architecture, 293.
Normanvill, Hugh de, 210.
Norsemen settled in France have some scruples about baptism, 39.
Northmen, Danes, or Vikingr, the terror of every coast in Europe, 9, 38, 110.
Northumbria, kingdom of, 49...Its extent, 82, 251.
Northumberland, Margaret of, 87.
Norway, maiden of, 211 ... Norwegians, 101.
Nottingham, slavery in, 54.
Notmogis (nutmegs), their price, 242.
Novogorod, 152.
Nuts, 330.

OAK, Augustine's, 60.
Oath of fealty used by the Saxons, 56.
Oatmeal, 123.
Oberwill, William de, of Pittencrieff; coal works, 235.
Obolus, a coin, 190.
Odilo and Tassilo, dukes of the Sclaves and Wends, 8.
Odin, 4...And Thor worshipped by the Saxons after they took possession of England, 57...Sons of, from Scandinavia, Jutland, and Saxony, 8.
Odo, abbot of Cluny, in Glasgow Cathedral library, 339.
Officers of the state, 224.
Oget-theyrn, value of, 181.
Ogga (a witness), 88.
Ohthere, an early traveller to the north of Europe, 66.
Oil duties, 237.
Olifard, David (a witness), 206.
Oggu, 89.
Onger, a coin, 243.
Ordeal, trial by fire and water, 186 ... Not known when abolished, 189... Falls into disrepute when law came into operation, 187.
Ores, a coin, value sixteen pence ; 3000 value of the king, 181.
Orkney islands; ancient dwellings, 279... "Druids' circles," 284-286...In possession of the Picts in eighth century, 82...Rent paid in wadmail, 229... Silver hoard discovered in 1857, 311.
Orm, John, son of (a witness), 202 ...And Ormiston, 89.
Orosius' History of the World translated by Alfred, 66...Quoted, 23.
Osbern, the priest (a witness), 88.
Osbert, abbot of Jeddeworde (a witness), 203.
Ossianic poetry, 255.
Ostrogoths' territory, 22.
Osulf, 89.
Oswald of Northumbria finds refuge at the court of the Scotch king, and is converted; the monks of Iona send a missionary, 102.
Oter (a witness), 88.
Ovid one of the books in Cathedral church of Glasgow in 1432, 270, 337.
Oxen, directions regarding, 322.
Oxford, evidence unsatisfactory as to its foundation by Alfred, 65... Its popularity in the fourteenth century, 273...Number of students, 267...Attended by crowds of Scotchmen, 274 ...Unpopularity of the northerns at the University; its causes, 274...The anti-pope, 274.
Oxfordshire, 54...Roman villa in, 44.

PAINTING, 291.
Paintings in illuminated charters, 310.
Paisley, Cluniac monks first planted at, 293 ...Abbey has thirty parish churches, 132...Chartulary, 130...Church an example of First Pointed style, 297... Burgh, 169.
"Pall," the; Cnut's displeasure at the Pope regarding its price, 70...Paulinus receives it, 59.
Palladius, the first missionary to Scotland, 97.
Pandects, in Glasgow Cathedral library, 337, 338.
Panic, 330.
Pannels, carved, in churches, 306.
Papas or patres, 19...Papæ, a name given by the Norsemen to the Iona missionaries, 101.
Paris, Mathew, cited, 234.
Paris Royal Library contains a few fragments of Scotch chronicles of the thirteenth century, 80.
Parishes, early, of Scotland arising from the settlement of the first Christian missionaries, 108...Division made in the reign of David, 132.
Parliament, or national assembly, 55... Committees of, 217...When the term was first used, 213...Earliest, 1266, 213...Earliest Scotch, 214...Defects of, 214...Of Bruce, 215...Of Scotland, constitution of, 224...At Scone; do. at Perth, 217.
Parliamentary usages, origin of, 199... Record of 1397 a specimen of Scottish language, 261.
Partridges, 328.
Pasque presents, etc., 133.
Passeleth, lands of, 205.
Patrick, son of Gospatrick. See Dunbar.
Patronage of the parish churches conferred gradually upon the great monasteries, 132.
Paulinus, the first Saxon bishop of York, converts Edwin, 58...Employed for 36 days in the river Glen baptizing the converts; receives the pall from Honorius, 59.

INDEX.   363

Peace of the king, 183, 191, 192...Of an earl, 192.
Peaches, 331.
Peafowl, 328.
Pear trees, 331.
Pearls, Scotch, much celebrated, 228.
Peasantry, 319.
Peats, 140...Peat-mosses, 330.
Peltry or Peloure, 286.
Penalties of theft and slaughter, 190-191.
Pepin, 5, 6...Bestows on the Roman see Romagna and Ancona, 5...Death, 21.
Pepper, its price in 1493, 242.
Percy, Alan de, 93...(A witness), 201.
"Perpendicular" style of architecture, 301.
Perry, 329.
Perth; its situation; fishings; great antiquity; commencement of its trading privileges dating from David I., 161...Earliest burgh charter preserved, one of William the Lion's; no tavern allowed in the sheriffdom of Perth, except where the lord of the place lives, and then only one, 162-163...Customs, 238...A residence of David, 120...Burgh school, 270, 271 ...Grammar school. Andrew Simson a teacher in, in the sixteenth century; number of pupils, 273.
Pertz, Monumenta Germaniæ historica, 14, 32, 331.
Peter of Pisa, 26.
Peter of Torento on the "Sentences," in Glasgow Cathedral library, 340.
Peter, friar, on the "Sentences," in Glasgow Cathedral library, 337.
Peter Lombard's Sentences, in Glasgow Cathedral library, 339.
Petrarca Francesco, De Remediis, in Glasgow Cathedral library, 337.
Petrie's round towers of Ireland, 290.
Pettincrieff coal works, 235.
Pewtar "veschalls," with three chargeours, imported in 1493; their price, 244.
Pheasants, 328.
Pictish mormaers of Buchan, 321-325.
Picts, described by Bede; their possessions, 82 ... Southern, converted by St. Ninian, 97.
"Picts' Houses," 282-3.
Pigeons, 328.
Pines, 331.
Pine forests in the Highlands, 234.
Pinkie House built in the reign of James VI., by Lord Chancellor Seton, 317.
Plein Cour of king William at Selkirk, and persons present, 209-10.
Plate imported; its cost, 248.
Plough, ancient Scotch, 139.
Plough-alms, 71.
Plum trees, 331.
Pluscardine, an example of "First Pointed" style, 297.
Poetry, early, 255.
Polloc, lands of, 205.

Portenmoch, a pertinent to St. Serf's, 333.
Poictiers, 5.
Pots and pans imported, 249.
Potyngary, 242.
Poultry, Charlemagne's, 327, 330.
Poysley, Mr. John's, book on the quodlibets, in Glasgow Cathedral library, 337.
Prayer to Woden by the Saxon army, 15.
Prebenda, Hugh de, 210.
Prendergest, Patrick de, purchases the freedom of Renaldus, a slave and alderman of Berwick, 142...Adam de, 142.
Preston and Tranent coalfields, 235.
"Probi homines," 208.
Processionaria in Glasgow Cathedral, 336.
Procopius on human sacrifices, 11.
Proof by witnesses gradually admitted, 189.
Pulse, 330.

QUEEN, or wife, Anglo-Saxon, 52.
Quinces, 331.

RACES, struggle of, 148.
Radbod; a Frisian chief's reason for "dying unbaptised," 82.
Raisins; their cost per cop, 237, 245.
Ralf, bishop of Doune in Ireland, 209.
Rape lands, 324.
Rauf, see Fitz.
Raul, a moneyer of Roxburgh, 308.
Red hand, law regarding the murderer taken, 182.
Redemption for "thyft," 188.
Reginald of Durham's description of a village school in Norham, 270.
Register of Dunfermline, 143, 144.
Register of Kelso quoted, 141.
Relief, among feudal casualties, 122.
Religion of the Northern and Eastern Teutons known from Frankish royal ordinances, 9.
Remi de Feschamp, Bishop of Lincoln, 73.
Renaldus, a slave redeemed, 142.
Rental of Kelso Abbey, 138.
Representation in the Parliament of Scotland, 211...Of small freeholders; system of, 223.
Restennot, an example of "First Pointed" style, 297.
Restitutus, bishop of London, at council of Arles, 46.
Revenue, sources of, 212.
Rhind, Rob, a correspondent of Haliburton, 213.
Rhine, the, 7.
Rice imported, 247...Price of, in 1493, 243.
Richard, Friar, on Aristotle, in Glasgow Cathedral library, 337.
Richard II. of England to the Chancellor of Oxford regarding Scotch students, 274.
Rickman, quoted, 297.
Ridel Jordan at Rokesburgh, 203.

Riddell, Hugh (a witness), 206.
Right of way frequently purchased, 146.
Roads in 13th century; green-road; highway; the king's road; caulsey, 146.
Robert I., parliaments of, 215...Law MS. of his reign, 81.
Robert II., parliaments of, 218.
Robert de Londin, natural son of king William the Lion, 210.
Robert of Brunne cited, 87.
Robert of St. Michael (a witness), 202.
Robert, son of David, an Aberdeen bailie, 157.
Roe, hart and hind, 129.
Roland, 128.
Rollo or Hrolf the Ganger's speech to envoys of French king, 38...Consents to become a vassal of French king; is baptized; and becomes Duke of Normandy, 39...Romance of "Rollo," 40.
Romagna, provinces of, 5.
Roman cities in Germany in the reign of Charlemagne; their effect upon the rude settlers of the open country; Romanised Gauls live with the Burgundians and Visigoths as brothers, 23 ...In the sixth century Alaric collected a body of Roman law, shewing the influence of Roman manners, long after the downfall of Roman power, 23 ...Romans in Britain had 46 military stations, and 28 cities, 42...Military force required for the colony; the head quarters of the sixth legion at York for 300 years, 43...Introduce Christianity, 45...Three British bishops, York, London, Lincoln, attend the Council of Arles, A.D. 314; and the same number, that of Ariminum, A.D., 359, 46 ...Colonization, defects of, 46 ... Leave Britain, A.D. 416, 47...Villas in Britain, 43.
Romances, metrical, 257.
Rome, Christian, made her existence felt, by sending her missionaries to the most distant and dangerous fields, 17.
Roofs of timber, 305...Of stucco, 306.
Ross, duke of, his account with Haliburton 243...His exports of salmon, 243... Second account, 245.
Rosmarkie burgh, 169.
Rothesay, duke of; complaint against him by the earl of Dunbar, 262.
Round towers at Brechin and Abernethy, 290...Of Ireland, 290.
Roxburgh; its burgh school, 270, 271... The munificence of its merchants, 234 ...William's court at; David's court at, 120...Burgh, fate of, 234.. Castle, 207, 314.
Roxburghe, duke of, 139.
Royal household, 121...Progresses, 119.
Rudolf, king, 70.
Runic inscription on a stone at the manse of Ruthwell, 289.

Rutherglen made a royal burgh by David; includes Glasgow; oldest charter one of William the Lion; its terms, 160... The rent paid to the Crown, 161... William's court at, 120.
Ruthwell, sculptured stone at, 289.
Ruthvens descended from Swain and Thor, 89.
Rutland, no slaves registered in, 53.
Ryssill. 245...Brown, imported; its price per ell, 244.

SABLE fur, 236.
Sacrifices, human, 11.
Saddlery of Alexander III., 122.
Saddlers, Charlemagne's, 330.
Saffron, its price in 1493, 242.
Sagas, 10.
St. Andrews, 132...Culdee establishment, 111...First foundation, 109...Bishop John erects a burgh at his see; Mainard first provost, 159...Bishop Robert grants to the priory, with the island abbey of Lochleven, the sixteen books belonging to the Culdees, 270... Particulars of the grant, 333...Church of, receives an estate from Alexander I., and with it an Arab horse, 228... Archdeacon of, a correspondent of Haliburton, 246...Cathedral of, some portions, examples of "First Pointed," 297...Choir of the Cathedral, Norman architecture, date, 295...Customs, 238, ...William's court at, 120... Ernald, bishop of (a witness), 203, 206; records, 263.
St. Augustine referred to in Aelfric's homilies, 269...His "City of God," 26... Works in Glasgow Cathedral library, 337, 339.
St. Bernard's "Sentences" in the Culdee house of St. Serf, 333...Sermons, "Epistles," in Glasgow Cathedral library, 337, 338.
St. Chad, 104.
St. Clair Henry buys serfs from Richard de Morvil, 142.
St. Columba, see Columba.
St. Cuthbert's Church at Edinburgh, 159.
St. Duthac's, Tain, an example of the Decorated or Flamboyant period, 302.
"St. Drostan's Day," 323.
St. Gregory referred to in Aelfric, 269... His pastoral, 339. See Gregory.
St Jerome on the Creed in Glasgow Cathedral library, 337 ... Referred to in Aelfric, 269.
St. Kentigern, 112...Life of, in Glasgow Cathedral, 336.
St. Machutus, 107...His church at Lesmahago a sanctuary, 286.
St. Magnus' Church, Kirkwall, Norman architecture; its date, 295.
St. Margaret at Edinburgh, 86, 159...Her

chapel in the castle of; Norman architecture, 295.
St. Ninian's Church at Whithorn, its age, 292.
St. Omers, monastery at, 5.
St. Paul's Cathedral, London, on the site of Diana's temple, 45.
St. Paul's epistles to Seneca in Glasgow Cathedral library, 339.
St. Peter's Church, Westminster, 45.
St. Prosper's text of the gospels, in Culdee, Library of St. Serf, 334.
"St. Peter's penny," 71, 311.
St. Pol and Blois, Earl of; ship building at Inverness, 234.
St. Rule's tower, Norman, its date, 295, 312.
St. Serf, or Servanus, 119...The little library of the Culdees at, in the twelfth century, 110, 269...Detailed list, 333... David's gift of the island to the canons of St. Andrews, 111...A life of, in Glasgow Cathedral library, 336.
St Thomas, *see* Aquinas.
St. Vigean's church in Angus, sculptured stone at, 288.
Salaries of the royal household, 121.
Sallust, copy in the library of Glasgow Cathedral, 270, 337.
Salmon, 124...An export, 243, 246, 247.
Salt, 123, 249...Duties, 237.
Sanctuary, law of, 190-198...Breach of, instance where the bishop of Durham causes Nicholas le Porter to do penance, 195.
Sanctuaries, 194...Lesmahago, 197, 286... Wedale, 196...Tyningham, 198...In English churches; "the stone seat beside the altar," still existing at Beverley and Hexham, 195.
Sanders of Lawder, 248.
"Sang school," or choral school, 136.
Satin, its value, 242...Cramyssit; its price, 244.
Saxnot, a Thuringian divinity, 14.
Saxons, 8...Their ideas of another state of being; eating horse-flesh, 10. Gregory enjoins Boniface to repress it; Christian converts sell slaves to their pagan brethren for sacrifice, 11..In the second century, inhabit islands at the mouth of the Elbe, 47...Occupy the south of Roman Britain, 50...Their favourite weapon the *saex*, or long knife, 9... Slaves under them, 53...Their religious and superstition; their virtues, 10, 12.
Saxon and Danish names, 88.
Saxon language of south and west England, 251.
Say imported, 244, 247.
Scandinavia, 8.
Scherar, John, an Aberdeen bailie, 157.
Scholar, the profession of, 274.
Schools in Scotland, in thirteenth century, 135...Schools for singing, 136...Kelso Abbey had schools in Roxburgh in reign of William the Lion; Lady of Molle's gift to secure the education of her son, 135...Burgh and convent, 270 ...Grammar, 272...Act of Parliament of 1496, requiring barons and others to put their eldest sons to schools, 271.
School life depicted in James Melville's diary, 340-342.
Schroschatis, price in 1493, 243.
Sclaves, Wends, and Bavarians, enemies of the Franks and Christianity, 8.
Scone; its beauty, 120...Abbey of, early charter granted by Alexander I, confers jurisdiction of trial by fire and water, 186... Abbey possessions in Caithness, 231...Abbot of, lease to the Hays of Leys, 254, 329.
Sconin mill, 333.
Scotch Christians as missionaries to north of England, 61...History, beginning of, 3...Language, 251-253.
Scots came from Ireland in fourth century, 82...Settle on the west coast and north of Firth of Clyde; join with Caledonians in ninth century, 82 ...At battle of Standard, 91.
Scott, Sir W, "Monkbarns and Sir Arthur," 84.
Screens, carved, in cathedrals, 306.
S. Crucis (register of Holyrood), cited, 230.
Sculptured monuments, 286-289.
Sea kings, 52...Or Norsemen, settle in Scotland in ninth century, 82.
Seals, ancient, seal engravers, 307.
Seal; the royal larder sometimes possessed "a side of seal," 125.
Selkirk, William's court at, 120.
Seat covers, 329.
Semple, Robert, ballads, 342.
Serfdom, 141-145.
Serfs made over and sold to the church, and to private individuals, 141-142... "Stud book," or genealogies of the stock of serfs in the Register of Dunfermline, mostly of Celtic nomenclature, 142...Earl Waldev of Dunbar, in a deed of 4 lines, makes over a whole tribe to the Abbot of Kelso, A.D. 1170, 141... The lowest class in Saxon society; their numbers greatest where the British population maintained itself longest, 53-4... Redeemed by Ædan, 105...The lowest of the inhabitants of the Grange, 141...Transferred with the land, 141... Legal name, nativus or neyf, 141...Price of serfs in thirteenth century, 142-143...Their emancipation by the church, 143...The latest case of slavery reported, 145.
Servants' wages, Alexander III.'s, 122.
Service trees, 331.
Service, feudal, of the roll les, 128.
Services, predial, commuted for money, 140.

Session, Lords of, 219.
Seton, Alex., Lord Dunfermline, builds Pinkie, etc., 317.
Severus, 43.
Shakspeare, 265.
Sheep, a man not to be hanged for less than the price of two, 190...shearing, 140.
Sheriff, presiding officer of the Gemot, 55.
Shetland islands, 82, 101...Rent paid in wadmail, 229...Picts' houses, 282.
Shield makers, 323-324.
Shingles, 330.
Shipbuilding, 234.
Shipping carried on by the great religious houses, 231...Employed in the reign of James IV., 249, 250.
Ships, "watchers" of king's (Alex. III.) in 1264, for 23 weeks, 123...Names of merchant vessels; "Cowasch," "Douglas," 242..." Eagle," a trader between Scotland and Flanders, 211..."The Julyan," a trader, 244.
Shires of England, formed from the Anglo-Saxon kingdoms and Episcopal sees, 54...And hundreds, 63.
Shoemakers, 329, 330.
Sicily, 91.
Silk imported; its price, 246.
Silver mines in Cumberland, of David I., 230...Hoard found in Orkney, 311.
Sinaar, plains of, 15.
Sir Gawain, 257...And the Green Knight, extract from, 260.
"Sir Mordrede," 257.
Siward, Earl of Northumberland, 86.
Skene, Sir John, on the authenticity of the laws of Malcolm M'Kenneth, 204.
Skins exported, 244, 245; value, 242.
Slave names, 144
Slaves, see Serfs.
Slavery in England, 53, 54.
"Squire Meldrum," 256.
Smollet, John, a correspondent of Halyburton; imports woad, 248.
Soap and soap-makers in Charlemagne's manors, 329, 330.
Soap an import, 243.
Soissons Parliament, 5.
Somervills, 89, 201.
Somme, 7.
"Son of the nation," cyning or king, 51.
Spain; the first country in modern Europe, where municipal institutions were revived, 150.
Spalding Club publications, 239.
Spices imported, 247.
Staffordshire, slavery in, 53.
Stained glass; its scarcity in Scotland, 304.
Stair, Lord, cited, 203.
Stalls, carved, in cathedrals, 306.
Standard, battle of the, 90.
State papers, earliest, 2.
Statutes of Council of Tours, in Glasgow Cathedral library, 337.
Statutes of the gild of Berwick, 156, 157.

Statutes of Alexander II., quoted, 188.
Steintun, 206.
Stennes in Orkney; "the standing stones," 281.
Steward, high, hereditary, 89, 210, 211.
Stewart charters, 202-205...Family holds the office of great steward, 120...Had from David all the barony of Renfrew, 127...Their other possessions, 128.
Stirling castle, 314, 317...David's residence there, 119...William's court at, 120...Its burgh school, 270...Customs, 238...Sheriff of, 125.
Stow, formerly Wedale, 196.
Strathannan granted to Robert Bruce, 201.
Strathclyde, 83.
Strath-Irewin, David's court at, 120.
Stratherne, earldom of, the only palatinate in Scotland, 126, 209...Earl Malis endows Inchaffray, 127...At battle of Standard, 93.
Strathmore, earl of, as architect, 317... Builds Castle Huntly and Glammis, 318.
Strathmore, sculptured stones in, 286... Valley of, the haunt of the wild boar, 124.
Strath Nith, 201.
Stucco, its use for roofs; the mouldings formed by the hand, 306.
Sturgeon, 124.
Subterranean abodes, 279.
Succar candy; "lacrissye;" "valans:" price in 1493, 243.
Suetonius, 26.
Suffolk, 54.
Sulis, Ralph (a witness), 206.
Sumervil, William of (a witness), 201, 206.
Surrey, 54.
Suttee among the Wends and Sclaves, 13.
Suze de Henri. cardinal bishop of Ostia; treatise on Decretals, in Glasgow Cathedral library, 338.
Swans, 328.
Swain and Thor, ancestors of the Ruthvens, 89.
Sweetheart abbey church, an example of "First Pointed" style, 297.
Swein, son of Ulfkill (a witness), 88.
Swenvel, its price in 1493, 242.
Swine; Charlemagne's directions regarding, 328.
Syr Gawayn and the Green Knight, the romance of, 257.

Table linens, 322.
Tacitus' mention of London, 43.
Talahee, lands of, 205.
Tallow and hides, 229...Charlemagne's directions, 328, 330.
Tanistry, law of, 176.
Tassilo and Odilo, dukes of Sclaves and Wends, 8.
Tavern, singular laws regarding their number in Perth, 162.

INDEX. 367

Taxes, 216...Borne by burghs in William's reign, 232...The power to impose, 212.
Tayllefer, Lawrence, a correspondent of Haliburton, 241.
Teazles, 323...Imported, 237.
Tenth Penny, law regarding, 215.
Tenures, early, 201.
Teodbald (a witness), 88.
Teutonic races, 7, 50.
Teviotdale, 128...Abbeys of, 147, 251.
Thane, value of, and a thane's nephew, 181 ...The title first acquired by service, 52.
Thierry quoted, 11.
Third estate, its first presence in Parliament, 216.
Thomas, Captain, his researches in Orkney, 280.
Thomson, Thomas, commentary upon the Ayr charter, 167.
"Thor aide," a war cry of the Norsemen, 40.
Thor worshipped by the Anglo-Saxons, 57...Worshippers of; preserved traditions of Asgard and Asaland, and an Asiatic origin, 8...Thor, Woden, and Saxnot, 14.
Thor the Long (a witness), 88.
Thorpe, Benjamin, laws and institutes of England, quoted, 56...Lappenberg, quoted, 67...Translation of Aelfric, 332.
Thuringians, 11, 14, 22; their catechism, 14.
Tigerne (a witness), 88.
Tiles, imported, 248...Paving, 307.
Timber roofs, 305.
Tithes, 54, 71, 132...Charlemagne's, 328.
Tod fur, 236.
Torfaeus cited, 232.
Torques, 311.
Tours, council of, Statutes of, 337.
Towelling imported; its price in 1493, 244.
Tower of London contains fine specimens of Early Norman, 296.
Trade and manufacture, 228-250.
"Trades" of towns, incorporated by Henry V., 151.
Traquair, David's court at, 120...William's court at, 120.
Transmutation of metals, 15.
"Treasure Trove," at Orkney, 311.
Trial by battle, 182-5...By fire and water, privilege granted to the great monasteries, 186.
Trinity church, Edinburgh, an example of Middle Pointed style, 302.
Trout exported, 246, 247.
Turnberry castle, 314.
Turners, 329, 330.
Turtles, 328.
Tyningham church a sanctuary, 198.
Tyningham park, a fragment of Norman architecture preserved in, 295.

Uhtred, Eilav's son (a witness), 88.
Ulf (a witness), 88.
Ulf Jarl, Cnut's brother-in-law; murdered in the church of St. Lucius, 68.
Umphramvill, de, 88, 203, 206.
Uniæt Hwite (a witness), 88.
Union, benefits of, 199.
Urquharts, family of, 318.

Valdev, or Waldev, son of Earl Gospatrick (a witness), 203, 206.
"Valerius Maximus" in Glasgow Cathedral library, 337.
Valoins, William de, 210.
Value, respective, of the king and of his subjects, 180.
Vaus, John, rector of the grammar school of Aberdeen in 1520, 272; his elementary work on Latin Grammar, 273.
Vatican MS. of Thuringian catechism, 13.
Vegetables used in Scotland in the thirteenth century, 125.
Velvet; its value in 1493, 242, 245.
Vermilion, 329.
Vescis, de, 89...Eustace, 209.
Via Scoticana, the Highland road, 146.
Vikingr, 9.
Villa, Roman, in Oxfordshire, its apartments, library, banqueting, and bathrooms, etc., 44.
Villas, Charlemagne's, 327-31.
Villein, see Serf, 138.
Vinegar, 330...An import, 242.
Vinget (a witness), 88.
Vineyards, 327, 330.
Visigothic territory, 22, 23.
Vitrified forts, 281-2.
Vortigern's story, 48.

Wad, manufacture of, 229.
Wager of battle in the reign of David, 182-3.
Waldev, Earl of Dunbar, gift of a tribe of serfs to the abbot of Kelso, 141. See Dunbar.
Waldev, son of Earl Gospatric (a witness), 203.
Waldev, son of Baldwin (a witness), 202.
Walghton, Nes de, 210.
Wales, Romans in, 42...Christianity preserved, 57...Bards of, 50...Monuments of, 289.
Wallace and Bruce, wars of, 313.
Walter the chancellor (a witness), 203, 206.
Wapentakes, division of counties adopted by the Anglo-Saxons, 49-54.
Ward among feudal casualties, 122.
Wardlaw, Henry, afterwards bishop of St. Andrews, and founder of its university at Oxford, 274.
Wardlaw, Walter, cardinal bishop of Glasgow, 337.
Warin, Hervi Fitz, 201.
Water, trial by, 187.
Wends, 8.

Wealh, the native Briton, 53.
Wearmouth, 64.
Weavers, 229.
Wedale church a sanctuary; now called "*The Stow*," 196, 198...Arthur's gift, 196.
Wedderburn's songs, mentioned by Melville, 342.
Weser, the, 7.
Wheat, 123 ... Grown in Moray in thirteenth century, 145.
Whithorn, St. Ninian's church at, 97, 292 ...Cathedral, an example of "First Pointed" style, 297.
Whitret fur, 236.
Wilbrord and Boniface, English missionaries to the Frisians, 18, 61.
William, abbot of Melrose (a witness), 203, 206.
William, Malcolm's brother, 203, 206.
William, son of Lethe, a serf, 141.
William of Copland (a witness), 202.
William of Hellebot (a witness), 202.
William of Normandy; crusade against England, 72.
William the Lion, 128, 135...Holds a court at Perth; statutes regarding the composition of king's court, 208-9... Provides against abuses in the barons' court of "lyf and lym;" statute respecting "ordeal by water," 187 ... Precept to the ministers of Wedale, 196...Statutes regarding ordeals, 188 Residences at Selkirk, Melrose, Traquair, Roxburgh, Lanark, Rutherglen, Stirling, Linlithgow, Clackmannan, Edinburgh, Haddington, Dunfermline, St. Andrews, and Kinghorn; at Forfar, Aberdeen, Elgin, Forres, Nairn, Inverness, 120...His two daughters and their dowries. 232.
William, a moneyer of Berwick; an artist of the reign of William the Lion, 308.
William de Monte Haudon; his book in Glasgow Cathedral library, 340.
Winchester cathedral; the crypt of Early "Norman," 296.
Winchester charters granted by Henry I.. models of burgh charters of England, 154.
Wine account of Alexander III., 122, 233 ...Gascon claret for his majesty's summer drink, from Dundee in the "king's wain," 124.

Wines, 237, 241, 244, 245...Charlemagne's directions regarding, 327, 329-331
Winfred, known afterwards as Boniface of Devonshire. 61.
Wintoun, *see* Wyntoun.
Witan, or king's high court of Parliament, constitution of, 55.
Witchcraft, trials for, 187.
Witenagemot at Langdene, 66.
Witham, Patrick de, 210.
Witikind, prince, 4, 15; baptized, 33.
Woad or madder imported, 237.
Woden, 52...Prayer to, by the Saxons; sacred hill of, 15. *See* Odin.
Wolves. 125, 331.
Wolf hunter at Stirling. 125.
Wolf of Badenoch, 297.
Women employed in harvest work, 140.
Woodwork, 307.
Wool, 163...Exported: litted; its price, 229, 237, 241, 242, 243, 246, 338, 330... Combs, 329.
Worsaäe, an authority on Danish antiquities, 283.
Writings, early Scotch, none extant so early as the reign of Malcolm Canmore, 78, 79...Except the marginal notes on the Gospel MS. of the Church of Deir, 321, 325.
Wulframn, a missionary, 32.
Wulfstan, an early traveller, 66.
Wyntoun, Andrew, prior of Lochleven, date of his chronicle, 81...Its value, 263...Compiled from records at St. Andrews; its literary merit, 264... Specimen; ballad on king Alexander preserved in it, 265...account of Alexander's gift to the church of St. Andrews, 228...First mention of Parliament, 214...On Macbeth's reign, 118.

Y, *see* Iona.
Yeoman or bonnet-laird, 140.
Yorkshire and Northumbrian barons, 90.
Yorkshire and Teviotdale abbeys, schools of polite letters, 251. 252.
York, no slaves in, 53....Sixth Roman legion stationed at. 43.
Ypre black gown imported, 247.

Zacharias dethrones Childeric III., the last of the Merovingian kings, 5.
Zealand, 248.

www.ingramcontent.com/pod-product-compliance
Lightning Source LLC
Chambersburg PA
CBHW030556300426
44111CB00009B/998